# ENGLISH HUMANISM

WORLD AND WORD SERIES
Edited by Professor Isobel Armstrong, University of Southampton

**Literature and the Social Order in Eighteenth Century England**
Stephen Copley

# English Humanism
## Wyatt to Cowley

Edited by Joanna Martindale

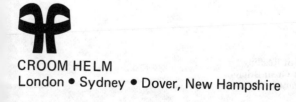

CROOM HELM
London • Sydney • Dover, New Hampshire

© 1985 Joanna Martindale
Croom Helm Ltd, Provident House, Burrell Row,
Beckenham, Kent BR3 1AT
Croom Helm Australia Pty Ltd, First Floor, 139 King Street,
Sydney, NSW 2001, Australia

British Library Cataloguing in Publication Data

English humanism.
1. Humanism
I. Martindale, Joanna
144       B821

ISBN 0-7099-2032-6
ISBN 0-7099-2067-9 Pbk


Croom Helm, 51 Washington Street,
Dover, New Hampshire 03820, USA

Library of Congress Cataloging in Publication Data
Main entry under title:

English humanism.

   (World and word series)
   Bibliography: p.282
   Includes index.
   1. English literature — Early modern, 1500-1700 — His-
tory and criticism — Sources. 2. Humanism in literature.
3. Humanism — History — Sources. 4. Erasmus, Desiderius,
d. 1536 — Translations, English. 5. English literature —
Early modern, 1500-1700. 6. European literature —
Renaissance, 1450-1600 — Translations into English.
7. English literature — Translations from foreign languages.
I. Martindale, Joanna. II. Series.
PR428.H8E5   1985      820'.8'0384      84-17667
ISBN 0-7099-2032-6 (U.S.)
ISBN 0-7099-2067-9 (U.S.:pbk.)


Typeset by Columns of Reading
Printed and bound in Great Britain
by Billing & Sons Limited, Worcester.

PARENTIBUS OPTIMIS

# CONTENTS

# GENERAL EDITOR'S PREFACE

The *Word and World* series, as its title implies, is based on the assumption that literary texts cannot be studied in isolation. The series presents to students, mainly of English literature, documents and materials which will enable them to have first-hand experience of some of the writing which forms the context of the literature they read. The aim is to put students in possession of material to which they cannot normally gain access so that they may arrive at an independent understanding of the inter-relationships of literary texts with other writing.

There are to be twelve volumes, covering topics from the Middle Ages to the twentieth century. Each volume concentrates on a specific area of thought in a particular period, selecting from religious, philosophical or scientific works, literary theory or political or social material, according to its chosen topic. The extracts included are substantial in order to enable students themselves to arrive at an understanding of the significance of the material they read and to make responsible historical connections with some precision and independence. The task of compilation itself, of course, predetermines to a great extent the kind of connections and relationships which can be made in a particular period. We all bring our own categories to the work of interpretation. However, each compiler makes clear the grounds on which the choice of material is made, and thus the series encourages the valuable understanding that there can be no single, authoritative account of the relationships between word and world.

Each volume is annotated and indexed and includes a short bibliography and suggestions for further reading. The *World and Word series* can be used in different teaching contexts, in the student's independent work, in seminar discussion, and on lecture courses.

Isobel Armstrong
University of Southampton

# PREFACE

Humanism is a large subject; an entirely different set of authors and themes from those included in this anthology could doubtless have been selected to illustrate it. For the reasons given in the Introduction, I have chosen to centre this volume on Erasmus, and have selected five topics which have an important bearing on English Renaissance literature. Following P. O. Kristeller and Frances Yates, I view the Florentine Neo-Platonism of Ficino and Pico as a different tradition from the philological and rhetorical humanism which is the subject of this book;[1] Neo-Platonism is therefore not treated here, important though its influence was on English Renaissance literature.

I hope that the format of this book is clear. The relevant section in the Introduction is intended to be read together with each group of extracts. A biographical note about each author will be found in the headnote to the first extract from him in the anthology, and similarly a note about each work is given the first time it appears. Latin titles have been translated throughout. All Greek has been transliterated. Books included in the Select Bibliography have been cited in the body of the text in abbreviated form only.

Richard Stoneman of Croom Helm kindly gave me the opportunity to write this book. I am very grateful to all those who have helped me with specific enquiries. Especial thanks are due to my brother, Charles Martindale, who read a draft of the Introduction and made many helpful criticisms, and who also translated the extracts from Erasmus' *Ciceronianus*. My greatest debt is to my husband, Robert Parker, who not only supplied translations from Erasmus but has also given unflagging advice, support and encouragement.

NOTE

1. See Frances A. Yates, 'No man's land' (review of P. O. Kristeller, *Eight philosophers of the Italian Renaissance*), *Renaissance and reform: the Italian contribution*, *Collected essays*, vol. II (Routledge and Kegan Paul, 1983), pp. 73-8.

# A NOTE ON THE TEXT

The texts given in this anthology are almost all based on the first edition of the particular work, and are given with modern spelling and punctuation. The following editions were used: Ascham, *The schoolmaster*, 1570; Castiglione, *The book of the courtier*, translated by Sir Thomas Hoby, 1561; Colet, *Aeditio*, 1527; Daniel, *Musophilus*, from *Poetical essays*, 1599; Elyot, *The book named the governor*, 1531; Hoole, *A new discovery*, 1660; Machiavelli, *The prince*, translated by Edward Dacres, 1640; North, *The lives of the noble Grecians and Romans*, 1579; Peacham, *The garden of eloquence*, 1577 and 1593 editions; Wilson, *The art of rhetoric*, 1553. Erasmus' *On giving children an early and a liberal education* is given in the translation included in Richard Sherry's *A treatise of schemes and tropes*, 1550; *The pious feast* is from Sir Roger L'Estrange's *Twenty select colloquies out of Erasmus Roterodamus*, 1680 (there entitled *The religious treat*); and the *Paraclesis* is in the anonymous translation, perhaps by William Roy, entitled *An exhortation to the diligent study of scripture*, 1529. (The other extracts from Erasmus, for which there were no Renaissance translations available, have been freshly translated for this volume.) The passage from Ben Jonson's *The New Inn* is from the 1631 octavo; the passage from *Volpone* from the 1616 Folio; and the passages from *Discoveries* from the 1640 Folio. In the latter case, some readings from the standard modern edition by Herford and Simpson have been adopted.

Syntax and vocabulary make texts from the early sixteenth century hard for the modern reader to understand; the added difficulty of the original spelling and punctuation can make them impenetrably opaque. For this reason, I have modernised punctuation, spelling and unfamiliar and confusing morphology. I have retained a few old forms for rhythmical and other reasons. Proper names are generally given in the standard modern English form, or in a regularised Latin form. For obsolete words, I have adopted the spelling used in the lemma in *OED*. Those who have struggled with the problems of modernising will know that consistency has continually to be juggled with expediency. With regard to punctuation, I have generally respected the unit of the sentence, except in the case of *An exhortation to the diligent study of scripture*, where the sentence divisions were incomprehensible in modern terms.

There are real disadvantages in modernising spelling and punctuation. Modern spelling helps to conceal the differences between the language of the past and that of the present. To give one example: in the sixteenth century 'travail' and 'travel' had not been differentiated in spelling; either spelling could imply either meaning and both senses could be present together; the moderniser must choose between them. Modern punctuation does not always harmonise well with old syntax; further, where there is ambiguity in the old punctuation, the moderniser cannot always be sure that the sense he imposes with his punctuation is the one which the author intended. An old text in modern spelling and punctuation is a hybrid, which may well cause offence to the linguistic purist. On balance, I think that the gains in comprehensibility outweigh the losses.

# INTRODUCTION

The title of this volume, *English humanism: Wyatt to Cowley*, is perhaps provocative. It expresses a conviction about the literature of Renaissance England, which I believe to have been deeply indebted to Continental humanism and the classical revival. In the past, some influential critics have denied that there was any fruitful connection:

> All the facts seem consistent with the view that the great literature of the fifteen-eighties and nineties was something which humanism, with its unities and *Gorboducs* and English hexameters, would have prevented if it could, but failed to prevent because the high tide of native talent was then too strong for it. Later, when we were weaker, it had its way and our pseudo-classical period set in.[1]

Shakespeare and the Metaphysical poets, we are told, base their poetry on 'the current colloquial speech of the age'; Ben Jonson imports an impersonal Latinate idiom and ushers in the pomposities of the 'Augustan' age of Waller, Dryden and Pope.[2] In the rhetoric of such accounts, the 'native' is accorded a high — and it seems to me unexamined — value; humanist classicism is represented as drying up the native sap. The humanists are portrayed as narrow pedants, obsessed by rules and concerned only with the cultivation of correct Latin style; imitation, a central humanist doctrine, is viewed as a deadening conformism, 'a feast of husks'.[3] I shall argue in this Introduction that such a picture is misdrawn, and that the literature of the whole period was affected in fundamental ways by humanist ideas. There is no great division between the sixteenth and seventeenth centuries in this respect; as Emrys Jones argues in *The origins of Shakespeare*, in a chapter which should be read by everyone considering this topic, these are both part of 'the classical, or neo-classical, phase of our literature', which embraces both Shakespeare and Ben Jonson, and does not end until after the death of Pope.[4]

But first the nettle must be grasped: what is meant by the term humanism? Modern senses of the word which have nothing to do with the historical movement must be dismissed from our minds:

*Humanism n.* Devotion to human interests; system concerned with human (not divine or supernatural) matters, or with the human race (not the individual), or with man as a responsible and progressive intellectual being. (*Concise Oxford dictionary*, 6th edn)

The force of 'human' in the sense of the word 'humanism' we are investigating is not primarily human as opposed to divine. Rather it is the same as in Cicero's use of *humanitas* and *studia humanitatis* to mean literary culture, the studies which are most appropriate to man and separate him from the animals, *humanitas* as opposed to *feritas* ('wildness'); in *On the republic*, Scipio says that the name of men should only be given to those who are 'accomplished in the arts appropriate to humanity' ('politi propriis humanitatis artibus').[5] Aulus Gellius, the literary antiquary, writing in the second century AD, says that the proper meaning of *humanitas* is not, as in the common usage of his day, *philanthropia*, kindness, but *paideia*, 'education and training in the liberal arts':

> Those who earnestly desire and seek after these are most highly humanized. For the pursuit of that kind of knowledge, and the training given by it, have been granted to man alone of all the animals, and for that reason it is termed *humanitas*, or 'humanity'.[6]

The Ciceronian phrase *studia humanitatis* was taken up by classical scholars and enthusiasts in the fourteenth century and applied to their studies; it was frequently used by Coluccio Salutati, the Florentine chancellor, friend of Petrarch and promoter of classical studies, and in Leonardo Bruni's *Dialogues* (1401), Petrarch is said to have restored the extinct *studia humanitatis*. The humanists liked to emphasise that their studies were concerned with man, as opposed to what they considered the futile speculations of scholastic scientists and metaphysicians. In the fifteenth century, *studia humanitatis* acquired a more technical meaning; used in the context of the university or the library, it denoted the study of grammar, rhetoric, poetry, history and moral philosophy, centred on Latin and Greek literature. Then, probably in the late fifteenth century, the Italian word *umanista* (in the Latin form, *humanista*) was coined in the universities, on the analogy of such words as *legista* and *canonista*, to describe the teacher of the *studia humanitatis*, the word being later extended to anyone interested in these studies. John Florio in his Italian-English dictionary, *A world of words* (1598) translates *umanista* as 'a humanist or professor of humanity', and the first use of the word in English in this sense given in the *Oxford English dictionary* is from Abraham Fleming's preface to the reader of his translation of Virgil's *Georgics* (1589), where he says that his work is intended for 'weak grammatists' rather than 'courtly humanists'.

The present-day use of the word 'humanist' to describe a participant in the historical movement seems to have begun by the eighteenth century (Gibbon, for example, speaks of the humanists of the fifteenth century), but the popularity of the term 'humanism' was brought about by German use of the term *humanismus*; Georg Voigt's influential book on the classical revival (1859) was subtitled *Das erste Jahrhundert des Humanismus*, 'the first century of humanism'. Since then, humanism has acquired all the imprecision of such general terms. Some recent scholars have tried to employ it more precisely, with reference to the Renaissance meanings of *umanista* and *studia humanitatis*, to denote a programme of studies and a set of attitudes associated with this programme.[7]

It certainly seems safer to define humanism by its characteristic pursuits and attitudes than to attempt an interpretation which may provoke disagreement — to view it as the triumph of the secular spirit, for example, or as the efflorescence of the new bourgeois individualism, or merely as a development of the traditional inter-faculty squabble of rhetoric and philosophy.[8] There is no need here to go into the question of whether the 'Renaissance' ever took place. Certainly, we can no longer accept the text-book stereotype of a pietistic, gloomy and heaven-centred Middle Ages, succeeded by a rational, optimistic and man-centred Renaissance. Most modern accounts of the Renaissance stress the many continuities with the Middle Ages, and view it as a new synthesis rather than as a complete break; the humanists are now seen as the heirs of the medieval *dictatores*, rhetoricians who taught the art of letter-writing.[9] The humanists' own stereotype of a dark age of Gothic barbarism succeeded by a new age illumined by antique wisdom is unacceptable as a statement of historical fact. It is worth noting, though, as a factor of psychological importance; that the humanists felt they were living in a Renaissance is a change in itself, and can be used to defend the concept of Renaissance.[10]

Humanism was a fresh attempt to rediscover and utilise the classical heritage; Petrarch (1304-74) was its first representative of major importance, if not its founder as used to be thought,[11] and it spread to Northern Europe in the fifteenth and sixteenth centuries. (Although there are differences between Italian and Northern humanism, there is recognisable continuity: certain ideas persist despite the changing cultural conditions.[12]) The humanists placed a very high value on classical studies, and viewed the ancient world as the highest point of civilisation, embodying the ideal way of life as well as of letters; the classics perhaps reached the zenith of their influence on European culture in this period.[13] Of course, the Middle Ages had not lost all knowledge of antiquity; the Latin language was at the centre of education and culture throughout the period, and individual poets could respond with appreciation and understanding to individual classical authors, as Dante to Virgil. Many aspects of the ancient world were embedded in European culture and taken for granted (indeed, the change in the Renaissance approach to the classics has been defined as an increasing sense of the separateness of the classical past, which led to the building up of a complete picture of a civilisation seen as distinct from the present).[14] There were also several deliberate attempts to revive the antique; various aspects of Roman art and literature were imitated in the movements known as the 'Carolingian Renaissance' and the 'Twelfth-century Renaissance'.[15] The most recent engagement with the ancient world was the triumph of scholastic philosophy, Thomas Aquinas' synthesis of Aristotle and Christianity. The Renaissance movement was in part a reaction to scholasticism, the intellectual system which dominated the schools and universities of the late Middle Ages and placed a high value on dialectic and logic.[16] The humanists pursued different kinds of interest in the classical world.

The central emphasis was literary; rhetoric was believed to hold the key to the good life.[17] The Roman ideal of the orator was revived, backed by the discovery of complete texts of Cicero's *On the orator*, *The orator* and *Brutus* and Quintilian's *The education of an orator*, all containing important definitions of the orator's role. The orator must be able to express his thought in appropriate speech in order to move his audience; hence the immense importance attached to the cultivation of style and 'correct', i.e. classical, Latin by the humanists. The recovery of manuscripts, textual criticism, the study of Latin idiom were all keenly pursued, and knowledge of Greek literature (largely unknown in the Middle Ages, unlike Greek philosophy) was added to that of Roman.[18] The humanists studied the classics not only in order to understand and to admire but also to imitate; they were prolific writers of speeches, letters, treatises and poems in Latin. Apart from literature, they had shared interests in history, education and ethics, and shared dislikes for metaphysics and logic; in general, they placed greater value on the concrete than on the abstract. Cicero's *On duties*, which puts philosophy at the service of life in the world, was a favourite of the humanists, and their twin slogans were *ad fontes* and *ad res*, to the sources and to reality.[19]

It must be stressed again that enthusiasm for the classics did not entail paganism. Despite George Eliot's portrayal of Bardo Bardi and Tito Melema in *Romola*, humanism was not an irreligious movement.[20] In Petrarch's thought, knowledge of man involved knowledge of God, which was the true end of philosophy.[21] Petrarch revered both Cicero and St Augustine, and was a deeply pious man:

> One of these feeble ones who believe in you is much happier than Plato, Aristotle, Varro and Cicero, who with all their learning did not know you . . .

> If to admire Cicero is to be a Ciceronian, I am a Ciceronian. I certainly admire him; I even wonder at those who do not . . . But when we come to think or speak about religion, that is about utmost truth and true happiness and eternal salvation, I am certainly not a Ciceronian, nor a Platonist, but a Christian. (*On his own ignorance and that of many others*)[22]

English humanist circles were characterised by pious interests as well as by enthusiasm for the ancient world,[23] and this is reflected in literature by the attempts to fuse Christian and classical.

Here, as elsewhere in this study, the most important figure is Erasmus (1466?-1536), the great synthesiser, populariser and mediator of Italian ideas to the rest of Europe. His conviction that the moral thought of the ancients was in harmony with Christianity, and his defence of classical learning as part of the Christian scheme in *The antibarbarians* are of great importance for English literature. Erasmus should not be viewed, anachronistically, as a forerunner of nineteenth-century rationalism; his thought was firmly based on Christianity (in this echoing Petrarch):

> The arts, moral philosophy, rhetoric are acquired to this end — that we may understand Christ and celebrate his glory. This is the target of all learning and eloquence. (*Ciceronianus*)[24]

Erasmus' ideas form a close-knit whole in which classical and Christian are inextricably intermeshed.[25] He sought a renewal in both learning and religion through a return to a pristine Christianity and a true classicism. He believed that the decline in knowledge of classical Latin and Greek had brought about a general decay: 'for the ignorance of tongues either hath marred all the sciences or greatly hurt them, even divinity itself, also physic and law'.[26] For Erasmus, the unclassical Latin of the scholastic theologians was a sign of their misguided thinking — the pursuit of inessentials in theology and of formalism in religion (i.e. the emphasis on such observances as pilgrimages and the worship of relics to which the reforming party in the Church was opposed). The early Church Fathers were his preferred ideal, especially St Jerome, who had put rhetoric and secular learning at the service of Christianity, and showed that one could be at once learned and a Christian. The true goal of theology was the study of the Scriptures, in which Christ's teaching was preserved. Erasmus christianised humanist ideas about the importance of language and the close links between eloquence and wisdom. Language is the basic civilising act, which distinguishes man from beast;[27] the spirit issuing in speech reflects the generation of the Son by the Father:

> What in the divine sphere is the Father generating the Son from himself is in us the mind, the fount of thoughts and speech; what there is the Son being born from the Father is in us speech (*oratio*) coming from the soul. The Son is said to be the image of the Father, so like that whoever knows one of the two knows both. So, too, in us speech is the mirror of the soul — hence the saying of Socrates, 'Speak that I may see you,' has become famous. (*Language or on usage and abusage*)[28]

Erasmus caused a furore by translating the Greek word *logos* at the beginning of St John's Gospel ('In the beginning was the Word') by *sermo*, speech, conversation, rather than the traditional *verbum* of the Vulgate, in order to emphasise the rhetorical role of the Son. The theologian is the Christian orator:

> The particular aim of theologians is to interpret the scriptures wisely, to offer explanations about faith not about frivolous questions, to treat of piety gravely and powerfully, to move us to tears, to inflame souls to celestial things. (*The proper system or method in brief of attaining true theology*)[29]

It seems to me somehow fitting that in explaining mysteries there should be a certain dignity of speech and that emotion should not be lacking. This has the result that the reader not only understands what is taught by a learned man but loves what is communicated by a man who loves. (*Letter to Balthasar Mercklin*)[30]

(The author of *Paradise Lost* would surely have appreciated such an aim.) Erasmus adapted to the study of the Bible humanist philological methods devised for classical texts; he believed that the theologian should know three languages, Latin, Greek and Hebrew, and should be versed in grammar and rhetoric.

Erasmus is of prime importance for English humanism.[31] Not only were his books widely read (in the list of books sold in 1520 by an Oxford bookseller, John Dorne, works by Erasmus predominate[32]) but he made several visits to England at the outset of his career as an international scholar, and formed fruitful links with English humanists, notably Colet and More. When Erasmus first visited England in 1499, John Colet (1467?-1519) was in Oxford, where he gave lectures on the epistles of St Paul. Rejecting the traditional method of scriptural exegesis, which was to suggest multiple allegorical and spiritual meanings in addition to the literal, Colet concentrated on the historical meaning, and used his knowledge of Roman history to explain the society in which St Paul lived. Colet was well versed in the classics and in the Church Fathers; he was hostile to scholastic theology and to such religious practices as the worship of relics. There was much to appeal to Erasmus here, and Colet probably influenced the development of his religious views and encouraged him in the pursuit of biblical study; the edition of the New Testament in Greek in 1516 was the eventual result. In 1510, Colet founded St Paul's school to provide a sound education in Christianity and good letters; here, it was Erasmus' ideas which, almost certainly, influenced Colet.[33] He sent Colet a revised version of *On the proper system of study* in 1511 (it was published in 1512); the school embodied the spirit and probably many of the details of the educational programme sketched in it. Erasmus revised and published for use in the school the influential *On abundance*, a manual for Latin composition; he also contributed to Lily's Latin grammar, which, commissioned by Colet for St Paul's, became the standard school grammar at least until the eighteenth century. St Paul's was to be the model for successive grammar schools, so that Erasmus' influence on English life and letters was here fundamental.

Thomas More (1478-1535), when Erasmus first met him in 1499, was a young lawyer with typical humanist interests in classical learning and church reform; the chancellorship and martyrdom lay in the future.[34] On Erasmus' second visit to England in 1505-6, the pair collaborated in translating from Greek into Latin some of the satiric sketches of Lucian, the late Greek author of the second century AD. Characteristically, Lucian appealed to them not just as a model for humour and satire but for his contemporary message; his attacks on the hypocrisy, superstition and quarrelsomeness of his chief target, philosophers, could be applied to the monks and to contemporary religious practices. Erasmus and More saw Lucian as a moralist, whereas today he is generally viewed as a light-hearted manipulator of stock rhetorical patterns. Lucian may be felt behind the two works written by mutual inspiration, Erasmus' *Encomium moriae* (*Praise of folly*, with a pun on his friend's name) and More's *Utopia*, which both set out from the characteristic humanist interest in society and the affairs of men in the world.[35]

Erasmus paid his last visit to England in 1517, but his thought continued to be influential after the Reformation. His religious ideas, indeed, played a part in the Henrician religious settlement, and Thomas Cromwell fostered interest in Erasmus and sponsored a programme of translation.[36] His books continued to be used in schools; Sir Thomas Elyot had recommended *On abundance* and *The education of a Christian prince* in *The governor* (1531), and the schoolmaster Charles Hoole, in the seventeenth century, is still recommending 'that excellent book' *On abundance*, the *Colloquies*, *On writing letters*, the *Adages* and the *Apophthegms*; he calls *On the proper system of study* a 'golden little book'. Erasmus' influence can be seen working on two English poets. Shakespeare almost certainly knew the *Adages*, Erasmus' enormous collection of proverbs; Hamlet's 'sea of troubles' probably recalls Erasmus' *mare malorum*. Shakespeare responded, too, to 'the Erasmian paradoxes of the wisdom of folly and the folly of wisdom'.[37] Ben Jonson utilises Erasmus' defence of *The praise of folly* from his letter to Martin Dorp both in *Discoveries* and in the dedicatory epistle to *Volpone*, and drew on some of the *Colloquies*; for example he used the colloquy *The alchemist* for his own play of the same name.[38] He shared Erasmus' veneration for classical wisdom, his dislike of romance, and his interest in ethical matters, men and manners. In the eighteenth century, we find Pope (whose *Dunciad* might be viewed as an updating of *The antibarbarians*) praising Erasmus for restoring learning after the barbarous Middle Ages, in an unashamedly biased vignette:

> With Tyranny then Superstition joined,
> As that the body, this enslaved the mind;
> Much was believed, but little understood,

And to be dull was construed to be good;
A second deluge Learning thus o'er-run,
And the monks finished what the Goths begun.
    At length, Erasmus, that great, injured name,
(The glory of the priesthood and the shame!)
Stemmed the wild torrent of a barb'rous age,
And drove those holy vandals off the stage.
(*Essay on criticism*)[39]

It is because of his special importance for English humanism that
Erasmus is allotted so much space in this anthology. In many cases, the
same ideas — for example on education or on imitation — could have
been illustrated from Italian humanists, but it was largely through
Erasmus that such ideas reached England. Erasmus is also the answer to
C. S. Lewis' caricature of the humanist. He cannot be accused of empty
formalism. He was passionately interested in the content of classical
literature and in its relevance for modern man; he wished to renew the
present by the past. He valued style not for its own sake but as a mirror
of thought; knowledge of language led to 'judgement and to the knowledge of all disciplines'.[40] He hated rules; 'the letter killeth but the spirit
giveth life' (II Corinthians, 3: 6) was his motto both in literary imitation and in religion.[41] He wished to imitate the spirit of Cicero, not his
verbal configurations, and he valued faith above ritual.

I want to look now in more detail at some influential humanist ideas
and to suggest ways in which they affected English literature. I shall
follow the order of the sections into which the anthology is divided.
The material given there will fill out the ideas expressed briefly here,
and the discussion will gain if read in conjunction with the passages.

### Education: theory and practice

Education was one of the chief humanist interests; from the time of
Vittorino da Feltre and Guarino, who had schools at Mantua (1423-46)
and at Ferrara (1429-36) respectively, humanists were often involved in
the teaching of children, and they wrote many educational treatises.
These stress the supreme importance of education: man cannot live by
the promptings of nature alone, 'doctrine' (knowledge, teaching) must
be added to experience, and the mind should be formed early. Three
classical works in particular influenced humanist educational ideas: the
pseudo-Plutarchan essay *The education of children*, from the *Moralia*,

Cicero's *On the orator* and above all Quintilian's *The education of an orator*.

Humanist treatises frequently stress the special importance of sound education for the ruler and the governing class: the *studia humanitatis* lead to knowledge and virtue, and hence to good government.[42] The English educational writers, Elyot and Ascham, both take this up, echoing the arguments of Erasmus and Castiglione (see further chapter 3). The standard example used to demonstrate the efficacy of education for the ruler was that of Alexander the Great, whose tutor was Aristotle and whose favourite author was Homer.[43] Humanists do seem to have contributed to bringing about a change of attitude here; the medieval idea of a different education for nobles and 'clerks' (ecclesiastics, who often held bureaucratic posts) fell into disfavour, and the upper classes began to send their sons to the grammar schools, the universities and the Inns of Court; education came to be seen as essential for public life.[44]

Complaints about the state of education and attacks on medieval teaching methods are common in humanist authors; Batt, in *The antibarbarians*, lavishes scorn on the ignorance of schoolteachers and on the stupidity of medieval grammars. Of course, there had been schools in the Middle Ages where classical authors were studied, for example the celebrated school of Chartres where Bernard taught the classics to John of Salisbury in the twelfth century.[45] But by Erasmus' day, there had been a decline.[46] Classes were often very large. Generally only the master was provided with a text-book, and so everything had to be dictated and then learnt by heart. (Renaissance schooling benefited both from the invention of printing and from the spread of cheap paper, which meant that the boy could preserve copious notes on the authors he was studying.) Logic was the dominant discipline; logical disputation was begun early in the schools and even the teaching of grammar was affected by it, so that the boys learnt complex definitions of grammatical cases. This kind of thing was anathema to the humanists, as was the Latin usage taught:

> All Latin adulterate, which ignorant blind fools brought into this world and with the same hath distained and poisoned the old Latin speech and the very Roman tongue which in the time of Tully and Sallust and Virgil and Terence was used, which also Saint Jerome and Saint Ambrose and Saint Austin and many holy doctors learned in their times — I say that filthiness and all such abusion which the later blind world brought in, which more rather may be called

blotterature than literature, I utterly abanish and exclude out of this school. (Colet, *Statutes*, 1518)[47]

Viewed by modern educational ideas, the education provided in the English grammar school of the Renaissance, which put into practice humanist ideas, was extraordinarily single-minded, perhaps even narrow-minded. The whole tenor was literary. Boys learnt to read and to write English, Latin and Greek, generally in that order and with the greatest attention being paid to Latin. Humanist educators believed that Latin grammar should be learnt not by rote but by observing and copying the practice of 'good authors'. In his influential *Elegancies of the Latin language* (1471), a study of classical usage, Lorenzo Valla had said, 'I accept for law whatever has pleased great authors.' The sentiment is echoed by English educationalists; 'without doubt', writes Ascham in *The schoolmaster*, 'grammatica itself is sooner and surer learned by examples of good authors than by the naked rules of grammarians'.[48] Latin literature was always read with an eye to imitating; particular authors were studied at the same time as particular kinds of composition were being mastered: for example, the relevant parts of Cicero were read while orations and epistles were being composed. The closest attention was paid to details of expression; the boy kept a notebook in which he jotted down phrases which he could employ in his own compositions.[49] The aim of the system was rhetorical expertise, the ability to express oneself fluently on any topic. Hence all the innumerable exercises in translating from one language into another (it is worth noting that boys sometimes translated into English verse), in varying one thought in different words, in composing themes and orations.

It can hardly be chance that an educational programme of this kind coincided with a tremendous outburst of literary activity.[50] Not only professional writers but men immersed in practical affairs could turn their hand to a poem and sometimes produce a masterpiece, as Sir Henry Wotton did in 'Ye meaner beauties of the night'. The emphasis on the cultivation of stylistic fluency had its effect. Shakespeare may laugh at pedantic schoolmasters in Holofernes (in *Love's labour's lost*), a trick of whose speech is *variatio*, the production of strings of synonyms:

> *Hol.* The deer was, as you know, *sanguis*, in blood; ripe as the pomewater, who now hangeth like a jewel in the ear of *coelo*, the sky, the welkin, the heaven; and anon falleth like a crab on the face of *terra*, the soil, the land, the earth.

> *Nath*. Truly, Master Holofernes, the epithets are sweetly varied, like
> a scholar at the least: but, sir, I assure ye, it was a buck of the
> first head,

but he is the supreme example in English literature of Erasmian *copia*,
stylistic abundance.[51] Reading habits learnt at school persisted in later
life; Ben Jonson marked phrases in his books with an eye to redeploy-
ment in his own poetry.[52] The teaching methods of the period may
seem to us soul-destroying and Latin compositions sometimes school-
boyish, but when the poets came to compose in English, they could
draw on a large stock of ideas and phrases. By the time the boy had left
school, he had read very widely in classical literature and learnt a good
part by heart; it is therefore not surprising if we find so many reminiscences of the classics in English Renaissance literature.

### Classicism and imitation

Against C. S. Lewis' view that the humanist approach to the classics was
too literary — grubbing for beauties, in Kinglake's words, rather than
pressing the siege[53] — must be set the constant emphasis from school
onwards upon the moral lessons to be learnt from classical literature.
This may seem naïve to us today, when few people would value the
*Iliad* for presenting 'the true image of all virtues and human government' (Chapman's phrase),[54] and it certainly led to some misunder-
standings of particular poems. Thus, Horace's witty ode 'Integer vitae'
(*Odes*, I. xxii), where he says that he was saved from a wolf by singing
about Lalage, was often read as a defence of moral purity.[55] However
unfashionable today, ethical fervour is characteristic of much
Renaissance writing at its best — the poetry of Spenser or of Ben
Jonson, for example; it was fostered by humanism.[56] Erasmus provided
the apologia for the fusion of Christian and classical morality which
colours much writing of the period. In *The antibarbarians*, he streng-
thened the traditional Christian apologetic for classical learning, and in
the colloquy *The pious feast* and several of the dedicatory letters to his
editions of classical authors, he commented on the closeness of pagan
and Christian ethics.

    Another of Lewis' charges against the humanists is that they over-
classicised the classics, making them grander and more marmoreal than
they really were. He points to the fact that the humanists invented the
notion that each language goes through a cycle of growth and decay,

with a classic period in the centre. Although this does seem to be a common Renaissance notion, found in Ascham's *Schoolmaster*, for example, it is also the case that the canon of classical authors was much less selective in the Renaissance than today, including many late writers both Greek and Latin. William Drummond of Hawthornden, whose library is well documented, owned copies of Lucian, the Greek romances, the *Anacreontea* and the *Greek anthology*, many Silver Latin authors and still later writers, such as Apuleius and Ausonius. Ben Jonson was devoted to Silver Latin authors, especially Martial, Juvenal and Seneca, and made extensive use of them in his poems and plays; to Drummond, he recommended Quintilian, Pliny the Younger, Tacitus, Juvenal, Martial, Petronius and Persius. Erasmus' fondness for Lucian has already been mentioned, and he admired an extensive range of classical authors.[57] It was the Romantics and Victorians who valued sublimity in classical authors, seeking for the qualities of noble simplicity and calm grandeur which Winckelmann had praised.[58] Renaissance authors were interested in every odd corner of the classical heritage, not only in the moral (although I have stressed this above) but in the playful and the erotic, witness Herrick and Marlowe. One reason for the breadth of the canon was that classical authors were still read for the technical and scientific information they contained, which has since been superseded; Erasmus could write in *On the proper method of study* that 'almost everything worth learning' was to be found in Greek and Latin writers. Who now would read Aelian's *Tactics* to learn how to fight, or study Oppian to learn about fishes?

Thus, when an English author set out to imitate the classics, he had a wide range of authors to choose from, certainly not just the Augustans.[59] Imitation was a central humanist doctrine, which affected vernacular literature; certain misconceptions about it perhaps still need dispelling. The counsel to imitate is not counsel to assume another's voice; it is rather to learn how to project one's own voice. Erasmus has something to say and he looks for a classical model to help him to express it; Ben Jonson turns to Roman writers to add authority to his own ideas.[60] It is a commonplace of imitation theory that one must digest what one borrows (the metaphor goes back to Seneca and Quintilian, and is employed by Erasmus and Jonson in the passages I have selected); Erasmus stresses that writing must bear the impress of the writer.[61] Slavish copying is always condemned. Again and again, we find Renaissance authors converting classical literature to their own uses, assimilating it to their own traditions of style and thought, and to the contemporary historical situation. The fortunes of Horace's Second

Epode in the seventeenth century provide a good example; the figure of the Roman countryman was successively recast as Jacobean landowner, fulfilling the responsibilities of his position (the Sir Robert Wroth of Jonson's poem), as Christian mystic, and as Restoration gentleman living a life of comfortable and cultured ease.[62] Imitation should not be viewed as a restrictive doctrine; writers may respond to the same model in many different ways, and classical authors offered inspiration for more than one kind of poetry. It is not true that Roman poetry only influenced the public strains of English poetry, in opposition to the individualism of the native tradition. Horace showed Ben Jonson how to give personal colouring to his poems and provided a model for private moods, witness Lovelace's *The grasshopper*, where friendship is opposed to the frosty political scene of the Interregnum; Ovid was used by Donne and others to cock a snook at conventional morality.[63] The impulse to imitate should be seen as an impulse to extend knowledge and the range of literary possibilities — not to deny native traditions but to add to them the wealth of classical experience. Thus Marvell in *An Horatian ode upon Cromwell's return from Ireland* fuses the forms of an ode by Horace and a Metaphysical lyric, classical and contemporary ideas, in order to express more than he could have done if he had confined himself to the traditions of his own period; something of the coldness and realism of the Roman political experience is added to the exaggerations and fatuities of the contemporary panegyric style.[64] It was for similar reasons, perhaps, that Shakespeare turned from Hall and Holinshed to Plutarch, from the religious interpretation of history, and the divinity that hedges the king and punishes rebellious subjects, to the power struggles of ancient Rome and the secular world of the fecund Nile.

'Classical' and 'native' should not be seen as necessarily opposed. Both Erasmus and Ben Jonson could easily relate their lives to the ancient world. Just as Erasmus saw Lucian's philosophers as the monks of his own age, so Jonson, in *Poetaster*, translated his own struggles with his enemies to the world of Horace's satires (so that Marston is recreated as the bore of Horace's famous poem, while Jonson is more flatteringly shadowed forth by Horace) and, in *To Penshurst*, viewed his relations with his patrons in terms of Juvenal's and Martial's with theirs.[65] Despite the growth of historicism, classical authors had not yet become museum pieces to be disinterred by careful scholarship but were still a part of living culture.[66]

A final point must be noted about the vernacular. The prescriptions of Erasmus and Ascham for imitation were of course for writing in

Latin; both thought that the vernacular languages were inferior to the learned languages (though Ascham was willing to experiment with English). At the beginning of the sixteenth century, this was the common attitude in England, but by the end of the century, views had changed; Richard Mulcaster, headmaster of Merchant Taylors' School and later of St Paul's, gave a spirited defence of the native tongue in *The first part of the elementary, which entreateth chiefly of the right writing of our English tongue* (1582), where he argued that no language was inherently more eloquent than another, and that all that was needed was to develop English more:

> And eloquence itself is neither limited to language nor restrained to soil, whose measure the whole world is, whose judge the wise ear is, not in greatness of state but in sharpness of people ... It is our accident which restrains our tongue and not the tongue itself, which will strain with the strongest and stretch to the furthest, for either government if we were conquerors or for cunning if we were treasurers, not any whit behind either the subtle Greek for couching close or the stately Latin for spreading fair. Our tongue is capable if our people would be painful.
>
> I love Rome but London better; I favour Italy but England more; I honour the Latin but I worship the English.[67]

However, the humanist doctrine of imitation was carried over quite naturally to the imitation of the classics in the vernacular; Ben Jonson clearly felt himself to be carrying out Erasmus' precepts.[68] Indeed, in general, the humanist emphasis on the study of Latin language and literature did not impede the growth of the vernaculars but suggested ways of developing them: by translating from the classics, with the consequent enrichment of vocabulary and expression, by systematising, by the means of dictionaries and the study of orthography, by paying close attention to details of diction and syntax.[69]

## Wisdom and eloquence

In the dedication of *The garden of eloquence* (1577), Henry Peacham speaks of 'wisdom and eloquence, the only ornaments whereby man's life is beautified'. The coupling is significant; wisdom and eloquence are two parts of one ideal.[70] Wisdom cannot express itself properly without eloquence; eloquence is so much empty verbiage without wisdom.[71] It should be stressed again that the emphasis on style in Renaissance literary theory is not formalism. The intimate connection between style and thought is often reiterated; in the *Apophthegms*, Erasmus recounts an anecdote about Socrates, who said to a youth who had been sent by his father to be seen by the philosopher, 'Speak that I may|see you',

> signifying that the mind of man is manifested less in his face than in his speech (*oratio*), because this is the surest and least lying mirror of the soul.[72]

Diseases of the mind issue in diseased speech; the idea is expressed in *Discoveries* and exemplified by the characters in Jonson's plays, in the bombast of Sir Epicure Mammon, for example.

Wisdom and eloquence are the properties of the true orator. Humanists revived the classical ideal of the orator, whose aim was not just to know the good but, through eloquence, to move others to the good; passages from Cicero and Quintilian expressed this ideal eloquently.[73] Humanists had what may seem an excessive faith in the power of the word and the persuasive force of language.

> How much eloquence can accomplish in the shaping of human life is known both from reading in many authors and from the experience of everyday life. How great is the number of those we recognise in our own day, to whom even examples were of no help, who have been aroused and turned suddenly from a most wicked manner of life to a perfectly ordered one simply by the sound of others' voices,[74]

wrote Petrarch. 'Nothing among humans is more powerful at stirring all motions of the soul than speech (*oratio*),' said Erasmus.[75] Such faith pervades Daniel's *Musophilus*. It is important to note that ideas about oratory were transferred to poetry; the argument of Sidney's *Defence of poesy* centres on the moving power of literature:

> Truly, I have known men, that even with reading *Amadis de Gaule* (which God knoweth wanteth much of a perfect poesy) have found their hearts moved to the exercise of courtesy, liberality, and especially courage. Who readeth Aeneas carrying old Anchises on his back, that wisheth not it were his fortune to perform so excellent an act?[76]

and Ben Jonson adapts Quintilian's definition of the orator to the poet in *Discoveries*. English poets made high claims for their art as a moral and cultural force: Spenser declared that the aim of *The fairy queen* was 'to fashion a gentleman or noble person in virtuous and gentle discipline', and Milton thought Spenser 'a better teacher than Scotus or Aquinas'.[77]

To define what the humanists meant by wisdom is a delicate matter.[78] If I may simplify a complex issue, they turned away from the Metaphysical ideal of the Middle Ages, when theology was queen of the sciences and its study was guided by logic, towards an ethical ideal, often with a bias towards the active life (the Neo-Platonism of Ficino and Pico in its advocacy of contemplation looks back to scholasticism; but many humanists did still feel the attraction of the life of contemplation). Such an ideal was in harmony with Cicero's ideas of wisdom. In hundreds of passages of Renaissance literature, we find pictures of wisdom as self-knowledge, self-rule, moderation, superiority to circumstance, constancy, rationality, which are thoroughly classical in spirit. Plutarch and Ben Jonson share a similar belief in reason. The humanist idea of wisdom tended to emphasise the part played by natural reason, with the caveat that such reason is implanted in us by God. 'I call nature an aptness to be taught and a readiness that is grafted within us to honesty,' wrote Erasmus,[79] whose belief in the co-operation of nature and grace (here, he was in harmony with Aquinas)[80] and in the natural tendency of men to the good ('Now doth every man's mind incline unto that which is wholesome and expedient for his nature'[81]) was one of the issues in which he clashed with Luther, who viewed the will as corrupt and who accused Erasmus of paganism.[82] Erasmus thought that the virtuous pagans might have been saved because of their behaviour (here, he was in harmony with Dante); Luther thought they were damned because they had no faith in Christ. Luther was, like St Augustine,[83] ambivalent in his attitude to pagan wisdom; both felt that it was in opposition to Christian wisdom and that it might be used but not enjoyed. Erasmus believed rather that it was in a continuum with the Christian revelation and that it must be used (see the passage from *The antibarbarians* in chapter 2). As far as English literature is concerned, it was Erasmus' view which was on the whole victorious (though there were sometimes tensions, as in the famous passage in *Paradise lost*, where Milton turns the pagan gods into devils, and there were attacks on pagan literature by both Catholics and Puritans throughout the Renaissance).[84]

Humanists have sometimes been accused of anti-intellectualism, because of their attacks on the scholastic metaphysicians.[85] There is certainly a trace of this in Petrarch's essay *On his own ignorance and that of many others*, with its attack on Aristotle and the atheism of some of his modern followers, and the famous declaration that it is better to will the good than know the truth. However, in rejecting abstract philosophical speculation and also sometimes scientific enquiry, humanists did not come down on the side of simple innocence. Philosophy was replaced by scholarship and erudition. Elsewhere, Petrarch writes, 'Ignorance, however devout, is by no means to be put on a plane with the enlightened devoutness of one familiar with literature.'[86] Erasmus speaks of 'good letters, without which what is human life?'[87] and his *Antibarbarians* is a defence of learning against those who felt that it had no part in the Christian life; in it, he defines wisdom as 'virtus cum eruditione liberali', virtue joined to liberal learning.[88] Many passages from Erasmus praising cultivation of mind and making the Socratic connection between knowledge and virtue could be collected. 'What is most pernicious to man? Stupidity', he writes in *On giving children an early and a liberal education*,[89] and in *The education of a Christian prince* he stresses the need of the ruler for knowledge:

> How can anyone who does not know what is best direct it? Or even worse, if he considers the wickedest things the most desirable, being utterly misled by his ignorance or personal feelings? . . . There is only one means of deliberating on a question, and that is wisdom. If the prince lacks that, he can no more be of material assistance to the state than an eye can see when sight is destroyed.[90]

Similar ideas are expressed by English writers. 'Oh no, he cannot be good that knows not why he is good,' says the wise councillor, Philanax, in the *Arcadia*, whose heroine, Pamela, is described as 'she in whose mind virtue governed with the sceptre of knowledge'. In an aside in *The defence of poesy*, Sidney writes, 'it is manifest that all government of action is to be gotten by knowledge, and knowledge best by gathering many knowledges, which is reading'.[91] In Spenser's poem, *The tears of the Muses*, Urania praises knowledge:

> What difference twixt man and beast is left,
> When th'heavenly light of knowledge is put out,
> And th'ornaments of wisdom are bereft?[92]

'Men have been great, but never good by chance,' wrote Jonson,[93] whose poems are full of praises of action joined to knowledge, the man 'that does both act and know' (Marvell's phrase from the *Horatian ode*), and attacks on the ignorant barbarians who oppose him (see the three odes to himself).

The humanist rejection of abstract reasoning may have influenced some writers in their presentation of ideas. Erasmus thought that truth could not be arrived at step by step, by the logical process; rather he preferred to suggest it obliquely. Hence his fondness for the dialogue form and for the ironies of Lucian; the reader has to make a synthesis which embraces all the complexities which the author has suggested.[94] *The praise of folly* and *Utopia* are notoriously elusive and complex works, and such qualities may be found in other Renaissance writers. Debate and alternative points of view play an important part in Shakespeare's history plays, and Ben Jonson knew the value of ambiguity, irony and indirection in presenting moral issues, witness *Volpone*.[95]

## Men and affairs: history and ethics

For that knowledge of histories is a very profitable study for a gentleman, read you the *Lives* of Plutarch and join thereto all his philosophy [i.e. the *Moralia*] which shall increase you greatly with the judgement of most part of things incident to the life of man. Read also Titus Livius and all the Roman histories which you shall find in Latin, as also all books of state both old and new, as Plato, *De republica*, Aristotle, *Politics*, Xenophon . . . orations.

And as in these the reading of histories as you have principally to mark how matters have passed in government in those days, so have you to apply them to these our times and states and see how they may be made serviceable to our age, or why to be rejected, the reason whereof well considered shall cause you in process of time to frame better courses both of action and counsel, as well in your private life as in public government, if you shall be called.[96]

So wrote Sir Francis Walsingham, Elizabeth's secretary of state, to his nephew. History and moral philosophy were two branches of study which the humanists approved of and made popular. They were both concerned with the affairs of men in the world: 'the one shews what men should do, the other what men have said and done in the past, and what practical lessons we may draw therefrom for the present day', wrote the Italian humanist Pier Paolo Vergerio.[97] Many humanists — the courtier and diplomat Castiglione, for example[98] — were engaged in practical affairs; they wrote histories of their city or country, and treatises about the family and the court. This in turn suggested themes for imaginative literature: Shakespeare made plays out of historical subject-matter, Ben Jonson wrote poems about the ethical relationships between men — friendship and patronage.

In the humanist writings on these themes, there is often a mixture of practicality and ethical idealism. *The courtier* is characteristic, discussing questions of dress and of good government. The ideal of the virtuous and knowledgeable ruler was elaborated in many works, Erasmus' *The education of a Christian prince* and Elyot's *The governor*, as well as *The courtier*, despite the challenge to it made in Machiavelli's *The prince*. (Here the humanists combined the medieval tradition of the advice-book with a wealth of illustration from classical historians and philosophers.[99])

History, too, was seen in an ethical as well as a practical light; as can be seen from the passage by Walsingham quoted above, it was valued for offering moral and practical lessons to the present. History was immensely popular in the Renaissance.[100] Many praises of history could be collected, most of which would cite Antonius' definition of history from Cicero's *On the orator*: 'the witness of the ages, the light of truth, the life of memory, the teacher of life, the messenger of antiquity'.[101] History is often praised for being based on actualities and for bringing us the wisdom of experience: 'History provides the light of experience — a cumulative wisdom fit to supplement the force of reason and the persuasion of eloquence' (Vergerio).[102] It presents not just precepts but concrete examples, which are much more persuasive (Valla).[103] The Renaissance saw the beginnings of the modern study of history, with a more scientific approach to sources and evidence, a better understanding of chronology, developing interests in epigraphy and archaeology and in the details of a past civilisation (witness *On the ass*, the study of the Roman coinage by the French humanist Guillaume Budé). By deploying philological and chronological arguments, the Italian humanist Lorenzo Valla showed that the Donation of Constantine, on which the Papacy based its claims to temporal sway, was a forgery.[104] But history also continued to be viewed in the time-honoured way as a source of moral lessons.[105] In the Middle Ages, there had been compilations of moral examples drawn from history for sermons, and the moral approach to history was also encouraged by some classical historians: for example, in the preface to his history of Rome, Livy said that history was the best study for a sick mind, presenting examples of good and bad to imitate or to shun.[106] The assumption that human nature remains the same, so that the lessons of history are applicable to the present, was shared by Machiavelli, Sir Thomas Elyot and the Spanish humanist Juan Luis Vives:

> It is true there are those men who persuade themselves that a know-ledge of antiquity is useless, because the method of living all over the world is changed, as e.g. in the erection of elegant dwellings, the manner of waging war, of governing people and states. Since this opinion is opposed to the judgement of wise men, it is a strong indication that it is against reason. To be sure, no one can deny that everything has changed, and continues to change, every day, because these changes spring from our volition and industry. But similar changes do not ever take place in the essential nature of human beings, i.e. in the foundations of the affections of the human mind, and the results which they produce on actions and volitions. This fact has far more significance than the raising of such questions as to how the ancients built their houses or how they clothed themselves. For what greater practical wisdom is there than to know how and what the human passions are: how they are roused, how quelled? (*On the transmission of knowledge*)[107]

'Next in importance [to history]', writes Vergerio, 'ranks Moral Philosophy, which indeed is, in a peculiar sense, a "Liberal Art", in that its purpose is to teach men the secret of true freedom.'[108] Moral philosophy was the one branch of philosophy which appealed to the humanists. Disliking the technical aspects of philosophy, they did not aim to treat ethical topics according to a rigorous philosophical method; they aimed at a general rather than a specialised audience (Elyot's discussion of the moral virtues in *The governor* is typical). As with history, they pursued a literary ideal; Plutarch's *Moralia* and Cicero's moral treatises, even more than Aristotle's *Ethics*, were their chief models.[109]

Humanists found discussions of many ethical topics of interest to them in classical writers: good and bad counsel, flattery, friendship, the conferment of benefits. This was partly because there were similarities between the two societies, in the realm of patronage, for example: Jonson can apply Seneca on benefits to modern life with hardly any change in *An epistle to Sir Edward Sackville*. Plutarch's essay from the

*Moralia, How to tell a flatterer from a friend*, provides a good example of the kind of moral discussion which appealed to the humanists. It is alluded to by Erasmus in *The education of a Christian prince*, Castiglione, Elyot, Budé in *The education of the prince* and Montaigne in *On the inconvenience of greatness*;[110] Erasmus translated it into Latin and sent it to Henry VIII; Ben Jonson imitates a paragraph from it in *Epigram to a friend and son* (*Underwood*, LXIX).

Plutarch gives several tests for distinguishing the friend, who has the true interests of the great man at heart and who will praise the good in him but criticise the bad, from the flatterer, who is serving his own interests and knows how to work on the great man's vanity. The difficult flatterer to detect is not the obvious parasite but the man who assumes a frank and even bitter tone. One trick is to catch him out by changing your opinions and watching him alter his response to suit yours; shape-changing is the mark of the flatterer. Such an essay may seem to us rather dull; it is perhaps hard to see any relevance to our lives. But the issue of good counsel was a pressing one to the humanists;[111] it is discussed by More in *Utopia*, Erasmus, Castiglione, Machiavelli and Sir Thomas Elyot; Bacon wrote an essay *Of counsel*; Amyot praises history as the prince's only true counsellor in the preface to his translation of Plutarch's *Lives*. Plutarch says that flattery often overturns kingdoms; Clarendon says that it was the Duke of Buckingham's chief misfortune to have no true friend to give him good advice, and implies that one of the causes of the Civil War was Charles I's lack of good counsellors. For a literary treatment, we may think of Shakespeare's Richard II surrounded by flatterers, 'the weeds which his broad-spreading leaves did shelter'.[112]

Plutarch's essay had much to offer the writer. It provided the kind of psychological interest that we would today expect to find in a novel. Plutarch may set up ethical ideals — self-knowledge and disinterested friendship — but he knows that people deviate from them. There are hints about human behaviour which could be worked up in detail by a creative writer such as Shakespeare. Indeed, Plutarch's characterisation of the frank flatterer may recall to us Shakespeare's picture of the abrasive Iago ('This fellow's of exceeding honesty'; what a pity Othello had not read Plutarch), while Hamlet's gulling of Polonius:

*Ham.* Do you see yonder cloud that's almost in shape of a camel?
*Pol.* By th'mass and 'tis — like a camel indeed.
*Ham.* Methinks it is like a weasel.
*Pol.* It is backed like a weasel.

*Ham*. Or like a whale.
*Pol*. Very like a whale

puts into practice Plutarch's trick for detecting a flatterer.[113]

Plutarch's essay is not just an abstract discussion; it is full of concrete details, examples and anecdotes. This feature was imitated by Castiglione and Elyot, who both drew on the many quotable anecdotes in the *Moralia* and the *Lives* (indeed, the chief interest of Elyot's discussion of the virtues lies in the examples). In *Discoveries*, Ben Jonson speaks of the literary quality of

> life and quickness, which is the strength and sinews, as it were, of your penning, by pithy sayings, similitudes and conceits, allusions to some known history or other commonplace, such as are in *The courtier* and the second book of Cicero, *De oratore* [*On the orator*].[114]

'He that mindeth to persuade', wrote Thomas Wilson in *The art of rhetoric*, 'must needs be well stored with examples.'[115] The emphasis on the concrete fostered by humanism is of great importance for Renaissance literature. Erasmus constantly stresses that abstract discussion is of no value without exemplification from human experience; in order to persuade one must present things in a concrete way. In *On writing letters*, he says that nothing inflames us to virtue as much as examples, especially those of the famous, the old and the domestic. In *On abundance*, he gives examples of how to fill out a theme by giving concrete details: thus, 'we shall blame you for the war' may be filled out by detailing the particular horrors of war — the trampling of the harvests, the burning of farm and village, the deserted fields, old men left childless, children fatherless, mothers widowed, the extinction of the arts, the total confusion of every divine and human value, and so on (we may recall Shakespeare's son who has killed his father and father who has killed his son from *3 Henry VI*, as well as Burgundy's speech on the despoliation of the French countryside in *Henry V*). Erasmus goes on to stress the ideal of *enargeia* or *evidentia*, vividness, the ability to present a concrete picture, something in which he thought Homer excelled.[116] His collections of materials, *Adages, Parallels, Apophthegms*, furnished writers with stocks of concrete details which they could employ. An example of what Shakespeare could do with a classical anecdote is given by Emrys Jones: Macbeth's behaviour at the banquet at which Banquo's ghost appears is worked up from a hint about the tyrannical behaviour of Claudius in Suetonius. Ben Jonson devised the plot of *Volpone* from details about the behaviour of fortune hunters given by Lucian and other classical authors.[117]

## Religion and vernacular Scripture

I have stressed above that humanism was not an irreligious movement. On the other hand, it was not primarily concerned with religion, as were Lutheranism and Calvinism, and the other religious movements of the period. One cannot speak of the humanist attitude to religion as one can of the humanist attitude to the classics (although hostility to scholastic theology was a common note), and after the Reformation humanists could be either Roman Catholic or Protestant. The same is true of the poets who were influenced by humanist ideas.

In England, humanism in the period before the Reformation was closely associated with Erasmus. As I have indicated above, Erasmus' humanist ideas did go hand in hand with his religious ideas in a reforming programme, and both were influential in England; indeed his religious ideas probably helped to make his ideas about the classics more acceptable. English humanist circles were characterised by Erasmian enthusiasms for moderate reform of the Church, good works, lay piety and Scripture reading; *The handbook of the Christian knight*, which advocates a religion of the spirit rather than of ceremonies, and urges the layman to read both the classics and the Bible, was very popular. Humanist patrons encouraged publication of devotional works and translations from the classics. The break with Rome split the humanist group, but a considerable number gave their support to the king, and Thomas Cromwell's policies carried on the Erasmian tradition: conservative theology, together with church reform, hostility to saints' days and pilgrimages, encouragement of Bible reading in the vernacular. In the 1530s, quite a number of Erasmus' religious works appeared in English translation, including Tyndale's version of *The handbook of the Christian knight*.[118] From the reign of Edward VI onwards, Calvinism became an ever more dominant force, and Erasmus' religious ideas are only one strand in a complex picture; but an Erasmian strain of moderate, undogmatic, laicist piety persisted throughout the century and became embedded in Anglicanism.[119] In the religious feeling of English poetry, we find both the pessimism about the will and human endeavour engendered by Calvinism and the doctrine of predestination, and the moderate optimism and rationalism of Erasmus, who believed in the freedom of the will to respond to divine grace and the co-operation of the human and the divine (witness the *Paraclesis*).

The importance for English poetry of Erasmus' belief in the compatibility of the classics with Christian teaching has already been sufficiently stressed. There is one other part of Erasmus' religious programme which was of great importance for English literature – his belief that the Bible should be translated into the vernaculars and placed in the layman's hands. This belief was eloquently expressed in the influential *Paraclesis* (the Greek word for 'exhortation'), the preface to Erasmus' edition of the New Testament in Greek in 1516. An anecdote about William Tyndale, which went into Foxe's *Book of martyrs*, shows the connection between his plan to translate the Scriptures into English and Erasmus' preface, with its famous wish that the ploughman should sing a portion of the Scriptures at the plough:

> Soon after, Master Tyndall happened to be in the company of a learned man, and in communing and disputing with him drove him to that issue, that the learned man said: 'We were better be without God's law than the Pope's.' Master Tyndall, hearing that, answered him: 'I defy the Pope and all his laws'; and said: 'If God spare my life, ere many years I will cause a boy that driveth the plough shall know more of the Scripture than thou dost.'[120]

When Tyndale's translation of the New Testament from Erasmus' Greek version first arrived in England from Worms in 1526, it met with trouble from the authorities, who were suspicious of Tyndale's Lutheran tendencies; Bishop Tunstall had it burnt at St Paul's Cross, and Sir Thomas More wrote against it in *A dialogue concerning heresies*, 1529 (where he argued, less radically than Erasmus, that though there was no reason why the Bible should not be translated into the vernacular, the laity should be allowed only limited access to it). However, the movement for vernacular Scripture gained ground after the break with Rome, and by 1538 Cromwell was setting out injunctions that a Bible in English should be placed in every church and that the clergy should encourage laymen to read it. The official version was the Great Bible of 1539; this was Miles Coverdale's revision of 'Matthew's Bible', which in turn was based on Tyndale's and Coverdale's earlier versions. The second edition of the Great Bible in 1540 appeared with a preface by Cranmer, in which he made a very strong plea for the primacy of the Bible:

Here may all manner of persons: men, women; young, old; learned, unlearned; rich, poor; priests, laymen; lords, ladies; officers, tenants, and mean men; virgins, wives, widows; lawyers, merchants, artificers, husbandmen, and all manner of persons, of what estate or condition soever they be; may in THIS BOOK learn all things, what they ought to believe, what they ought to do, and what they should not do, as well concerning Almighty God, as also concerning themselves, and all others.[121]

He urges all men to read 'the whole story', and to commit to memory the passages they understand and to brood over what they do not understand, until God sends illumination.[122] Biblical story and phraseology became central to English literature. All later translations, including the Authorised Version, were influenced by the phrasing of Tyndale's version, and so here the Erasmian religious programme bore important literary fruit.

In all these areas, then, humanist ideas had an important influence on English life and letters. Humanism was certainly not just a question of school exercises and of a purely literary imitation of classical writers. Classical ideas affected people's thought and behaviour, and their interpretation of their lives; this in turn interacted with the literature of the period. One could choose one of the first English humanist poets, Sir Thomas Wyatt, to illustrate the interaction of life and literature. He participated in public life and undertook several difficult embassies; he was twice imprisoned, as a result of his friendships with Anne Boleyn and Thomas Cromwell. It is easy to see why the classical theme of quiet of mind appealed to him so deeply and recurs in his writings.[123] In his poem, 'Who list his wealth and ease retain', he backs up the moral maxims about the quiet life from the chorus from Seneca's *Phaedra* which he is imitating with a reference to his own experience: he recalls watching the execution of Anne Boleyn's 'lovers' out of his window in the Tower:

> The bell-tower showed me such sight
> That in my head sticks day and night:
> There did I learn out of a grate,
> For all favour, glory or might,
>     That yet *circa Regna tonat*.

By proof, I say, there did I learn
Wit helpeth not defence to earn,
Of innocency to plead or prate:
Bear low, therefore, give God the stern.
    For sure, *circa Regna tonat*.[124]

In 1527, he published *Quiet of mind*, the first English translation from Plutarch to appear in print, which was done from Budé's Latin version. In it he captures the tempered optimism of Plutarch's advocacy of a rational response to life's uncertainties:

> Therefore, as painters are wont in tables to underlay dim colours to the eyes and to interline and draw fair and bright colours upon them, so should men in their own minds all heavy and dark chances overcover and overthrow with glorious and fair chances worthy to be remembered ... For so variable, diverse and reboundable is the tune of this world as of an harp, nor in mortal things is there anything that is pure, clear and simple. But as music standeth by high and low sounds, and grammar by letters, vowels and mutes, and that he is not a musician or a grammarian whom eitherlike of these doth offend but he that can use them and temper them most accordingly, no notherwise it seemeth that he wisely hath stablished his life that most diverse chances contrary among themself hath learned to mingle handsomely, weighing prosperity with adversity. For clearly to set apart good or ill, mortal commodity will not suffer, but it behoveth to make a temper with both, if we will determine right of these things. It is not therefore according in the tone of these to plain, and fainting in the mind, to fall down as it were under too heavy a burden, but the power and the impression of every worst chance to repulse with the remembrance of better things, always wrapping up discommodities in commodities, as it were in a napkin, to make the tenor of the whole life made and gathered with prosperities and adversities, as a certain accord tempered with cunning reason.[125]

We can see the appeal of Plutarch's ideas to the Christian Wyatt: a good conscience is said to be the key to a quiet mind, and gloomy behaviour ingratitude to God. In the two very personal and Christian letters Wyatt wrote to his son in 1537, he recommends a similar moral constancy in the face of 'the chances of this troublesome world', and advises him to read the Stoic philosophers, Seneca and Epictetus, as well as keeping his grandfather's life in mind.[126] In all these writings, there is an Erasmian blend of classical and Christian, of literature and life.

One could equally well choose an example from later on in the period under consideration, that of Sir Richard Fanshawe, humanist translator of Horace and Virgil, and royalist soldier and diplomat. In his volume of translations from Horace, Fanshawe praises the Roman poet's rational morality, his tranquillity of mind and 'happy moderation';[127] he is himself presented as an embodiment of the Horatian virtues by his wife in her memoir of him. She says that he was 'ever much esteemed by his two masters, Charles the First, and Charles the Second ... he being so free from passion',[128] and she narrates several incidents to illustrate this Horatian tranquility. When he had been imprisoned after the battle of Worcester and had been granted an interview with her, she recounts how he 'was very cheerful in appearance' and said,

'Pray let us not lose time, for I know not how little I have to spare. This is the chance of war: nothing venture, nothing have; and so let us sit down and be merry whilst we may.' Then taking my hand in his, and kissing me, said 'Cease weeping. No other thing upon earth can move me. Remember we are all at God's dispose.'[129]

After recording his death, Lady Fanshawe quotes his translation of Horace's lines praising Lollius as the man upright in propitious and unpropitious times (*Odes*, IV. ix. 34-44).[130]

The need to rise above Fortune's blows through moral courage and 'a breast of proof' (Lovelace's phrase from his imitation of Horace, *Odes*, II. x, in *Advice to my best brother*) is one of the great classical/ Renaissance themes. It was the uncertainty of life in the period which made it so popular; Guicciardini said that when he considered all the hazards of life, he was always surprised to see an old man or a fertile season (*Ricordi*, CLXI).[131] In addition to the hazards of war and disease, there was no secure career structure for the upper classes; patronage was essential, and changes of ruler could bring about a complete reversal in a man's position. This is vividly brought to life in the very readable memoirs of Robert Carey, youngest son of Elizabeth's lord chamberlain.[132] Perhaps the most poignant expression in English literature of the dangers of great place and the need for moral uprightness is to be found in Sir Henry Wotton's brilliant epigrams upon the sudden restraint of James I's favourite, the Earl of Somerset:

Dazzled thus with height of place,
Whilst our hopes our wits beguile,
No man marks the narrow space
'Twixt a prison and a smile.

Then since Fortune's favours fade,
You that in her arms do sleep,
Learn to swim and not to wade;
For the hearts of kings are deep.

But if greatness be so blind,
As to trust in towers of air,
Let it be with goodness lined,
That at least the fall be fair.

Then though darkened you shall say,
When friends fail and princes frown,
Virtue is the roughest way,
But proves at night a bed of down.

At the end of our period, Abraham Cowley, who had lived through the Civil War and met disappointment in his hopes of preferment, embroiders in his *Several discourses by way of essays in verse and prose* (1668), in a lucid and relaxed vernacular, the themes of freedom of mind and content with little, drawing both on classical authors and on his own tastes and experiences for illustration.

NOTES

Works included in the Select Bibliography are cited here in abbreviated form only. References to Erasmus, *Opera omnia*, are to the Leyden edition; see p. 283. For Erasmus' letters I give the numeration in P. S. Allen's edition of the letters, *Opus epistolarum*; see p. 284. Translations in the Introduction are my own unless otherwise stated in the notes.

    1. Lewis, *English literature in the sixteenth century*, pp. 19-20. Lewis' attack on humanism was partly motivated by his feeling that medieval literature was undervalued by the literary establishment.

    2. Patrick Cruttwell, *The Shakespearean moment* (Vintage Books, 1960), chapter 8. Cruttwell's hostility to classical imitation should doubtless be seen in the context of the Leavisite movement to establish English as an independent discipline.

    3. Lewis, *English literature in the sixteenth century*, p. 281.

    4. Chapter 1, pp. 8-10.

    5. Cicero, *On the republic*, I. xvii. 28. For his use of *humanitas*, see e.g. *On the orator*, I. ix. 35; xvi. 71; lx. 256; II. xvii. 72; for *studia humanitatis*, see

*On behalf of Archias*, ii. 3; *On behalf of Murena*, xxix. 61.

6. *Attic nights*, XIII. xvii. 1 (Loeb translation).

7. On the meanings of *umanista*, *studia humanitatis* and humanism, see Campana, 'The origin of the word humanist'; Kristeller, *Renaissance thought and its sources*, pp. 21-3, 98-9, and notes, pp. 282-4; Kristeller, *Eight philosophers*, p. 16, and note 24, pp. 170-1; Pfeiffer, *History of classical scholarship*, pp. 15-17, who gives the quotation from Bruni. Skinner, *The foundations of modern political thought*, vol. I, pp. xxiii-xxiv, follows Kristeller in restricting the word 'humanist' to its Renaissance sense.

8. See Rice, *The Renaissance idea of wisdom*; Bolgar, *The classical heritage*; Kristeller, *Renaissance thought and its sources*, respectively. Gray, 'Renaissance humanism', gives an excellent account of humanist attitudes and pursuits.

9. For some accounts of the Renaissance which stress the continuity with the Middle Ages, see e.g. Bush, *The Renaissance and English humanism*; Dresden, *Humanism in the Renaissance* (especially chapter 5); Walter Ullmann, 'The medieval origins of the Renaissance' in *The Renaissance: essays in interpretation* (Methuen, 1982), pp. 33-82. On *dictatores* and humanists, see Kristeller, *Renaissance thought and its sources*, pp. 91ff; Seigel, *Rhetoric and philosophy in Renaissance humanism*, chapter 7; Skinner, *The foundations of modern political thought*, vol. I, pp. 28-41. Perhaps it should be noted here that when I speak of 'the humanist belief' in something, I do not necessarily mean that no one in the Middle Ages had had the same idea.

10. A point made by Panofsky, *Renaissance and renascences*, pp. 36-8. For examples of humanist praises of a new dawn, see Panofsky, pp. 9ff; Skinner, *Foundations of modern political thought*, vol. I, pp. 109-12; Ross and McLaughlin, *The portable Renaissance reader*, pp. 65-162.

11. On Petrarch's predecessors, see Reynolds and Wilson, *Scribes and scholars*, pp. 110-13; Pfeiffer, *History of classical scholarship*, pp. 3-5, who regards them as pre-humanists. On Petrarch, see also Hay, *The Italian renaissance in its historical background*, pp. 77-86; Kristeller, *Eight philosophers*, chapter 1; Seigel, *Rhetoric and philosophy in Renaissance humanism*, chapter 2.

12. On the spread of Italian humanism to the North, see the helpful accounts by Skinner, *Foundations of modern political thought*, vol. I, chapters 7-9, and Hay, *The Italian Renaissance in its historical background*, chapter 7. On the progress of humanism in England, see Caspari, *Humanism and the social order*, chapter 1.

13. See Kristeller, *Renaissance thought and its sources*, pp. 19-20, 25-8.

14. See e.g. Skinner, *Foundations of modern political thought*, vol. I, pp. 85-8; Seigel, *Rhetoric and philosophy in Renaissance humanism*, chapter 6. But see Eisenstein, *The printing press as an agent of change*, pp. 163-225, who, in a very interesting passage, argues that the intimacy felt by Petrarch and others with classical writers precludes the modern rational and historical interpretation of antiquity. Both ways of looking at the past were possible, see further pp. 36f.

15. See Panofsky, *Renaissance and renascences*, chapter 2; Bolgar, *The classical heritage*, chapters 3 and 4.

16. Scholasticism is another term of loose definition; most broadly it covers the aims and methods of the medieval educational system, but it is commonly applied to the characteristic thought of the key disciplines, philosophy and theology, in particular to the rational approach to religious doctrines. On scholasticism, see further Bolgar, *The classical heritage*, chapter 5. On the relationship between humanism and scholasticism, see Kristeller, *Renaissance thought and its sources*, chapter 5; Gray, 'Renaissance humanism', pp. 200-4; Skinner, *Foundations of modern political thought*, vol. I, pp. 103-9 (the latter two with

some criticisms of Kristeller's account).

17. Seigel, *Rhetoric and philosophy in Renaissance humanism*, examines the ideal of the orator in Petrarch, Salutati, Bruni and Valla, and gives many relevant quotations praising rhetoric; see also Gray, 'Renaissance humanism'.

18. It is often said that Greek culture was not really important for the Renaissance, and that knowledge of the language was not widespread. No doubt it is true that the humanists did not have the historical understanding of the Greek world attained in the nineteenth century, and they did not know about the oral element in the Homeric poems. Nevertheless, some Greek authors were very influential in the medium of Latin and vernacular translations, for example Plutarch (see pp. 37f). Aristotle's *Nicomachean ethics* and *Politics* were widely read in Leonardo Bruni's Latin translations. Emrys Jones argues convincingly that Shakespeare may have known Erasmus' Latin versions of Euripides' *Hecuba* and *Iphigenia in Aulis* (*Origins of Shakespeare*, chapters 3 and 4). Many excerpts from Greek writers were made known by Erasmus' *Adages* and *Apophthegms*.

19. See Kelley, *Foundations of modern historical scholarship*, p. 23.

20. See e.g. Bush, *The Renaissance and English humanism*, *passim*; Hay, *The Italian Renaissance in its historical background*, pp. 21-2, 132-3, 181-3; Skinner, *Foundations of modern political thought*, vol. I, pp. 92f; Eisenstein, *The printing press as an agent of change*, pp. 294-9.

21. See Kristeller, *Eight philosophers*, pp. 16-17.

22. *Opere latine*, ed. Antonietta Bufano (Classici UTET, 1975), vol. II, pp. 1046, 1122. An English translation of this essay will be found in Cassirer *et al.*, *The Renaissance philosophy of man*.

23. See further McConica, *English humanists*, especially chapter 3.

24. Erasmus, *Opera omnia*, vol. I, col. 1026B.

25. My discussion here is indebted to Boyle, *Erasmus on language and method in theology*. See also Hall, 'Erasmus: biblical scholar and reformer'; Pfeiffer, *History of classical scholarship*, chapter 7.

26. *On giving children an early and a liberal education*, *Opera omnia*, vol. I, col. 501D (Sherry's translation).

27. *On right pronunciation*, *Opera omnia*, vol. I, col. 913D.

28. *Opera omnia*, vol. IV, col. 698B-C. On the saying of Socrates, see p. 32, and p. 49, note 72.

29. Ibid., vol. V, col. 83F-84A.

30. Allen no. 2284.

31. In sixteenth-century English accounts, Erasmus, rather than Petrarch, is often credited with initiating the revival of learning (as he still is in the passage from Pope quoted below); see Elizabeth Mackenzie, 'What about Petrarch', *Review of English studies*, n.s., XXXIV (1983), pp. 458-63. For the importance of Erasmus for England, see Jones, *Origins of Shakespeare*, pp. 9-13, 96-7; Kaiser, *Praisers of folly*, pp. 19-24.

32. *The Cambridge history of English literature*, ed. A. W. Ward and A. R. Waller, vol. III, *Renascence and Reformation* (Cambridge University Press, 1908), pp. 19-21. The list of books which Alexander Nowell had when at Oxford in 1539 also includes much Erasmus (see Baldwin, *William Shakspere's small Latine*, vol. I, p. 174).

33. On Erasmus and the founding of St Paul's, see Baldwin, vol. I, chapters 4-6; Simon, *Education and society*, pp. 73-80.

34. On the friendship with More, see McConica, *English humanists*, pp. 36-42.

35. On Lucian, Erasmus and More, see Duncan, *Ben Jonson and the Lucianic tradition*, pp. 9-76, and Robinson, *Lucian and his influence*, pp. 165-97.

36. See further McConica, *English humanists*, especially chapters 5 and 6.

37. Jones, *Origins of Shakespeare*, pp. 11-12. For some further reminiscences of Erasmus by Shakespeare, see Kenneth Muir, *The sources of Shakespeare's plays* (Methuen, 1977), *passim*; L. T. Woodbridge, 'Shakespeare's use of two Erasmian colloquies', *Notes and queries*, n.s., XXX (1983), p. 122.

38. For the letter to Dorp, see Ben Jonson, ed. C. H. Herford, Percy and Evelyn Simpson, vol. VIII, pp. 633-4, and notes, vol. XI, pp. 280-1; vol. V, pp. 18f, and notes, vol. IX, pp. 678f. For *The alchemist*, see vol. II, p. 99.

39. Lines 687-96. For Pope's interest in Erasmus and the Renaissance, see Jones, 'Pope and dullness', pp. 234-8.

40. *On giving children an early and a liberal education*, *Opera omnia*, vol. I, col. 501D (Sherry's translation).

41. See Gray, 'Renaissance humanism', p. 216.

42. See Skinner, *Foundations of modern political thought*, vol. I, pp. 122, 241-3.

43. For Alexander and Aristotle, see Plutarch, *Lives*, *Alexander*, vii. 2-9, viii. 4-5; Quintilian, *The education of an orator*, I. i. 23; Cicero, *On the orator*, III. xxxv. 141; Aulus Gellius, *Attic nights*, IX. iii. 5-6; for Alexander and Homer, see Plutarch, *Alexander*, viii. 2-3; Cicero, *On behalf of Archias*, x. 24. Both examples are used by Castiglione in his defence of letters, see below, p. 165.

44. See Caspari, *Humanism and the social order*, chapters 1 and 6; Charlton, *Education in Renaissance England*; Simon, *Education and society*, *passim*.

45. See Bolgar, *The classical heritage*, pp. 196-7, 417-18.

46. For accounts of late medieval education, see P. S. Allen, *The age of Erasmus* (Clarendon Press, 1914), chapter 2; Watson, *The old grammar schools*, chapter 1.

47. Quoted Baldwin, *William Shakspere's small Latine*, vol. I, p. 128.

48. On the new grammar, see Jones, *Henry Howard, Earl of Surrey*, pp. xi-xiii.

49. On the importance of the notebook method, see Bolgar, *The classical heritage*, pp. 265-75.

50. See Jones, *Origins of Shakespeare*, pp. 5-8, 12-13, 18.

51. *Love's labour's lost*, IV. ii. 3-10, and see Baldwin, *William Shakspere's small Latine*, vol. II, chapter 36. For some other ways in which school exercises influenced Shakespeare, see Trousdale, *Shakespeare and the rhetoricians*, pp. 17-20.

52. See Herford and Simpson, vol. I, p. 254, and David McPherson, 'Ben Jonson's library and marginalia: an annotated catalogue', *Studies in philology*, LXXI (1974). I do not accept the latter's argument that the underlinings in Jonson's copy of Horace are probably not his own.

53. *English literature in the sixteenth century*, pp. 26-7.

54. From the preface to the Earl of Essex of the *Seven books of the Iliads*.

55. See e.g. the commentary of Bernardino Partenio (Parthenius) on Horace's *Odes and Epodes* (Venice, 1584), p. 43 (this is of interest as a book owned by Ben Jonson).

56. On Renaissance moralism, see Trousdale, *Shakespeare and the rhetoricians*, chapter 6.

57. For Drummond, see *The library of Drummond of Hawthornden*, ed. Robert H. Macdonald (Edinburgh University Press, 1971); for Jonson, see Herford and Simpson, vol. I, pp. 132, 136; for Erasmus, see Phillips, 'Erasmus and the classics'.

58. On Winckelmann, see Hugh Honour, *Neo-classicism*, (Style and Civilisation, Penguin, 1977), pp. 57-62; on the Victorians, see Richard Jenkyns, *The Victorians and ancient Greece* (Blackwell, 1980), p. 78 and *passim*.

59. *Pace* Cruttwell, *The Shakespearean moment*, pp. 209-10.

60. On Erasmus, see Robinson, *Lucian and his influence*, p. 179; on Jonson, see George Parfitt, *Ben Jonson: public poet and private man* (Dent, 1976), pp. 104-10.

61. For Seneca, see *Moral letters*, lxxxiv, 5-8; for Quintilian, see *The education of an orator*, X. i. 19; on Erasmus on imitation, see Cave, *The Cornucopian text*, pp. 36-54.

62. See Maren-Sofie Røstvig, *The happy man: studies in the metamorphoses of a classical idea*, vol. I (2nd edn, Oslo, Universitetsforlaget, 1962).

63. On Horace, see Erskine-Hill, *The Augustan idea in English literature*, pp. 169-74; on Ovid, see R. M. Ogilvie, *Latin and Greek: a history of the influence of the classics on English life from 1600 to 1918* (Routledge and Kegan Paul, 1964), chapter 1 (but he underestimates the influence of Horace's *Odes* in the period).

64. On Roman colour in the *Horatian ode*, see A. J. N. Wilson, 'Andrew Marvell, *An Horatian ode upon Cromwell's return from Ireland*; the thread of the poem and its use of classical allusion', *Critical quarterly*, XI (1969), pp. 325-41; on English panegyric, see Ruth Nevo, *The dial of virtue: a study of poems on affairs of state in the seventeenth century* (Princeton University Press, 1963), chapters 1, 3 and 4.

65. On *Poetaster*, see E. W. Talbert, 'The purpose and technique of Jonson's *Poetaster*', *Studies in philology*, XLII (1945), pp. 225-52; on *To Penshurst*, see the notes in Ian Donaldson's Oxford Standard Authors edition of Jonson's poems (Oxford University Press, 1975), p. 90, and Introduction, p. xvii.

66. See further Eisenstein, *The printing press as an agent of change*, pp. 181-225.

67. From *The peroration*, pp. 257, 259, 254. On changing attitudes to the vernacular in England, see Jones, *The triumph of the English language*.

68. On imitation in the vernaculars, see Bolgar, *The classical heritage*, pp. 317-29.

69. See further Simon, *Education and society*, pp. 121, 204; Jones, *Henry Howard, Earl of Surrey*, pp. xi-xxv.

70. The complexities of this ideal are charted by Seigel, *Rhetoric and philosophy in Renaissance humanism*, in the thought of Petrarch, Coluccio Salutati, Bruni and Valla, with many relevant quotations, e.g. pp. 79, 83-4, 101, 107-8, 140.

71. Cicero, *On the orator*, III. xxxv. 142-3, is a much quoted source for this ideal.

72. *Opera omnia*, vol. IV, col. 162D. A slightly different version of this anecdote is told by Apuleius, *Florida*, ii, which is referred to by Erasmus in the *Adages*, *Opera omnia*, vol. II, col. 602C. See also *Letters*, Allen no. 3141; *Language*, *Opera omnia*, vol. IV, col. 698C; *Adages*, *Opera omnia*, vol. II, col. 243B. For the idea of speech as the mirror of the soul, see also *Adages*, *Opera omnia*, vol. II, col. 67B-C (in the Toronto translation, vol. XXXI, pp. 141-2); *Paraphrase on St John's gospel*, *Opera omnia*, vol. VII, col. 499A-B. Ben Jonson also quotes the saying of Socrates, see below, p. 206.

73. E.g. Cicero, *On the orator*, I. viii. 30-4; xlvi. 202; II. i. 5; viii. 33-ix. 35; III. xxxv. 142-3; Quintilian, *The education of an orator*, I. Pr. 9-20. On the orator in the Renaissance, see Gray, 'Renaissance humanism'.

74. Quoted by Seigel, *Rhetoric and philosophy in Renaissance humanism*, p. 34.

75. *Paraphrase on St John's gospel*, *Opera omnia*, vol. VII, col. 499B.

76. Sir Philip Sidney, *An apology for poetry*, ed. Geoffrey Shepherd (Manchester University Press, 1973), p. 114.

77. For Spenser, see the letter to Raleigh about *The fairy queen*, *Spenser's Faerie queene*, ed. J. C. Smith (Clarendon Press, 1909), vol. II, p. 485; for Milton, see *Areopagitica*, ed. K. M. Lea (Oxford paperback English texts, Clarendon Press, 1973), p. 15.

78. See Rice, *The Renaissance idea of wisdom*.

79. In *On giving children an early and a liberal education* (Sherry's translation); see below, p. 57.

80. But see Bradshaw, 'The Christian humanism of Erasmus', pp. 442-3, who discusses the differences in the theological positions of Erasmus and Aquinas.

81. From the *Paraclesis* (Roy's translation); see below, p. 275.

82. See further Boyle, *Christening pagan mysteries*, chapter 3; Rice, *The Renaissance idea of wisdom*, chapter 5; Phillips, *Erasmus and the Northern Renaissance*, chapter 5.

83. On St Augustine's attitude to pagan wisdom, see Boyle, *Christening pagan mysteries*, chapter 1; Rice, *The Renaissance idea of wisdom*, chapter 1.

84. For some attacks on the classics, see Baldwin, *William Shakspere's small Latine*, vol. I, pp. 78, 108-13; Charlton, *Education in Renaissance England*, p. 64.

85. Lewis, *English literature in the sixteenth century*, pp. 29-31.

86. Quoted by Rice, *The Renaissance idea of wisdom*, p. 33.

87. Allen no. 1973.

88. *Collected works of Erasmus* (Toronto translations), vol. XXIII, p. 100.

89. *Opera omnia*, vol. I, col. 497E.

90. Born's translation, p. 174. See further Pfeiffer, *History of classical scholarship*, p. 74; Rice, *The Renaissance idea of wisdom*, pp. 156-63 (on Erasmus and Vives).

91. *Arcadia*, ed. Maurice Evans (Penguin, 1977), pp. 82, 520; *An apology for poetry*, ed. Geoffrey Shepherd, pp. 126-7.

92. *Spenser's minor poems*, ed. Ernest de Selincourt (Clarendon Press, 1960), p. 168.

93. In *An epistle to Sir Edward Sackville*, Herford and Simpson, vol. VIII, p. 156.

94. See Trousdale, *Shakespeare and the rhetoricians*, pp. 31-8; Gray, 'Renaissance humanism', pp. 207, 214.

95. On Shakespeare, see Jones, *The origins of Shakespeare*, pp. 14-15; on Ben Jonson, see Duncan, *Ben Jonson and the Lucianic tradition*, chapters 7 and 8, and also pp. 6, 69, 96. See also on the Erasmian subtlety of *The defence of poesy* Dorothy Connell, *Sir Philip Sidney: the maker's mind* (Clarendon Press, 1977), pp. 5-8.

96. From a transcript given in Conyers Read, *Mr Secretary Walsingham and the policy of Queen Elizabeth* (Clarendon Press, 1925), vol. I, p. 18.

97. Translated by Woodward, *Vittorino da Feltre*, p. 106.

98. Woodhouse, *Baldesar Castiglione*, relates the message of *The courtier* to the diplomatic life of its author.

99. Skinner, *The foundations of modern political thought*, vol. I, pp. 33-5, 40, 116-18, 213-15.

100. On history in the Renaissance especially in England, see further Charlton, *Education in Renaissance England*, pp. 246-52; Simon, *Education and society*, pp. 113, 385-6; Lily B. Campbell, *Shakespeare's 'histories': mirrors of Elizabethan policy* (University paperback, Methuen, 1964), pp. 18-116.

101. *On the orator*, II. ix. 36.

102. Translated by Woodward, *Vittorino da Feltre*, pp. 106-7.

103. See Kelley, *Foundations of modern historical scholarship*, p. 27.

104. See Skinner, *The foundations of modern political thought*, vol. I, p. 202.

105. See Frances A. Yates, *Renaissance and reform: the Italian contribution*,

*Collected essays*, vol. II (Routledge and Kegan Paul, 1983), chapter 8.

106. Livy, *From the founding of the city*, I. Pr. 10.

107. Translated Watson, *Vives: On education*, p. 232. On Machiavelli, see Skinner, *The foundations of modern political thought*, vol. I, p. 169.

108. Translated Woodward, *Vittorino da Feltre*, p. 106.

109. See Vives, *On the transmission of knowledge*, Watson, *Vives: on education*, pp. 253-4. On the importance of Plutarch, see further Charlton, *Education in Renaissance England*, pp. 241f.

110. *The education of a Christian prince*, trans. Born, p. 196; Castiglione, *The book of the courtier*, trans. Hoby, (Everyman edn)'p.72; Elyot, *The governor*, Book II, chapter xiv, 'The election of friends and diversity of flatterers'; Bude, see Skinner, *The foundations of modern political thought*, vol. I, p. 216

111. See further Skinner, vol. I, pp. 213-21.

112. Clarendon, *The history of the rebellion and civil wars in England*, ed. W. Dunn Macray (Clarendon Press, 1888), vol. I, pp. 42-3; 5, 59f, 182; vol. IV, pp. 4, 490; *King Richard II*, III. iv. 50.

113. *Othello*, III. iii. 262; *Hamlet*, III. ii. 368-73.

114. Herford and Simpson, vol. VIII, pp. 632-3.

115. See the whole section on example from Book III.

116. *On writing letters*, *Opera omnia*, vol. I, col. 387E; *On abundance*, *Collected works of Erasmus* (Toronto translations), vol. XXIV, pp. 576-7, 577f; *3 Henry VI*, II. v. 55-122; *Henry V*, V. ii. 23-67.

117. On Shakespeare, see Jones, *Origins of Shakespeare*, pp. 26-8; on Jonson, see Herford and Simpson, vol. II, pp. 50-3.

118. McConica, *English humanists*, chapters 1-6.

119. McConica, pp. 280-1; Simon, *Education and society*, p. 401.

120. Quoted Bruce, *The English Bible*, p. 29.

121. Quoted Bruce, p. 71.

122. See Simon, *Education and society*, p. 176.

123. See further Kenneth Muir, *Life and letters of Sir Thomas Wyatt* (Liverpool University Press, 1963), pp. 253-4; Patricia Thomson, *Sir Thomas Wyatt and his background* (Routledge and Kegan Paul, 1964), chapter 4.

124. *Collected poems*, ed. Joost Daalder (Oxford University Press, 1975), p. 186.

125. A text of Wyatt's translation will be found in *Collected poems of Sir Thomas Wyatt*, ed. Kenneth Muir and Patricia Thomson (Liverpool University Press, 1969), pp. 440-63.

126. A text of these will be found in Muir, *Life and letters of Sir Thomas Wyatt*, pp. 38-43.

127. *Selected parts of Horace, prince of lyrics* (1652), pp. 56-7, 71.

128. *The memoirs of Anne, Lady Halkett and Ann, Lady Fanshawe*, ed. John Loftis (Clarendon Press, 1979), p. 103.

129. Ibid., p. 134.

130. On Fanshawe, see further John Buxton, *A tradition of poetry* (Macmillan, 1967), chapter 6.

131. Quoted Woodhouse, *Baldesar Castiglione*, p. 195.

132. *The memoirs of Robert Carey*, ed. F. H. Mares (Clarendon Press, 1972).

EDUCATION: THEORY AND PRACTICE

**Erasmus:** *On giving children an early and a liberal education*

*Three passages on the importance of education*

*Erasmus was born in or near Rotterdam, some scholars think in 1466, others in 1469, the illegitimate son of a priest (although his father may not yet have been ordained at the time of his birth). He went to school in Deventer, and after his parents died in his teens, he was persuaded by his guardian to enter the monastery of the Augustinian canons at Steyn, although he had no vocation and was already keenly interested in humanistic studies. Sometime in the early 1490s, he escaped from the monastery to be secretary to the Bishop of Cambrai, and then to study in Paris at the university. It was not until 1517, when he had gained an international reputation as a scholar, that he obtained official dispensation from the Pope to live outside his monastery. Though courted on all sides with offers of employment, he preferred to remain independent; he accepted the nominal post of Councillor of the Empire in 1515. Erasmus was an apostle of peace (he wrote an essay on the adage 'dulce bellum inexpertis', 'war is sweet to those who have not tried it') and believed in tolerance and compromise; his later life was saddened by the split in the Church, and he was unwillingly drawn into controversy with Luther. Despite his criticism of many aspects of the Roman Catholic Church, he remained within it at the Reformation, subject to attacks from both conservatives and reformers. He died in Basle in 1536. Erasmus' output was prodigious; his complete works fill ten large folio volumes of double columns.*

De pueris statim ac liberaliter instituendis (On giving children an early and a liberal education) *was not published until 1529, but, as Erasmus explains in his dedication to William Duke of Cleves (Allen no. 2189), it belongs to the earlier period of his visit to Italy in 1506 to 1509, and was written to accompany the newly drafted* On abundance, *as an example of how to develop the same theme both briefly and copiously. A copyist in Rome had destroyed part of the manuscript, and it was only on the persuasion of friends, he writes, that he reconstructed it and had it published.*

*The essay is a strong plea that society should pay more attention to education. Following Quintilian, Erasmus argues for the importance of first impressions and the need to start forming the minds of the young early; he favours gentle persuasion rather than coercion. As well as Quintilian, the Plutarchan* The education of children *contributes to the discussion. The three passages given here, in the translation included in Richard Sherry's* A treatise of schemes and tropes *(1550), show eloquently Erasmus' belief in the educability of man, who has the seeds of virtue implanted within him, in the importance of knowledge, which cannot be gained solely from experience, and in the value of the intellect, without which man is a beast. The English writers on education, Elyot and Ascham, adopt many of the same arguments.*

*(i)*

And what living thing or what plant will be as the owner or husbandman would have it to serve for, except our diligence help nature? The sooner it is done, the better will it come to pass.

Indeed, to many dumb beasts, nature, the mother of all things, hath given more help to do their natural offices, but because the providence of God hath of all creatures unto men only given the strength of reason, she hath left the greatest part to education, in so much that one[1] hath written very well the first point, the middle and the third – that is, the chief of all man's felicity – to be good instruction and right bringing up. Which praise Demosthenes gave to right pronunciation,[2] and that indeed not falsely, but right bringing up helpeth much more to wisdom than pronunciation to eloquence. For diligent and holy bringing up is the fountain of all virtue; as, to folly and mischief, the first, second and third point is undiligent and corrupt education. This is the thing that is chiefly left unto us. That is the cause why unto other beasts nature hath given swiftness, flight, sharpness of sight, greatness and strength of body, scales, fleeces, hairs, horns, nails, venom, whereby they may both defend their health and provide for their living and bring up their young, and bringeth forth man only soft, naked and unfenced;[3] but, instead of all this, hath given him a mind able to receive all discipline,[4] because in this only are all things if a man will exercise it. And every living thing, the less meet it is to learning, so much the more it hath of native prudence. Bees learn not to make their cells, to gather juice and to make honey. The emmets[5] are not taught to gather into their holes in summer whereby[6] they should live in winter, but all these things be done by instruction of nature. But man neither can eat, nor go,[7] nor speak except he be taught. Then, if the tree bring forth either no fruit or unsavoury without the diligence of grafting, if the dog be unmeet to hunt, the horse unapt to joust, the ox to the plough, except our diligence be put to, how wild and unprofitable a creature would man become except diligently and in due time he should be fashioned by good bringing up! I will not here rehearse unto you the example of Lycurgus, known of every man, which bringing out two whelps, one of a gentle kind but evil taught that ran to the meat, that other of sluggish sires but diligently brought up that left the meat and leapt upon the beast.[8] Nature is an effectual thing, but education, more effectual, overcometh it.

NOTES

1. *One*: so far unidentified; the expression, 'first, middle and third' is a commonplace.

2. Quintilian, *The education of an orator*, XI. iii. 6. *Pronunciation*: delivery.

3. *Unfenced*: undefended, unprotected. There is perhaps an allusion here to Plato, *Protagoras*, 320D-321C.

4. *Discipline*: learning, branch of learning.

5. *Emmets*: ants.

6. *Whereby*: i.e. that whereby.

7. *Go*: walk.

8. Plutarch, *Moralia*, *The education of children*, 3A-B. (This sentence seems to lack a main verb. Or perhaps *that* . . . *that* are subjects, not relatives; if so, we should put commas after *taught* and *brought up*.)

*(ii)*

As they be scant half mothers which only bring forth and not up their children, so be they scant half fathers which, when they provide necessaries for their children's bodies, even so much that they may riot withal, provide not that their minds may be garnished with honest disciplines. Trees peradventure will grow, though either barren or with wild fruit; horses are foaled, though perchance they be good for nothing; but men, trust me, be not born but fashioned. Men in old time, which by no laws nor good order led their lives in woods in wandering lusts of body, were rather wild beasts than men.[1] Reason maketh a man, that hath no place where all things are governed after affection.[2] If shape and fashion should make a man, images also should be counted among men. Elegantly said Aristippus, when a certain rich man asked him what profit learning should bring to a young man; 'And it be no more but this', quoth he, 'that in the playing place one stone sit not upon another.'[3] Very properly another philosopher, Diogenes, I trow, bearing in the midday a candle in his hand, walked about the marketplace, that was full of men; being asked what thing he sought, 'I seek', quoth he, 'a man.' He knew that there was a great company, but of beasts and not men.[4] The same man, on a day, when standing on an high place he had called a great sort[5] together and said nothing else but 'Come hither men; come hither men.' — Some, half angry, cried again, 'We are here men; say what thou hast.' Then quoth he, 'I would have men come hither and not you, which are nothing less than men,'[6] and therewith drove them away with his staff.[7] Surely, it is very true that a man not instructed with philosophy nor other good sciences[8] is a creature somewhat worse than brute beasts. For beasts follow only the affects of nature; a man, except he be fashioned with learning and precepts of philosophy, is raught[9] into affections more than beastlike. For there is no beast more wild or more hurtful than a man whom ambition driveth, desire, anger, envy, riot and lust. Therefore, he that provideth not that his son may by and by be instructed in the best learning, neither is he a man nor the son of a man. Were it not an abominable sight that the mind of a man should be in a beast's body? As we have read that Circe, when she had enchanted men with her witchcraft, did turn them into lions, bears and swine, so that yet there should be still in them the mind of a man;[10] which thing Apuleius wrote[11] to have happened to himself, and Austin[12] also hath believed that men have been turned into wolves.[13] Who could abide to be called the father of such a monster? But it is a more marvellous monster that a beast's mind should be in a man's body; and yet do very many please themselves in such children, and both the fathers seem and the common people think such to be very wise.

It is said that bears cast out a lump of flesh without any fashion, which with long licking they form and bring into a fashion;[14] but there is no bear's young one so evil-favoured as a man is born of a rude mind.[15] Except with much study thou form and fashion this, thou shalt be a father of a monster and not of a man. If thy son be born with a copped head[16] or crook-shouldered or splay-footed or with six fingers in one hand, how loath wouldest thou be for it, how art thou ashamed to be called the father not of a man but of a monster! — and art thou not ashamed of so monstrous a mind? How discouraged be the fathers in their hearts if their wife bring forth a natural[17] and an infant of a brute mind. For they think they have begotten not a man but a monster and, except fear of the law did let[18] them, they would kill that that is born. Thou blamest nature, which hath denied the mind of a man to thy child, and thou causest by thine own negligence that thy son should be without the mind of a man. But thou wilt say, 'Better it is to be of a brutish rather than of an ungracious[19] mind.' Nay, better it is to be a

swine than an unlearned and evil man. Nature, when she giveth thee a
son, she giveth nothing else than a rude lump of flesh. It is thy part to
fashion after the best manner that matter that will obey and follow in
every point. If thou wilt slack to do it, thou hast a beast; if thou take
heed, thou hast, as I might say, a god. Straightway, as soon as thy
infant is born, it is apt to be taught those things which properly belong
to a man. Therefore, after the saying of Virgil,[20] bestow diligent labour
upon him even from his tender age. Handle the wax straightway while
it is very soft, fashion this clay while it is moist, season this earthen
vessel with very good liquor while it is new, dye your wool while it
cometh white from the fuller and is not defiled with any spots.

NOTES

1. Compare Plato, *Protagoras*, 322B-D; Cicero, *On invention*, I. ii. 2.
2. *Affection*: passion.
3. Diogenes Laertius, *Lives of eminent philosophers*, II. 72. *Playing place*:
i.e. theatre; in the Greek theatre, the seats were of stone.
4. Diogenes Laertius, VI. 41, 60.
5. *Sort*: number.
6. I.e. like nothing so little as men.
7. Diogenes Laertius, VI. 32, 60.
8. *Sciences*: branches of learning.
9. *Raught*: past participle of reach.
10. Homer, *Odyssey*, X. 233ff.
11. In *The golden ass*, a Latin novel (second century AD).
12. *Austin*: St Augustine.
13. *The city of God*, XVIII. xviii.
14. Pliny, *Natural history*, VIII. liv. 126. *Fashion*: shape.
15. A poor translation of the original: 'There is no bear cub so unformed in
shape as a man's mind is unformed at birth.'
16. *Copped head*: high, tapered head.
17. *Natural*: half-wit.
18. *Let*: prevent.
19. *Ungracious*: a poor translation. The Latin means 'wicked'.
20. *Georgics*, III. 74.

*(iii)*

Do we not see how that every beast not only doth beget young but also
fashion them to do their natural office? The bird is born to fly. Dost
thou not see how he is taught thereunto and fashioned by his dame? We
see at home how the cats go before their kitlings and exercise them to
catch mice and birds because they must live by them. They show them
the prey while it is yet alive, and teach them to catch it by leaping and
at last to eat them. What do harts? Do they not forthwith exercise their

fawns to swiftness and teach them how to run? — they bring them to high, steep-down[1] places and show them how to leap, because by these means they be sure against the trains of the hunters. There is put in writing as it were a certain rule of teaching elephants and dolphins in bringing up their young. In nightingales, we perceive the offices of the teacher and learner, how the elder goeth before, calleth back and correcteth, and how the younger followeth and obeyeth. And as the dog is born to hunting, the bird to flying, the horse to running, the ox to ploughing, so man is born to philosophy and honest doings; and as every living thing learneth very easily that to the which he is born, so man with very little pain perceiveth the learning of virtue and honesty, to the which nature hath grafted certain vehement seeds and principles, so that[2] to the readiness of nature is joined the diligence of the teacher. What is a greater inconvenience[3] than beasts, that be without reason, to know and remember their duty toward their young, man, which is divided from brute beasts by prerogative of reason, not to know what he oweth to nature, what to virtue and what to God? And yet no kind of brute beasts looketh for any reward of their young for their nursing and teaching, except we list to believe that the storks nourish again their dames forworn[4] with age and bear them upon their backs. But among men, because no continuance of time taketh away the thank of natural love, what comfort, what worship, what succour doth he prepare for himself that seeth his child to be well brought up! Nature hath given into thy hands a new-fallowed field, nothing in it, indeed, but of a fruitful ground, and thou through negligence sufferest it to be overgrown with briars and thorns, which afterwards cannot be pulled up with any diligence. In a little grain[5] how great a tree is hid; what fruit will it give if it spring out!

All this profit is lost except thou cast seed into the furrow, except thou nourish with thy labour this tender plant as it groweth, and, as it were, make it tame by grafting. Thou awakest in taming thy plant, and sleepest thou in thy son? All the state of man's felicity standeth specially in three points: nature, good ordering and exercise.[6] I call nature an aptness to be taught and a readiness that is grafted within us to honesty. Good ordering or teaching I call doctrine, which standeth in monitions[7] and precepts. I call exercise the use of that perfectness which nature hath grafted in us and that reason hath furthered. Nature requireth good order and fashioning; exercise, except it be governed by reason, is in danger to many perils and errors. They be greatly therefore deceived which think it sufficient to be born, and no less do they err which believe that wisdom is got by handling matters and great affairs without

the precepts of philosophy. Tell me, I pray you, when shall he be a
good runner which runneth lustily indeed but either runneth in the
dark or knoweth not the way? When shall he be a good sword-player
which shaketh his sword up and down winking?[8] Precepts of philosophy be, as it were, the eyes of the mind, and, in manner, give light
before us that you may see what is needful to be done and what not.
Long experience of diverse things profit much indeed, I confess, but to
a wise man that is diligently instructed in precepts of well-doing. Count
what they have done and what they have suffered all their life which
have gotten them by experience of things a silly[9] small prudence, and
think whether thou wouldest wish so great mischiefs to thy son. Moreover, philosophy teacheth more in one year than doth any experience
in thirty, and it teacheth safely, when by experience more men wax
miserable than prudent; in so much that the old fathers not without a
cause said a man to make a peril or be in jeopardy which assayed a
thing by experience.[10] Go to, if a man would have his son well seen in
physic, whether[11] would he rather he should read the books of physicians or learn by experience what thing would hurt by poisoning or
help by a remedy? How unhappy prudence is it when the shipman hath
learned the art of sailing by often[12] shipwrecks, when the prince by
continual battles and tumults and by common mischiefs hath learned
to bear his office! This is the prudence of fools, and that is bought too
dearly that men should be wise after they be stricken with mischief. He
learneth very costly which by wandering learneth not to wander.
Philippus wisely learned his son Alexander to show himself glad to learn
of Aristotle, and to learn philosophy perfectly of him to the intent he
should not do that he should repent him of.[13] And yet was Philip
commended for his singular towardness of wit. What think ye then is
to be looked for of the common sort? But the manner of teaching doth
briefly show what we should follow, what we should avoid; neither
doth it after we have taken hurt monish us, 'This came evil to pass;
hereafter take heed,' but or ever[14] ye take the matter in hand it crieth,
'If thou do this, thou shalt get unto thee evil name and mischief.' Let
us knit, therefore, this threefold cord, that both good teaching lead
nature and exercise make perfect good teaching. Moreover, in other
beasts we do perceive that every one doth soonest learn that that is
most properly belonging to his nature and which is first to the safeguard of his health — and that standeth in [avoiding][15] those things
which bring either pain or destruction. Not only living things but plants
also have this sense. For we see that trees also in that part where the
sea doth savour or the northern wind blow to shrink in their branches

and boughs, and where the weather is more gentle there to spread them further out.

And what is that that properly belongeth unto man? Verily to live according to reason, and for that is called a reasonable creature and divided from those that cannot speak. And what is most destruction to man? Foolishness. He will therefore be taught nothing sooner than virtue and abhor from nothing sooner than foolishness, if so be the diligence of the parents will incontinent[16] set awork the nature while it is empty.

NOTES

1. *Steep-down*: precipitous.
2. *So that*: provided that.
3. *Inconvenience*: incongruity, absurdity.
4. *Forworn*: worn out.
5. *Grain*: seed.
6. Plutarch, *The education of children*, *Moralia*, 2A-B.
7. *Monitions*: instructions, warnings.
8. *Winking*: with his eyes shut.
9. *Silly*: pitiable, miserable, poor.
10. An etymological point: *periculum* and *experientia*, danger and experience, are linked etymologically.
11. *Whether*: omit for modern syntax.
12. *Often*: adjectival, i.e. frequent.
13. Plutarch, *Lives*, *Alexander*, vii. 1-2.
14. *Or ever*: before.
15. *Avoiding* seems to have been missed out: it may be supplied from the Latin: 'ea sita est in vitandis iis'.
16. *Incontinent*: straightway, immediately.

## Erasmus: Letter to John and Stanislaus Boner

*Reading Terence*

*This letter (Allen no. 2584), a portion of which is omitted, is the dedication of an edition of Terence's comedies published in 1532. John Boner, the son of the governor of Cracow castle, together with his tutor, Anselm Ephorinus, had stayed with Erasmus in Freiburg in 1531. Erasmus here expresses characteristic sentiments about the importance of a good education, and outlines the way in which an author should be read at school level.*

'Habit formed in tender years is important,'[1] says the poet, and so we try to accustom the young from the start to what's best. That's the way to ensure that things which are naturally excellent come, through familiarity, to be what they like most. Nothing is better for a man than religious faith, and its first seeds should be instilled in babes with their mother's very milk. Next come the liberal arts; though they are not virtues in themselves, they prepare the mind for virtue by making it gentle and pliable instead of savage and cruel.[2] Aristotle says that the young are unsuited to learning moral philosophy,[3] which may be in some sense true. But it's less the fault of the subject or of the human mind than of bad teachers who either introduce it too late, when their pupils' minds have already been corrupted by a bad education and are full of evil desires, or teach it in an unpleasant and laborious way, more interested in showing off their own acuteness than in making their charges better men. But in fact there's nothing more natural than virtue and learning; if you take these two qualities from man, then he's ceased to be a man. Every animal finds it easiest to learn whatever skill it's been formed for by nature: horses are adept at galloping, dogs at hunting, birds at flying, monkeys at playing. There is no need, there-fore, to accuse nature. What matters is the source from which the first rudiments of religion and learning are drawn, and then the character of the guide who introduces the child to them, particularly in those tender years when the mind is still pure from vice, pliant as wax, ready to accept and to follow in everything the character of the person who moulds it.

And so, my excellent young men, I consider you fortunate on many counts: first, because you've been born in an age in which the pure forms of true religion and also of good literature have revived remark-ably. When I was a boy, religion was full of superstition, and almost everything that the young learnt at school with such torment was only fit for unlearning. Secondly, because you have a father who thinks that merely to make his children heirs to his wealth and position, which give him pre-eminence among persons of rank in Poland, is to do too little for their well-being, unless he can also make them rich and accom-plished in the true goods of the mind. He thinks he hasn't fulfilled the whole of a parent's duty unless he shapes your minds just as he begat your bodies; he knows that this is the better part of a man and his most precious possession. As a religious man, he is educating you not so much for himself as for Christ and the state. Your begetting was nature's work; but in ensuring that as soon as you left your mother's arms you were steeped in the best disciplines, he showed a true sense of duty; and in the choice of Anselm Ephorinus for the task he showed his sagacity, since Anselm's integrity, sense, loyalty, learning and care have been found in practice to be of the highest order. And so you must work all the harder to ensure that you aren't seen to let yourselves down, when every provision has been made for your happiness. The world has great expectations of you, and particularly of you, John Boner . . .

Sometimes before now I've written to urge you on, and I will do so again when the opportunity offers. But now, as a way of applying a kind of spur (even if you're already going at the gallop), I've formed the desire of publishing Terence's comedies in a much correcter form than before, under the auspices of the Boner name. It was your skill (yours and that of your servant Stanislaus Aychler) that made me want to do this; you've been in the habit of performing certain scenes before us so splendidly that everyone present has been full of admiration for your powers of imitation (as Quintilian says, the first sign of intelligence in a child[4]) and your memory. There's no writer from whom one can better learn a pure Latin style, and there's none more delightful to read or more suitable for young minds. Your teacher Ephorinus' skill will ensure that Terence proves beneficial both for your writing and for your character. On the one hand, a knowledge of men's varying characters and minds is an important part of wisdom, and, on the other, no rhetorician can teach propriety in characterisation better than Terence, or how to treat emotions, which are a principal source of charm in writing (Greeks call them *ēthē*). And again, the art of devising arguments is the most important of the divisions of oratory, and reading Terence is very helpful for developing skill at this for every kind of case. Not without reason have the critics praised this writer for his technique. If it's not too bold to say so, a single comedy of Terence shows more precise judgement than the whole works of Plautus. But with the work of such an author, as with a painting by Apelles,[5] it makes a great difference who you have to point out its qualities. If the critic is himself a true artist, reading Terence won't just amuse you, purify your style and improve your fluency and abundance; it will also teach you no small amount of moral philosophy – the only subject Socrates thinks that a man who wants to live happily ought to study thoroughly.[6]

And so, if I couldn't see that you were already full of enthusiasm, my dear John, I would be constantly urging you to think how much you are indebted to God, who in his generosity gave you such talents and such readiness to learn, and to whom you owe your father, Severinus Boner, and Anselm, your second father; I would urge you to remember what great expectations the eminent men who are watching your progress have of you, and finally to bear in mind how suited your time of life is for the liberal disciplines. You've not yet completed your fourteenth year, I think. In acquiring learning, one year of childhood is more valuable than ten years when the mind is busied with other cares and has lost its first openness to knowledge. And further, nothing sticks in the memory throughout life so firmly as what we learn as children.

I'll let you go now, after just advising you to practise hard at every kind of poetry, because those who neglect this area of learning derive less profit and less pleasure from the time they spend on writers who wrote in verse. They are also more liable to be misled by errors in the manuscripts, which the metrical scheme often reveals. But since the verse forms in Terence are rather confused and free, I've made a few notes which will, I trust, shed some light on them for the inexperienced. Farewell and make good use.

NOTES

1. Virgil, *Georgics*, II. 272.
2. Compare Seneca, *Moral letters*, lxxxviii. 20.
3. *Nicomachean ethics*, 1095A. (Aristotle's actual word here is *hē politikē*, politics, but for him ethics was a subdivision of politics.)
4. *The education of an orator*, I. iii. 1.
5. *Apelles*: famous Greek painter, fourth century BC.
6. See e.g. Xenophon, *Memorabilia*, I. i. 11-16; Cicero, *Academica*, I. iv. 15, *On the republic*, I. x. 15-16; Plato, *Phaedo*, 96B-99D, *Gorgias*, 507C-E, 526C-527E.

## Erasmus: *On abundance*

### The ideal of verbal dexterity

*Erasmus published* De duplici copia verborum ac rerum commentarii duo *(Two books of commentary on the twofold abundance of words and things) together with* On the proper system of study *in 1512 as 'a small literary contribution to the equipment' of the newly founded St Paul's. Several revised and enlarged editions followed, the fullest in 1534, and the book was indeed much used in English schools. It is a vast collection of methods of expression and ways of manipulating both words and themes; though devised for Latin, much of it is applicable to composition in English.*

*In this introductory section to the work, Erasmus sets out the ideal of verbal control, when a speaker or writer can say as much or as little as he likes, and suggests some exercises which help to attain it. Later in the book, he gives a virtuoso performance of two sets of variations on two short themes; from his several hundred variations on the second one, 'semper dum vivam tui meminero', 'always as long as I live I shall remember you', Shakespeare may have gained some ideas for Hamlet's speech to the ghost promising remembrance (Hamlet, I. v. 95-104) and for sonnet 24 (see Jacobsen, Translation, pp. 117-18).*

*That brief and copious speech are aspects of the same art*
There may be those who greatly admire Homer's Menelaus, 'not a man of many words',[1] and dislike his Ulysses, who 'flowed like a river swollen with the snows of winter'.[2] But even such people with a real relish for the Laconic style[3] and brevity ought not to object to this work of mine; they too should find it useful, because successful brevity and successful abundance seem to be governed by the same principles. Plato's Socrates argues neatly that the same individual should be good at both lying and telling the truth;[4] in the same way, no craftsman in words will be as skilful at keeping what he says within narrow limits as one who's equally expert at expanding it with every kind of embellishment. If conciseness of language is the aim, who can speak more briefly than someone who can pick out at once, from a vast cohort of words and the whole range of figures, whatever will contribute most to brevity? And as for brevity of thought, who will find it so easy to deal with a subject in the minimum number of words as someone who is well aware what are the main points and, as it were, pillars of a case, what the next most important points and which points have just been brought in to flesh it out? Certainly no one can see what can be left out without damage as quickly and reliably as someone who's seen what can be added and how.

*On those who make a foolish affectation either of brevity or abundance*
But if we find ourselves drawn in either of these directions, there's a danger of our making a mistake that one sees certain misguided admirers of the Laconic style falling into. These people use few words, but even of the few many (one might almost say all) are superfluous. On the other hand, inexperienced speakers who aspire to abundance are sometimes excessively verbose but still say too little, because they leave out many essential points. So the aim of my precepts will be to show how to encapsulate the essence of a subject in as few words as possible, without leaving anything out, or how to develop it with an expansiveness that none the less introduces nothing superfluous. So after learning the principles, you'll be free to strive after the Laconic, if you want,

or to imitate the Asiatic exuberance, or to embody the middle way of Rhodes.[5]

### That abundance is of two kinds

It is clear, I think, that abundance is of two kinds. We have, for instance, the evidence of Quintilian, who expresses particular admiration among Pindar's qualities for his most happy abundance in both matter and expression.[6] Abundance of expression consists in the use of synonyms, heterosis or alteration of grammatical forms, metaphor, changes in sentence form, equivalent expressions and other such techniques of variation. Abundance of subject-matter lies in assembling, expanding and amplifying arguments, examples, contrasts, similarities, dissimilarities, oppositions and other such features, which will be described more fully in their proper place. The two forms can sometimes appear so inter-linked that it's hard to separate them, since the one is often so impor-tant to the other that the distinction seems to be one of theory rather than practical experience; for teaching purposes, however, I shall divide them, but in a way that ought to guard me against charges both of pedantic hair-splitting and of sloppiness.

### What this training is useful for

To encourage students to tackle this subject with more enthusiasm, I shall now briefly explain what it is useful for. First, to practise varying one's speech will have considerable influence on one's style in general. More specifically, it will help in avoiding tautology, an ugly and objec-tionable fault. This is 'the repetition of the same word or phrase'.[7] It often happens that we have to make the same point several times. If we falter when this happens, because we lack resources of style, or keep on chanting the same thing like cuckoos and can't put different colours and semblances on the thought, we'll not just make fools of ourselves by revealing our infantile incompetence in speech but also kill our poor audience with boredom. Worse than tautology, as Quintilian says,[8] is 'homoeology', a style with no charm of variety to relieve boredom but all of the same tone. Who has such long-suffering ears that he can put up even for a short time with a style that never varies? Variety is so important in every sphere that nothing, however splendid, can avoid seeming dull without its aid. Nature herself delights perhaps above all else in variety; in the whole immense array of things, there is nothing she has left out and not adorned with some wonderful device of variety. Just as the eyes linger longer where they have varied things to look at, so the mind is always looking round for new objects, as it were, for its attention. If everything that strikes it from every side is just the same, it quickly turns away in boredom, and so the whole effect of the speech is lost. But this disaster is easy to avoid for anyone who knows how to turn the same idea into more shapes than even Proteus[9] transformed himself into. Further, this training will contribute greatly to facility in speaking or writing extempore, and will ensure that we don't keep hesitating in confusion or lapsing into humiliating silences. It won't be difficult to turn even a rashly undertaken speech neatly to the end we desire, when we have so many formulae ready for use. And it will be of considerable help to us in interpreting authors, translating from foreign languages and in writing verses; in all of these areas, without a training in these techniques, we'll often produce work that proves over-complicated or wooden, or we just won't be able to produce any.

*What system of exercise develops this skill*

Next it remains for me to indicate briefly what forms of exercise develop this skill. Once the rules have been carefully learnt by heart, we should often take an idea and deliberately express it in as many different ways as possible; Quintilian advises this, and compares the way in which a single piece of wax can be moulded into innumerable different shapes.[10] This exercise will prove even more useful if several students compete with one another, orally or in writing, on a theme set for them all. Individuals will benefit from one another's ideas, and each student, with the help of this handle, as it were, will have more ideas himself. Next we will treat a whole subject in several ways. Here it will help to imitate Milo of Croton's[11] technique, first treating a theme in two different ways, then three, then more and more, until finally we achieve such fluency that we can produce a hundred or two hundred variations without any difficulty. We can also improve the abundance of our style greatly by translating Greek writers, because the language is extremely rich in matter and words. Sometimes it may prove more useful to compete with them by paraphrasing their works. It's extremely worth while to reshape poems in prose, or to confine free prose within the limits of metre, or to treat the same subject in different verse-forms. It's also very helpful to take as a model a passage from a particular author that seems absolutely bursting with abundance and to try to match or even surpass it on our own account. And we will benefit enormously from 'handling good authors by both night and day',[12] particularly those such as Cicero, Aulus Gellius and Apuleius[13] who were outstanding for the abundance of their style. We should observe all the figures in their works attentively, memorise them when we've observed them, imitate them when we've memorised them, and so by frequent use come to have them at our fingertips.

## NOTES

1. *Iliad*, III. 214.
2. Erasmus seems here to be misquoting *Iliad*, III. 222. The Homeric passages were traditionally cited as providing examples of the plain and grand styles; see e.g. Quintilian, *The education of an orator*, XII. x. 64-5.
3. *Laconismus*, a word used by Cicero, *Letters to his friends*, XI. xxv. 2.
4. Plato, *Lesser Hippias*, 366E-369B.
5. The three styles of oratory were the Attic or plain style, the Asiatic or ornate style and the Rhodian or intermediate; see Cicero, *Brutus*, xiii. 51; Quintilian, *The education of an orator*, XII. x. 16-19.
6. Ibid., X. i. 61.
7. Ibid., VIII. iii. 50.
8. Ibid., VIII. iii. 52.
9. *Proteus*: the old man of the sea, who used to change his shape to avoid questioning, see Homer, *Odyssey*, IV. 384ff.
10. *The education of an orator*, X. v. 9.
11. An athlete who trained himself to carry a bull by lifting it every day from when it was a calf (ibid., I. ix. 5).
12. Horace, *The art of poetry*, 268-9.
13. *Aulus Gellius*: (second century AD) the author of an influential compendium, *The Attic nights*; *Apuleius*: his contemporary, the author of the prose tale, *The golden ass*.

## Erasmus: *On the proper system of study*

*The germination of the ideas in* De ratione studii ac legendi inter-pretandique auctores liber *(A book on the proper system of study and of reading and interpreting authors) goes back to the time when Erasmus was teaching pupils in Paris; in 1512, he set them out fully in print (there had been earlier drafts and an earlier pirated edition). The programme sketched in it is very close to the practice of English schools in the sixteenth century as it can be gauged from the curricula: the same set of authors was used and the same sequence of grammar, authors and compositional forms was followed (see further Baldwin,* William Shakspere's small Latine, *chapters 4, 6, 7).*

*In the first passage, we may note the emphasis on the importance of language, the approach to grammar through simple rules and the study of authors, rather than complex rules, and the recommendation to keep a notebook to enter details of expression. The second passage gives examples of the kind of exercises to set, and brings home to us the intensive training in literary skills received at school. For explanations of the rhetorical terms found in these passages, I would recommend looking at the Loeb edition of the pseudo-Ciceronian* To Herennius, *or at Thomas Wilson's* The art of rhetoric; *explanations of the themes given in the second passage will be found in the notes to the version of* On the proper system of study *in the Toronto translation of Erasmus (vol. XXIV).*

## (i) The school programme

First, all learning seems to be divided into two parts: learning of things and of words. That of words comes first, that of things is more important. But some people neglect the study of language as they rush in 'without wiping their feet', as the saying is, to learn about things, and by this mistaken attempt to make a saving they incur a heavy loss. For since no knowledge of things can be gained except through the verbal signs that denote them, anyone who isn't expert in the force of language inevitably is also constantly blind, deluded and like a madman in his judgement of things. Further, one finds in fact that nobody quibbles about trivial points of language more often than people who boast of not troubling about words but just considering the subject. And so it's essential to get the best teaching in both areas from the start and from the best teachers. For what could be sillier than to learn with great effort something that you'll have to unlearn later with even greater effort? Nothing is easier to learn than what's right and true. But if false beliefs once get fixed in the mind, it's astonishing how hard they are to remove.[1]

So Grammar can claim first place for itself, and it must be taught to children from the start in two forms, Greek and Latin. This isn't just because almost everything that's worth knowing is recorded in these two languages, but also because they're so closely related that it's easier to learn them both together than one without the other (certainly than learning Latin without Greek). Quintilian prefers us to start with Greek, but on condition that we go quickly on to Latin as soon as we know some Greek; at all events he advises us to take equal trouble over both, since then neither will interfere with the other.[2] So the rudiments of both languages must be learnt immediately, and from a really good teacher; if such a teacher isn't available, then — the next best thing — the best text-books should certainly be used; I think these should be few in number but very carefully chosen. Among Greek grammarians everyone grants first place to Theodore Gaza; in my view Constantine Lascaris can rightfully claim second place.[3] Of the earlier Latin grammarians, Diomedes.[4] Among the more modern ones I don't see much to choose, except that Niccolò Perotti seems to be the most thorough, though avoiding pedantry.[5] But though I admit rules of the kind they teach to be necessary, I'd like them to be kept to the minimum possible, provided of course that they're good. I've never approved of the common run of teachers who delay pupils for years while they drum rules into them.

In fact the best way of acquiring a real ability to speak without mistakes is, on the one hand, to talk and associate with people who speak correctly and, on the other, to read good writers constantly; the first ones to absorb are those who, as well as being thoroughly correct stylists, can also entertain the student by the attractiveness of their subject-matter. In this class, I would grant first place to Lucian, second to Demosthenes, third to Herodotus. And in poetry first place to Aristophanes, second to Homer, third to Euripides. (I might have put Menander[6] even first, but his works are lost.) And among Latin authors what better model of style is there than Terence? – pure, polished, close to colloquial speech, and popular with the young by the very nature of his subject-matter. If anyone thinks that some selected comedies of Plautus, free from obscenity, should also be included, I certainly don't object. Second will come Virgil, third Horace, fourth Cicero, fifth Caesar. If anyone thinks Sallust should be added, I wouldn't dispute the point strongly. I think these writers are sufficient to learn both languages from. I don't approve of people who spend their whole lives in going through writers of whatever quality with this in mind, and consider anyone who's missed the least scrap of writing as a mere speechless child.

Once some power of speaking correctly (if not ornately) has been achieved, attention must be turned to learning about things. One can acquire quite a considerable acquaintance with things *en passant* from the writers we read to polish our style, but it's traditionally to Greek authors that we should turn for almost all knowledge of this kind. For what purer, quicker or more delightful source could you find to draw from than the fountain itself? But perhaps it's more appropriate for me to discuss elsewhere the order the disciplines should be learnt in and the best choice of teachers. Let's revert for the moment to the programme for beginners. In order to get greater and swifter benefit from the authors I've named as stylistic models, I think you should read with care Lorenzo Valla's book, which is very elegant itself, *On the elegance of the Latin language*.[7] With the help of his rules, you'll make a number of observations yourself. For I don't want you to follow Valla's precepts in everything as though you were his slave. It will also be worth while to learn the figures of speech recorded by Donatus[8] and Diomedes, to memorise the rules of the various forms of poetry, and to be quite familiar with the main points of rhetoric, i.e. propositions, topics used in proof, embellishment, amplification, formulas of transition. All this is helpful for imitation as well as for criticism.

Equipped in this way you'll take careful note in your reading of any striking word that occurs, of anything expressed in an archaic or novel way, arguments that are cleverly devised or neatly turned, any outstanding elegance of style, any adages, historical parallels and general statements that are worth remembering. These passages should be indicated by some appropriate mark. (You should use several kinds of mark specially designed to show immediately what the point of interest is.) If anyone decides that Dialectic ought to be added to all this, I won't resist too much, provided it's learnt from Aristotle and not from the babbling tribe of Sophists,[9] and provided the student doesn't stop there and as it were grow old (in Gellius' phrase[10]) by these Sirens' rocks.

But remember all the while that 'the best teacher of style is the pen'.[11] It should be given constant practice in verse, in prose and on every kind of subject.

NOTES

1. See Quintilian, *The education of an orator*, II. iii. 1-3.
2. Ibid., I. i. 12-14. In English schools, Greek was taken up at a later stage than Latin.
3. Theodore Gaza and Constantine Lascaris were Greek scholars who lived in Italy in the fifteenth century.
4. *Diomedes*: grammarian of the fourth century AD.
5. Perotti's *Rudiments of grammar*, 1468, ousted the medieval Latin grammars.
6. *Menander*: writer of New Comedy, fourth century BC.
7. Valla's *Elegancies*, 1471, a detailed study of classical Latin usage, was a very influential book; over fifty editions were published by 1550. Erasmus admired it greatly and published an epitome in 1531, which became a popular schoolbook.
8. *Donatus*: the most famous grammarian of the fourth century AD.
9. *Sophists*: itinerant teachers of ancient Greece who claimed to impart the art of success and became proverbial for arguing any point of view; the term is here applied as one of abuse to the scholastic theologians.
10. *Attic nights*, XVI. viii. 17.
11. Cicero, *On the orator*, I. xxxiii. 150, quoted by Quintilian, X. iii. 1.

## (ii) Rhetorical exercises

From this point, they should be given themes for discussion as exercises. The main point to guard against here is that these shouldn't (as often happens) have silly subjects or be badly expressed, but should contain some clever or attractive thought (not too far removed, however, from a child's natural interests): in this way, while they're busy on the exercise, they can also learn something that will help them later in more serious studies. So a theme set for children should perhaps relate to some striking incident. For instance: the rash impetuousness of Marcellus endangered Rome's fortunes but the cautious delays of Fabius restored them. (Though there's a moral too here, that plans made in haste seldom work out well.) Or: it's hard to decide who was more foolish, Crates who threw gold in the sea or Midas who thought there was nothing better than gold. Or: excessive eloquence brought ruin to Demosthenes and Cicero. Or again: no praise can match the deserts of King Codrus, who thought that his people's safety was worth buying at the cost of his own life. It won't be difficult to collect instances of this kind from historians, particularly Valerius Maximus.[1] Alternatively, it should contain a myth, as for instance: Heracles won himself immortality by slaying monsters; the Muses take especial delight in springs and groves, and shun smoky cities. Or a fable: it was a good lesson the lark taught, that one shouldn't rely on one's friends to do a job one can do oneself.[2] Or: everyone sees the bag hanging on his front but nobody the one behind his back.[3] Or: it was sensible of the fox to prefer keeping the mosquitoes which were almost full, rather than squashing them and making room for some more that were empty and thirsty to drink all the blood it had left. Or a maxim such as: how different from most people today was he who preferred a man without money to money without a man.[4] Or: Socrates was right to despise those who don't eat to live but live to eat. Justly did Cato disapprove of those whose palates are sharper than their minds. Or a proverb, such as: let the cobbler stick to his last. Or: not everyone can sail to Corinth.[5] By publishing so many thousands of them myself I've ensured that they aren't hard to find. Or a moral saying, such as: nothing costs more than what is bought with prayers. And: flattery produces friends, truth hatred. And: friends at a distance are no friends. Or the remarkable properties of some object, as for instance: the magnet attracts iron, naphtha attracts fire. Or: such is the nature of the palm-tree that when a weight is put on it, far from being bent towards the ground, it thrusts upwards and raises itself higher. Or: the remarkable ability of the polypus to change its colour to match the ground beneath it and so escape the fisherman's wiles. Or perhaps some impressive figure of speech, such as a 'ladder': wealth leads to luxury, luxury to satiety, satiety to ferocity, ferocity to widespread hatred, hatred to destruction. Or a simile, such as: just as, if you use iron, it gets rubbed away, but if you don't it's devoured by rust, so too, if you use your mind, it's ground down by effort, but if you don't it comes to worse harm through idleness and decay. Or an allegory, such as: don't add fire to fire, don't pour oil on a conflagration. Or a rhetorical reversal, such as: I don't hold this opinion of you because I love you dearly, but I love you dearly because I've formed this opinion of you. Or a rhetorical division, as: he's too stupid to be able to keep silent but too much a child to be able to speak. He's too simple to be able to lie, too moral to want to. It's enough for me just to give these hints. Or some particularly elegant turn, which is something I needn't give examples of. But there's no reason why the same exercise shouldn't contain several of these features (for instance a moral maxim, a historical incident, a proverb and a figure of speech). And so the teacher, who ought to be constantly reading good authors, will collect such 'flowers' everywhere and will set a selection of them to his pupils as themes, or perhaps adapt them to a form that's suitable for young minds.

Once the child has acquired some skill in speech from these exercises, he can be recalled, if it seems appropriate, to more advanced rules of grammar; these should be taught so arranged that the easiest rules, briefly expressed, come first; more complicated rules should be added, each in its proper place, as the students' minds grow more mature. You can find an example of such arrangement in Theodore Gaza's grammar. Pupils shouldn't, however, be detained long on these topics, but quickly moved on to more serious authors, particularly if they've already learnt the main points of rhetoric that I mentioned earlier, and also figures of speech and verse-forms. At this stage, they should be given harder themes as exercises, and to choose and explain these a conscientious and learned teacher is needed. But a teacher of only moderate ability, provided he's modest, won't mind asking for some from a more learned colleague. Here are some possible kinds of theme. Sometimes the teacher should state in the vernacular a clever subject for a short letter, to be treated in Greek or Latin or both. On other occasions, a fable, or an interesting anecdote, or a general statement made up of four parts (two statements with a comparison or explanation attached to each). Or a demonstration to be handled in five sections or a dilemma in two, or an 'elaboration' as it's called, to be developed in seven parts.[6]

Sometimes, as a kind of preparation for rhetoric, they should handle one of its divisions on its own. (Aphthonius[7] wrote preliminary exercises of this kind.) For instance, praise, blame, a legend, a comparison, a contrast, or a figure of speech, a description, a division, an imaginary dialogue, a suggested answer, a characterisation through concrete details. Sometimes they should be told to turn a poem into prose, or a piece of prose into verse. Sometimes they should imitate a letter of Pliny or Cicero, in vocabulary and figures. Sometimes they should express the same idea several times in different words and figures; or in both Greek and Latin, in both verse and prose. Sometimes they should set out the same idea in five or six different verse-forms prescribed by the teacher. Sometimes they should reshape one idea with as many commonplaces and rhetorical figures as possible. But the most useful exercise is translating from Greek. They should be made to practise this constantly and with great care. For once one applies one's mind to catching the force of the writer's ideas and looks closely at the force and special characteristics of each of the two languages, one also comes to appreciate what we have in common with the Greeks and what we don't. And to reproduce Greek's power of implying more than it says all Latin's resources have to be put to use. Children may find all this hard at first, but practice will make it easier, and the teacher's intelligence and care will spare the children a good part of the difficulty by helping them with the parts he thinks are too difficult for them.

These exercises should be interspersed with frequent reading of authors, to provide a model for imitation. Nevertheless, after setting a theme, the teacher also ought to suggest a good number of possible words and figures. But subsequently, by just setting bare subjects, he ought also to give them the task of finding their own material, so that each of them has to discover for himself the resources needed to handle the theme and to enrich and embellish it. Here, too, choice and variety of theme depend on the care of a learned teacher, but I can give a specimen now. He will often set a subject for different kinds of letter: letters of persuasion, dissuasion, encouragement or discouragement, narration, congratulation, expostulation, recommendation, consolation. First, he will describe the general character of each and list some commonplaces and generally applicable formulas; then he will set a subject and suggest particular points. Sometimes he will give them a kind of theme for declamation in the different genres of oratory:[8] he might tell them, for instance, to criticise Julius Caesar or praise Socrates in the epideictic manner. Likewise, in the persuasory manner: that one should study the best subjects from the start; happiness doesn't consist in wealth; a mother should feed the child she has borne with her own milk; one should, or one shouldn't, study Greek literature; one should, or shouldn't, take a wife; one should, or shouldn't, travel. Or in the judicial style: Marcus Horatius does not deserve punishment. With pupils who are entering this arena for the first time, the person who has undertaken the responsibility of teaching them will not object to stating first how many main propositions the case can be handled under; then he will show what the proper order for the propositions is and how one follows from another; then how many arguments should be used to support each proposition and how many proofs for each argument; then the circumstances and the commonplaces that proofs can be based on; then the similarities, dissimilarities, examples, comparisons, general statements, proverbs, legends and fables that can be used to enrich each section. He should point out any rhetorical figures that he thinks could be effective in making the speech more forceful, ampler, clearer and more pleasing. If amplification is necessary, he should explain the technique, whether by commonplaces or by those methods that Quintilian divides into four classes.[9] If appeals to the emotions are relevant, he should advise them on how to deal with them too. And he should also teach the techniques of connection and the best ways of handling transitions: from the introduction to the narrative, from the narrative to the division, from the division to the argumentation, from one proposition to another, from one argument to another, from the argumentation to the epilogue or peroration. He should also mention some formulas that would be helpful for use in the introduction or even the peroration. Finally he should show them, if he can, some passages in writers that they could take points to imitate from because of the similarity in subject-matter. Once this has been done seven or eight times, they will begin, in Horace's image, to 'swim without floats',[10] and it will be enough just to set a theme, without as it were putting ready-chewed food in their mouths, as if they were babies.

I do not disapprove of a form of exercise that I see the ancients used, that of sometimes choosing themes from Homer, Sophocles, Euripides, Virgil or even history. As for instance: how Menelaus before the Trojan assembly seeks the restitution of Helen. Or: how Phoenix urges Achilles to return to battle. Or: Ulysses urges the Trojans to hand Helen back rather than face war. There survive some declamations of Libanius[11] and Aristides[12] of this kind. Or further: how a friend urges Cicero not to accept the terms offered by Antony (a subject that is found in Seneca);[13] how Phalaris urges the Delphians to consecrate his bronze bull to their god. The letters that circulate under the names of

Brutus and Phalaris[14] belong to this category. In correcting the exercise, the teacher will praise any successful piece of invention, treatment or imitation; he will point out anything that has been missed out or misplaced, and any expression that's redundant or sloppy or obscure or just not very elegant. He will show them how changes can be made and he will insist that they keep on making them. Above all, he'll spur his pupils on, starting with a comparison between them and so creating a kind of rivalry.

NOTES

1. *Valerius Maximus*: a Roman historian of the first century AD, whose *Nine books of memorable deeds and sayings* is a handbook of illustrative examples for rhetoricians, arranged under moral and philosophical headings.

2. The lark didn't move her nest of children until the farmer said that he was coming to plough the field himself, after his friends and relatives had failed to do it, Aulus Gellius, *Attic nights*, II. xxix.

3. The equivalent of the biblical proverb about the mote and the beam.

4. Themistocles, who preferred that his daughter should marry a good rather than a rich man, see Erasmus, *Apophthegms, Opera omnia*, vol. IV, col. 243C, drawing on Plutarch, *Moralia, Sayings of kings and commanders*, 185E.

5. I.e. one shouldn't try to do more than one is capable of.

6. These types of exercises are described in detail in *On abundance*, drawing on *To Herennius*.

7. *Aphthonius*: a Greek rhetorician of the fourth to fifth century AD; in his *Progymnasmata*, or preliminary exercises, he provided accounts of fourteen different types of theme with examples; it was a standard school text-book in the Renaissance, generally in Latin translation.

8. There were three types of speech in ancient rhetoric: the epideictic or demonstrative, for display purposes, generally to praise or blame; the deliberative, for political and other purposes, to persuade or dissuade; the judicial, for court cases, to prosecute or defend, see for example *To Herennius*, I. ii. 2.

9. *The education of an orator*, VIII. iv. 3ff.

10. Horace, *Satires*, I. iv. 120.

11. *Libanius*: Greek rhetorician of the fourth century AD, who wrote speeches and declamations.

12. *Aristides*: Aelius Aristides, second century AD, also wrote model declamations in Greek.

13. *Seneca*: i.e. the elder Seneca, *Suasoriae*, vi.

14. In the period 200 BC to AD 200, many letters in Greek purporting to be by famous men were written by rhetoricians. Sometimes these were deliberate forgeries; more often they were school exercises which were not meant to deceive. In the Renaissance, they were often thought to be genuine letters. Erasmus refers here not to the Latin letters of Brutus which are preserved with the correspondence of Cicero (as the Toronto Erasmus suggests) but to the probably spurious Greek letters of Brutus, which were printed in early editions along with the letters of Phalaris. In suggesting that the latter were declamations rather than genuine letters by the tyrant of the sixth century BC, who used to roast his enemies alive in a bronze bull, Erasmus anticipates the famous demonstration by Richard Bentley in 1697.

## Colet: *Aeditio*

*The best way to learn Latin*

*Colet's short Latin accidence, the* Aeditio, *was probably written in 1509; the first known edition is dated 1527. The concluding paragraph nicely summarises the humanist attitude to grammar: the best way to learn Latin is to read and imitate Latin authors; rules should be kept to a minimum. (On Colet, see Introduction, p. 23.)*

Of these eight parts of speech in order well construed be made reasons and sentences and long orations. But how, and in what manner, and with what construction of words, and all the varieties and diversities and changes in Latin speech, which be innumerable, if any man will know, and by that knowledge attain to understand Latin books and to speak and to write the clean Latin, let him above all busily learn and read good Latin authors of chosen poets and orators, and note wisely how th[e]y wrote and spake, and study alway to follow them, desiring none other rules but their examples. For in the beginning men spake not Latin because such rules were made, but contrariwise, because men spake such Latin, upon that followed the rules were made. That is to say, Latin speech was before the rules, not the rules before the Latin speech. Wherefore, well-beloved masters and teachers of grammar, after the parts of speech sufficiently known in your schools, read and expound plainly unto your scholars good authors, and show to them every word and in every sentence what they shall note and observe, warning them busily to follow and to do like both in writing and in speaking, and be to them your own self also speaking with them the pure Latin very present, and leave the rules. For reading of good books, diligent information of taught masters, studious advertence and taking heed of learners, hearing eloquent men speak, and finally busy[1] imitation with tongue and pen more availeth shortly to get the true eloquent speech than all the traditions, rules and precepts of masters.

NOTE

1. *Busy*: supplied from the 1534 edition. 1527 reads *easy*.

**Elyot:** *The governor*

Sir Thomas Elyot *(c. 1490-1546) is typical of the English humanist tradition in that he combined extensive writing on humanist subjects with a career in public life. The son of a judge, and a protégé of Wolsey and Thomas Cromwell, he served as a clerk in the law courts until 1526, and was chief clerk to the King's Council from 1523 to 1530; in 1531-2, he was ambassador to the Emperor, Charles V. Afterwards, he held local appointments only, as sheriff, justice of the peace and commissioner visiting monasteries in Oxford, and he sat in two parliaments. After the break with Rome, he was suspected of being a papist, and he probably favoured, like Erasmus, moderate ecclesiastical but not extreme doctrinal reform. Not much is known about his education; in the preface to his Latin-English dictionary, he says that he had no teacher after he was twelve, and was self-taught in liberal studies; he went to the Middle Temple in 1510 and perhaps later to Oxford. Stapleton, the biographer of More, says that Elyot was a member of More's circle and that his wife studied in More's school, and it was probably More who fostered his interest in the* studia humanitatis. *He may also have known Linacre, the humanist physician.*

*He was a productive author. Departing from the example of Erasmus and More, who were the chief influences on him, he turned exclusively to the vernacular; in the preface to* The knowledge which maketh a wise man, *he says that his aim is to develop English so that it can express complex ideas abundantly and translate adequately from Greek and Latin. He published several translations from classical authors into English, including a version of Isocrates' oration* To Nicocles, *one of* The education of children *from the* Moralia *(though it is probably not by Plutarch), and possibly versions of the pseudo-Lucianic* The cynic *and Plutarch's* How to profit by one's enemies *– all Renaissance favourites. He also wrote a Latin-English dictionary, a book of adages, a treatise on health and two dialogues on counsel.*

The book named the governor *was written in 1530, after Wolsey's fall from power, when Elyot was out of favour at court and had retired to Cambridgeshire; it was published in 1531. It takes the form of an advice-book addressed to the servants of the prince (the 'governor' of the title is not primarily the monarch but those who assist him to govern, though sometimes Elyot's advice is appropriate to both); its most famous predecessors in this genre were Castiglione's* The courtier *and Guevara's* The dial of princes. *It covers a characteristic humanist complex of subjects – political theory, education and ethics – which combine to make up a pattern for an ideal way of life. Elyot draws on many sources, both classical and modern; his selection is partly determined by his own interests and by those of his English audience. Like Ascham, he believes that humane learning should be put to the service of the state. As Caspari writes:*

> *His great achievement was the adaptation of the humanistic ideal of man and society to English needs and conditions: he created a new social norm which the English ruling class, then in its most formative period, could and did adopt as its own. (*Humanism and the social order, *p. 86)*

The governor *was a popular book, going through seven editions in fifty years; James I had it as a school-book, and Shakespeare drew on it for two passages about the ordered commonwealth (*Henry V, *I. ii. 180-203;* Troilus and Cressida, *I. iii. 75-137; see also Jones,* Origins of Shakespeare, *pp. 164-78, on* The governor *as a source for* 2 Henry VI*).*

*Book I gives the first detailed account in English of the aims and methods of humanist education, and draws its inspiration from Quintilian, 'Plutarch' and Erasmus. In the first passage, Elyot laments the state of education, which, like Batt in* The antibarbarians, *he blames on the shortage of good teachers, and with the help of Quintilian defines the ideal schoolmaster. In the second passage, he begins his sketch of the ideal curriculum, which starts with the classical poets, whose moral and practical utility is strongly emphasised. Compare his approach to Homer as the fountain of eloquence and learning with that of Ben Jonson (see below, pp. 132-3). The Renaissance view of Homer looks back to Quintilian, who said that Homer provided the model for every department of eloquence (*The education of an orator, *X. i. 46).*

*(i) 'For what cause at this day there be in this realm few perfect school-masters' (from Book I)*

Lord God, how many good and clean wits of children be nowadays perished by ignorant schoolmasters! How little substantial doctrine[1] is apprehended by the fewness of good grammarians![2] Notwithstanding I know that there be some well learned which have taught and also do teach, but, God knoweth, a few, and they with small effect, having thereto no comfort, their aptest and most proper scholars, after they be well instructed in speaking Latin and understanding some poets, being taken from their school by their parents, and either be brought to the court and made lackeys or pages, or else are bound prentices, whereby the worship that the master above any reward coveteth to have by the praise of his scholar is utterly drowned; whereof I have heard schoolmasters very well learned of good right complain. But yet, as I said, the fewness of good grammarians is a great impediment of doctrine (and here I would the readers should mark that I note to be few good grammarians and not none). I call not them grammarians which only can teach or make rules whereby a child shall only learn to speak congrue[3] Latin or to make six verses standing in one foot,[4] wherein perchance shall be neither sentence[5] nor eloquence. But I name him a grammarian by the authority of Quintilian[6] that, speaking Latin elegantly, can expound good authors, expressing the invention[7] and disposition[8] of the matter, their style or form of eloquence, explicating the figures as well of sentences as words, leaving no thing, person or place named by the author undeclared or hid from his scholars. Wherefore Quintilian saith it is not enough for him to have read poets, but all kinds of writing must also be sought for, not for the histories only but also for the property[9] of words, which commonly do receive their authority of noble authors. Moreover, without music, grammar may not be perfect, forasmuch as therein must be spoken of metres and harmonies, called *rythmi* in Greek. Neither if he have not the knowledge of stars he may understand poets, which in description of times (I omit other things) they treat of the rising and going down of planets. Also he may not be ignorant in philosophy,[10] for many places that be almost in every poet fetched out of the most subtle part of natural questions.[11] These be well nigh the words of Quintilian; then behold how few grammarians after this description be in this realm!

Undoubtedly there be in this realm many well learned which, if the name of a schoolmaster were not so much had in contempt and also if their labours with abundant salaries might be requited, were right sufficient and able to induce their hearers to excellent learning, so[12] they be not plucked away green and ere they be in doctrine sufficiently rooted. But nowadays, if to a bachelor or master of art study of philosophy waxeth tedious, if he have a spoonful of Latin, he will show forth a hogshead[13] without any learning, and offer to teach grammar and expound noble writers and to be in the room of a master; he will for a small salary set a false colour of learning on proper wits, which will be washed away with one shower of rain. For if the children be absent from school by the space of one month, the best learned of them will uneath[14] tell whether *fato*[15] whereby Aeneas was brought into Italy were either a man, a horse, a ship or a wild goose, although their master will perchance avaunt himself to be a good philosopher. Some men peradventure do think that at the beginning of learning it forceth not[16] although the masters have not so exact doctrine as I have rehearsed, but let them take good heed what Quintilian saith, that it is so much the better to be instructed by them that are best learned, forasmuch as it is difficulty to put out of the mind that which is once settled, the double burden being painful to the masters that shall succeed, and verily much more to unteach than to teach; wherefore it is written that Timotheus, the noble musician, demanded alway a greater reward of them whom other had taught than of them that never anything learned. These be the words of Quintilian or like.[17]

Also common experience teacheth that no man will put his son to a butcher to learn ere he bind him prentice to a tailor, or if he will have him a cunning goldsmith will bind him first prentice to a tinker; in these things, poor men be circumspect, and the nobles and gentlemen who would have their sons by excellent learning come unto honour, for sparing of cost or for lack of diligent search for a good schoolmaster, wilfully destroy their children, causing them to be taught that learning which would require six or seven years to be forgotten; by which time the more part of that age is spent wherein is the chief sharpness of wit, called in Latin *acumen*, and also then approacheth the stubborn age where the child brought up in pleasure disdaineth correction.

NOTES

1. *Doctrine*: instruction, knowledge, learning.
2. *Grammarians*: the Latin word *grammaticus* means a teacher of language and literature; Elyot gives a definition after Quintilian later in the passage.
3. *Congrue*: grammatically correct.
4. *Standing in one foot*: i.e. without effort, see Horace, *Satires*, I. iv. 10, where Lucilius is reproached for dictating two hundred lines in an hour, 'stans pede in uno', 'standing on one foot'.
5. *Sentence*: meaning.
6. *The education of an orator*, I. iv. 1-5; viii. 13-18.
7. *Invention*: 'the finding out of apt matter, called otherwise invention, is a searching out of things true, or things likely, the which may reasonably set forth a matter and make it appear probable' (Thomas Wilson).
8. *Disposition*: 'an apt bestowing and orderly placing of things, declaring where every argument shall be set and in what manner every reason shall be applied for confirmation of the purpose' (Thomas Wilson).
9. *Property*: aptitude, fitness.
10. *Philosophy*: the term includes natural philosophy, i.e. science.
11. *Natural questions*: scientific questions.
12. *So*: provided that.
13. *Show forth a hogshead*: either 'pretend to a greater knowledge of Latin than he actually has' (hogshead = large cask) or 'reveal himself a booby' (hogshead

= term of abuse).
    14. *Uneath*: with difficulty.
    15. *Fato*: in the opening lines of the *Aeneid*, Aeneas is described as 'the man who first from the shores of Troy, exiled by fate (*fato profugus*), came to Italy'.
    16. *It forceth not*: it doesn't matter.
    17. *The education of an orator*, II. iii. 1-3.

### (ii) 'What order should be in learning and which authors should be first read' (from Book I)

Now let us return to the order of learning apt for a gentleman, wherein I am of the opinion of Quintilian[1] that I would have him learn Greek and Latin authors both at one time; or else to begin with Greek, forasmuch as that it is hardest to come by, by reason of the diversity of tongues,[2] which be five in number, and all must be known or else uneath[3] any poet can be well understood. And if a child do begin therein at seven years of age, he may continually learn Greek authors three years and in the meantime use the Latin tongue as a familiar language; which in a nobleman's son may well come to pass, having none other persons to serve him or keeping him company but such as can speak Latin elegantly. And what doubt is there but so may he as soon speak good Latin as he may do pure French, which now is brought into as many rules and figures and as long a grammar as is Latin or Greek? I will not contend who among them that do write grammars of Greek (which now almost be innumerable) is the best, but that I refer to the discretion of a wise master. Alway I would advise him not to detain the child too long in that tedious labour,[4] either in the Greek or Latin grammar. For a gentle wit is therewith soon fatigate.[5]

    Grammar being but an introduction to the understanding of authors, if it be made too long or exquisite[6] to the learner, it in a manner mortifieth his courage; and by that time he cometh to the most sweet and pleasant reading of old authors, the sparks of fervent desire of learning is extinct with the burden of grammar, like as a little fire is soon quenched with a great heap of small sticks, so that it can never come to the principal logs, where it should long burn in a great pleasant fire. Now to follow my purpose, after a few and quick rules of grammar, immediately, or interlacing it therewith, would be read to the child Aesop's fables in Greek, in which argument children much do delight. And surely it is a much pleasant lesson and also profitable, as well for that it is elegant and brief (and, notwithstanding, it hath much variety in words and therewith much helpeth to the understanding of Greek) as also in those fables is included much moral and politic wisdom; where-fore, in the teaching of them, the master diligently must gather together those fables which may be most accommodate[7] to the advancement of some virtue whereto he perceiveth the child inclined or to the rebuke of some vice whereto he findeth his nature disposed. And therein the master ought to exercise his wit as well to make the child plainly to understand the fable as also declaring the signification thereof com-pendiously and to the purpose, foreseen alway that[8] as well this lesson as all other authors which the child shall learn, either Greek or Latin, verse or prose, be perfectly had without the book; whereby he shall not only attain plenty of the tongues, called copy,[9] but also increase and nourish remembrance wonderfully. The next lesson would be some quick[10] and merry dialogues elect[11] out of Lucian which be without ribaldry or too much scorning; for either of them is exactly to be eschewed, specially for a nobleman, the one annoying the soul, the other his estimation concerning his gravity. The comedies of Aristophanes may be in the place of Lucian, and by reason that they be in metre they be the sooner learned by heart. I dare make none other comparison between them, for offending the friends of them both, but thus much dare I say, that it were better that a child should never read any part of Lucian than all Lucian.

I could rehearse divers other poets which for matter and eloquence be very necessary, but I fear me to be too long from noble Homer, from whom as from a fountain proceeded all eloquence and learning. For in his books be contained and most perfectly expressed not only the documents[12] martial and discipline of arms but also incomparable wisdoms and instructions for politic governance of people, with the worthy commendation and laud of noble princes; wherewith the readers shall be so all inflamed that they most fervently shall desire and covet by the imitation of their virtues to acquire semblable[13] glory. For the which occasion, Aristotle, most sharpest-witted and excellent learned philosopher, as soon as he had received Alexander from King Philip, his father, he before any other thing taught him the most noble works of Homer; wherein Alexander found such sweetness and fruit that, ever after, he had Homer not only with him in all his journeys but also laid him under his pillow when he went to rest, and oftentimes would purposely wake some hours of the night to take, as it were, his pastime with that most noble poet.[14] For by the reading of his work called *Iliad*, where the assembly of the most noble Greeks against Troy is recited with their affairs, he gathered courage and strength against his enemies, wisdom and eloquence for consultations and persuasions to his people and army. And by the other work called *Odyssey*, which recounteth the sundry adventures of the wise Ulysses, he by the example of Ulysses apprehended many noble virtues, and also learned to escape the fraud and deceitful imaginations of sundry and subtle, crafty wits. Also, there shall he learn to ensearch and perceive the manners and conditions of them that be his familiars, sifting out, as I might say, the best from the worst, whereby he may surely commit his affairs and trust to every person after his virtues.

Therefore, I now conclude that there is no lesson for a young gentleman to be compared with Homer, if he be plainly and substantially expounded and declared by the master.

Notwithstanding, forasmuch as the said works be very long and do require therefore a great time to be all learned and conned, some Latin author would be therewith mixed, and specially Virgil, which in his work called *Aeneid* is most like to Homer and almost the same Homer in Latin. Also, by the joining together of those authors, the one shall be the better understood by the other. And verily, as I before said, none one author serveth to so divers wits as doth Virgil. For there is not that affect or desire whereto any child's fantasy is disposed but in some of Virgil's works may be found matter thereto apt and propice.[15] For what thing can be more familiar than his *Bucolics*?[16] Nor no work so nigh approacheth to the common dalliance[17] and manners of children, and the pretty controversies of the simple shepherds therein contained wonderfully rejoiceth the child that heareth it well declared, as I know by mine own experience. In his *Georgics*, Lord, what pleasant variety there is, the divers grains, herbs and flowers that be there described, that reading therein it seemeth to a man to be in a delectable garden or paradise! What ploughman knoweth so much of husbandry as there is expressed? Who delighting in good horses shall not be thereto more enflamed, reading there of the breeding, choosing and keeping of them? In the declaration whereof, Virgil leaveth far behind him all breeders, hackney-men[18] and scorsers.[19] Is there any astronomer that more exactly setteth out the order and course of the celestial bodies, or that more truly doth divine in his prognostications of the times of the year in their qualities, with the future estate of all things provided by husbandry, than Virgil doth recite in that work?

If the child have a delight in hunting, what pleasure shall he take of the fable of Aristaeus![20] — semblably in the hunting of Dido and Aeneas, which is described most elegantly in his book of *Aeneid*.[21]

If he have pleasure in wrestling, running, or other like exercise, where shall he see any more pleasant esbatements[22] than that which was done by Euryalus and other Trojans which accompanied Aeneas?[23]

If he take solace in hearing minstrels, what minstrel may be compared to Iopas, which sang before Dido and Aeneas, or to blind Demodocus, that played and sang most sweetly at the dinner that the king Alcinous made to Ulysses,[24] whose ditties and melody excelled as far the songs of our minstrels as Homer and Virgil excel all other poets?

If he be more desirous, as the most part of children be, to hear things marvellous and exquisite[25] which hath in it a visage of some things incredible, whereat shall he more wonder than when he shall behold Aeneas follow Sibyl into hell?[26] What shall he more dread than the terrible visages of Cerberus, Gorgon, Megaera and other furies and monsters? How shall he abhor tyranny, fraud and avarice when he doth see the pains of Duke Theseus, Prometheus, Sisyphus and such other, tormented for their dissolute and vicious living! How glad soon after shall he be when he shall behold in the pleasant fields of Elysium the souls of noble princes and captains, which for their virtue and labours in advancing the public weals of their countries do live eternally in pleasure inexplicable![27] And in the last books of *Aeneid* shall he find matter to minister to him audacity, valiant courage and policy to take and sustain noble enterprises, if any shall be needful for the assailing of his enemies. Finally, as I have said, this noble Virgil, like to a good nurse, giveth to a child, if he will take it, everything apt for his wit and capacity; wherefore he is in the order of learning to be preferred before any other author Latin.

I would set next unto him two books of Ovid, the one called *Metamorphoses*, which is as much to say as changing of men into other figure or form, the other is entitled *De fastis*, where the ceremonies of the gentiles and specially the Romans be expressed — both right necessary for the understanding of other poets. But because there is little other learning in them concerning either virtuous manners or policy, I suppose it were better that, as fables and ceremonies happen to come in a lesson, it were declared abundantly by the master, than that in the said two books a long time should be spent and almost lost, which might be better employed on such authors that do minister both eloquence, civil policy and exhortation to virtue.

Wherefore, in his place, let us bring in Horace, in whom is contained much variety of learning and quickness[28] of sentence.[29]

This poet may be interlaced with the lesson of *Odyssey* of Homer, wherein is declared the wonderful prudence and fortitude of Ulysses in his passage from Troy.

And if the child were induced to make verses by the imitation of Virgil and Homer, it should minister to him much delectation and courage to study; nor the making of verses is not discommended in a nobleman, since the noble Augustus and almost all the old emperors made books in verses.

The two noble poets, Silius[30] and Lucan,[31] be very expedient to be learned; for the one setteth out the emulation in qualities and prowess of two noble and valiant captains, one enemy to the other, that is to say, Silius writeth of Scipio the Roman and Hannibal, duke of Carthaginenses;[32] Lucan declareth a semblable matter but much more lamentable, forasmuch as the wars were civil and, as it were, in the bowels of the Romans, that is to say, under the standards of Julius Caesar and Pompey.

Hesiod[33] in Greek is more brief than Virgil where he writeth of husbandry, and doth not rise so high in philosophy, but is fuller of fables and therefore is more illecebrous.[34]

And here I conclude to speak any more of poets necessary for the childhood of a gentleman; forasmuch as these I doubt not will suffice until he pass the age of thirteen years. In which time childhood declineth, and reason waxeth ripe and deprehendeth[35] things with a more constant judgement.

Here I would should be remembered that I require not that all these works should be thoroughly read of a child in this time, which were almost impossible, but I only desire that they have in every of the said books so much instruction that they may take thereby some profit. Then the child's courage, inflamed by the frequent reading of noble poets, daily more and more desireth to have experience in those things that they so vehemently do commend in them that they write of.

Leonidas, the noble king of Spartans, being once demanded of what estimation in poetry Tyrtaeus, as he supposed, was, it is written that he answering said, that for stirring the minds of young men he was excellent, forasmuch as they, being moved with his verses, do run into the battle, regarding no peril, as men all inflamed in martial courage.[36]

NOTES

1. *The education of an orator*, I. i. 12-14.
2. *Tongues*: dialects.
3. *Uneath*: scarcely.
4. *Labour*: the first edition reads *labours*.
5. *Fatigate*: fatigued.
6. *Exquisite*: abstruse.

7. *Accommodate*: suited.
8. *Foreseen alway that*: provided that.
9. *Copy*: *copia*, abundance.
10. *Quick*: lively, acute.
11. *Elect*: chosen.
12. *Documents*: lessons.
13. *Semblable*: like.
14. Plutarch, *Lives*, *Alexander*, viii. 2-3.
15. *Propice*: suitable.
16. *Bucolics*: the *Eclogues*.
17. *Dalliance*: talk, play.
18. *Hackney-men*: men who hire out horses.
19. *Scorsers*: dealers.
20. *Georgics*, IV. 315ff.
21. *Aeneid*, IV. 129ff.
22. *Esbatements*: amusements, diversions.
23. *Aeneid*, V. 286ff.
24. *Aeneid*, I. 740ff; *Odyssey*, VIII. 62ff.
25. *Exquisite*: out of the way.
26. *Aeneid*, VI. 255ff.
27. *Inexplicable*: indescribable.
28. *Quickness*: liveliness, acuteness.
29. *Sentence*: thought.
30. *Silius*: Silius Italicus, Roman epic poet of the first century AD, who wrote the *Punica*, a historical epic on the Second Punic War.
31. *Lucan*: AD 39-65, author of the historical epic *The civil war*, which treats the conflict between Julius Caesar and Pompey.
32. *Carthaginenses*: Carthaginians.
33. *Hesiod*: early Greek poet, whose didactic poem the *Works and days* was the model for the *Georgics*.
34. *Illecebrous*: enticing, attractive.
35. *Deprehendeth*: understands, apprehends.
36. Plutarch, *Lives*, *Cleomenes*, ii. 3. (Tyrtaeus was an early Greek poet who wrote war songs.)

## Hoole: *A new discovery*

### The programme for the fifth form

A new discovery of the old art of teaching school *by Charles Hoole (1610-67) was published in 1660. Hoole had taught at the free school in Rotherham and then at various private schools in London; the book describes his own practice as a teacher. It shows the continuity of the educational programme instituted by Colet and Erasmus and of 'the good old way of teaching by grammar, authors and exercises'; Hoole's programme employs the same sequence of authors and compositional forms, and though there is more emphasis on grammatical rules, Hoole still stresses the importance of reading and imitation for the formation of a proper style: 'nothing is more available to gain a good style than frequent imitation of select pieces out of Isocrates and Demosthenes'.*

*In the programme for the fifth form, we may note again the atten-*
*tion to detail in reading and the use of the notebook to record stylistic*
*minutiae, the endless exercises in translation, variation and composi-*
*tion, and the monolithic concentration on one end – the formation of*
*the orator (Hoole still speaks of 'perfect orators and poets' and defines*
*the aim of the scholar as expertise 'in speaking and doing').*

*I do not have the space to annotate all the textbooks mentioned by*
*Hoole; the reader is referred to the list given at the end of Campagnac's*
*edition of* A new discovery *and to Watson,* The English grammar
schools.

Though it may seem a needless labour to prescribe directions for the
teaching of the two upper forms, partly because I find more written
concerning them than the rest, and partly because many very eminent
and able schoolmasters employ most of their pains in perfecting them,
everyone making use of such authors and such a method as in his own
discretion he judgeth meetest to make them scholars; not to say that
the scholars themselves, being now well acquainted with the Latin and
Greek grammar, and having gotten a good understanding (at least) of
the Latin tongue by the frequent exercise of translating and speaking
Latin, and writing colloquies, epistles, historical and fabulous narrations and the like, besides reading some school authors and other helpful and profitable books, will be able in many things to proceed without a guide, addicting their minds chiefly to those studies which their
natural genius doth most prompt them to, either concerning oratory or
poetry; yet, I think it requisite for me to go on as I have begun, and to
show what course I have constantly kept with these two forms to make
them exactly complete in the Greek and Latin tongues and as perfect
orators and poets in both as their young years and capacities will suffer,
and to enter them so in the Hebrew as that they may be able to proceed
of themselves in that holy language, whether they go to the university
or are otherwise disposed on to some necessary calling which their
parents or friends think fitting for them.

And first, I most heartily entreat those – especially that are my
loving friends and acquaintance – of my profession whose years and
experience are far beyond mine that they would candidly peruse and
kindly interpret what I have written, seeing I desire not by any means
to impose anything too magisterially upon them or others, but freely
to communicate to all men what I have for many years kept private to
myself and hath by some whose single judgement may sufficiently

satisfy me been importunately thus haled to the press; and if in any particular I seem to them to deviate from or fall short of what I aim at, *viz.* a facilitating the good old way of teaching by grammar, authors and exercises, I shall take it as a singular token of love that they acquaint me with it, and if by this rush-candle of mine they please to set up their own tapers, I shall rejoice to receive greater light by them and be ready to walk in it more vigorously. In the interim, I go on with my discovery touching the fifth form, which I would have employed in this manner:

(1) Let them and the form above them read daily a dozen verses out of the Greek Testament before the saying of parts.

(2) Let them reserve the Latin and Greek grammars and *Elementa rhetorices* for weekly parts, to be said only on Thursday mornings, and so divided that they may be sure to go over them all once every quarter. By this means, they will keep them in constant memory, and have more time allotted them for perusing authors and despatch of exercises. You must not forget at every part to let them have your help of explication of the most obscure and difficult places before they say, and, after they have said, to make such diligent examination as that you may be sure they understand what they learn.

And to make them more fully acquainted with the accents and dialects of the Greek tongue, you may (besides those few rules in their grammar) let them daily peruse a chapter in Mr Francklin's little book, *De orthotonia*, which is excellently helpful to young Grecians, and when they grow stronger, that appendix *De dialectis* at the end of Scapula will be worth their reading and observing. It would be good sometimes to make them compare the Latin and Greek grammar together, and to see wherein they agree and wherein they differ, but especially in the rules of syntaxis, and for this purpose Vechneri *Hellenolexia* will be of excellent use.

And as I have directed before how scholars should have a commonplace book for the Latin grammar, so I do here also for the Greek desire that after it is learnt it may be drawn into a synopsis, and that digested into commonplace heads, to which they may easily refer whatever they read worth noting out of any Greek grammar they peruse. And that they may more freely expatiate in such books, it were good if they had Mr Busby's grammar, Cleonard, Scotus, Chrysoloras, Ceporinus, Gaza, Urbanius, Caninius, Gretserus, Posselii *Syntaxis* and as many as can be gotten, both ancient and modern, laid up in the school library to collect annotations out of, as their leisure will best permit; and you will scarce imagine to what exactness a boy will attain and what a treasure of good notes he will have heaped up in these two years' time, if he be moderately industrious and now and then employ himself in collecting of his own accord – and I may add that scholars of any ordinary ingenuity will delight more to be doing something at their book, which they well understand, than to be trifling and rambling up and down about idle occasions.

(3) Forasmuch as it is usual and commendable to bring on children towards perfection in the Greek tongue as they proceed in oratory and poetry in the Latin, I think it not amiss to exercise these two forms in such authors as are commonly received and may prove most advantageous to them in all these; yet herein I may seem to differ from some others that, instead of grammar parts (which I reserve to be constantly repeated every Thursday), I would have this form to learn some lively patterns of oratory, by the frequent and familiar use whereof and the knowledge of the histories themselves to which they relate, they may at last obtain the artifice of gallant expression and some skill to manage future affairs, it being requisite for a scholar more than any man 'muthōn te rhētēr emenai prēktēra te ergōn',[1] to be expert in speaking and doing.

At first, therefore, for morning parts on Mondays, Tuesdays and Wednesdays, I would have them exercised in Aphthonius,[2] if it can be gotten, as I desire it may be reprinted, both in Greek and Latin. Out of which book I would have them translate the fables and themes, so as to finish at least every week one, into pure English, and to repeat them, being translated, in both languages, that by that means they may gain the method of these kind of exercises and inure themselves to pronunciation. When they have gone over them, they may next translate Tully's six *Paradoxes*,[3] and pronounce them also in English and Latin as if they were their own. And afterwards, they may proceed in those pithy orations which are purposely collected out of Sallust, Livy, Tacitus and Quintus Curtius,[4] having the histories of their occasions summarily set down before them. And of these I would have them constantly to translate one every day into English, beginning with those that are the shortest, and once a week to strive amongst themselves who can best pronounce them both in English and Latin. I know not what others may think of this task, but I have experienced it to be a most effectual mean to draw on my scholars to emulate one another who could make the best exercises of their own in the most rhetorical style, and have often seen the most bashful and least promising boys to outstrip their fellows in pronouncing with a courage and comely gesture; and for bringing up this use first in my school I must here thank that modest and ingenious gentleman, Mr Edward Perkins, who was then my usher, for advising me to set upon it. For I found nothing that I did formerly to put such a spirit into my scholars, and make them, like so many nightingales, to contend who could *malista ligeōs*,[5] most melodiously, tune his voice and frame style to pronounce and imitate the fore-mentioned orations.

(4) Their forenoon lessons on Mondays and Wednesdays may be in Isocrates,[6] and, to make them more attend the Greek,

(i) Let them, at first especially, translate every lesson by way of interlineary writing according to the grammatical order.
(ii) Let them parse the whole lesson in that order, and give you the variation and derivation of the most difficult nouns and verbs throughout, and the rules of syntax and of the accents.
(iii) Let them pick out the phrases and more elegant words as they go along and write them in a paperbook, and transcribe what sentences they meet withal into their commonplace book.

After they are well entered, you may cause them to translate the Greek into elegant Latin, and on Fridays, when they come to repeat, to render their own Latin into Greek, which they should endeavour to write down very true and fair without any help of their author, who is then to be thrown aside but afterwards compared with what they have done.

Three-quarters of a year, I conceive, will be sufficient to exercise them in Isocrates, till they get a perfect knowledge of etymology and syntax in Greek; which they will more easily attain to, if, out of this author especially, you teach them to translate such examples most frequently as may serve to explicate those rules which are not to be found in their Latin grammar and very seldom occur in the Greek one which they commonly read. And then you may let them translate a psalm out of English into Latin and out of Latin into Greek, and compare them with the Septuagint Psalter. Afterwards you may give them some of Demosthenes' sentences or similes, collected by Loinus, or of Posselius' *Apophthegms*[7] in Latin only, and let them turn them into Greek, which when they have done you may let them see the authors, that by them they may discover their own failings and endeavour to amend them.

Their lessons then for the fourth quarter, on Mondays and Wednesdays, should be in Theognis,[8] in which most pleasing poet they may be taught not only to construe and parse, as formerly, but also to mind the dialects, and to prove and scan, and to try how to make hexameter and pentameter Greek verses, as they formerly did Latin

ones out of Ovid *De tristibus*. And here I must not forget to give notice
to all that are taken with this author that Mr Castilion's *Praelectiones*
(which he sometimes read at Oxford, in Magdalen College, and Mr
Langley, late schoolmaster of Paul's, transcribed when he was student
there) are desirous to see the light, were they but helped forward by
some stationer or printer that would a little consider the author's pains.
I need give the work no more commendations than to say that, besides
Mr Langley that writ it long ago, Mr Busby, Mr Dugard, Mr Singleton
and some others of note have seen the book, and judged it a most
excellent piece not only to help young scholars in the understanding of
Theognis but also to furnish them with abundant matter of invention,
and to be a precedent to students in the universities, whereby they may
learn to compose such kind of lectures upon other poets, either for
their own private recreation or more public reading. Schrevelii *Lexicon
manuale* will be very useful to this form for parsing their lessons, and
Garthii *Lexicon*, which is annexed to it, Rulandi *Synonymia*, Morellii
*Dictionarium*, Billii *Locutiones*, Devarius *De Graecis particulis*, Posselii
*Calligraphia*, for translating Latin into Greek, but nothing is more
available[9] to gain a good style than frequent imitation of select pieces
out of Isocrates and Demosthenes, and translating one while out of the
Greek into Latin and another while out of Latin into Greek.

(5) For forenoon lessons on Tuesdays and Thursdays, I make choice
of Justin[10] as a plain history and full of excellent examples and moral
observations, which, for the easiness of the style, the scholars of this
form may now construe of themselves; and as you meet with an historical passage that is more observable than the rest, you may cause
every one of them to write it down in English as well as he can possibly
relate it without his book, and to return it again into good Latin. By
this means, they will not only well heed the matter but also the words
and phrases of this smooth historian. And after half or three-quarters of
a year, you may make use of Caesar's *Commentaries* or Lucius Florus[11]
in this manner, intermixing some of Erasmus' *Colloquies* now and then,
for variety's sake.

(6) Their afternoons' parts on Mondays and Wednesdays may be in
*Janua linguarum Graeca*, translated out of Latin by Theodorus
Simonius, which they may use as they formerly did the *Janua Latinae
linguae*: *viz.* after they have construed a chapter and analysed some
harder nouns and verbs, you may let them try who can recite the most
Greek names of things, and tell you the most Greek words for one
Latin word, and show their derivations and differences, and the rules
of their several accents. And to acquaint them the better with all the

Greek and Latin words comprised in that book, you may cause them at every part to write out some of the Latin index into Greek and some of the Greek index into Latin, and to note the manner of declining nouns and verbs, as the dictionaries and lexicons will show them.

(7) Virgil, the prince and purest of all Latin poets, doth justly challenge a place in school-teaching, and therefore I would have him to be constantly and thoroughly read by this form on Mondays and Tuesdays for afternoon lessons. They may begin with ten or twelve verses at a lesson in the *Eclogues*, which they may,

(i) First repeat *memoriter*[12] as well as they can possibly.

(ii) Construe and parse, and scan and prove exactly.

(iii) Give the tropes and figures with their definitions.

(iv) Note out of the phrases and epithets and other elegancies.

(v) Give the histories or descriptions belonging to the proper names and their etymologies.

But after they are well acquainted with this excellent poet, let them take the quantity of an eclogue at once, not minding so much to con their lessons by heart as to understand and examine them well and often over, according to the directions which Erasmus gives *De modo repetendae lectionis*,[13] which Mr Langley caused to be printed at the end of Lily's *Grammar*, by him corrected, and Mr Clarke hath worthily inserted in his *Dux grammaticus*. There are several translations of Virgil into English verse by the reading whereof young scholars may be somewhat helped to understand the Latin better, but of all the rest Mr Ogilby hath done it most completely,[14] and if his larger book may be procured to the school library, the lively pictures will imprint the histories in scholars' memories, and be a means to heighten their fancies with conceits answerable to the author's gallant expressions. After they have passed the *Georgics* by the master's help, he may leave them to read the *Aeneid* by themselves, having Cerda or Servius[15] at hand to resolve them in places more difficult for them to construe, though Mr Farnaby's notes upon Virgil will assist them ever and anon.

As they read this author, you may cause them sometimes to relate a pleasing story in good English prose and to try who can soonest turn it into elegant Latin, or into some other kind of verses which you please for the present to appoint them, either English or Latin or both.

(8) On Tuesdays, in the afternoons, you may cause them sometimes to translate one of Aesop's fables and sometimes one of Aelian's[16] histories, or a chapter in Epictetus,[17] out of Greek into English, and

then to turn its English into Latin and out of Latin into Greek. And on Thursdays, in the afternoons, they may turn some of Mr Farnaby's *Epigrammata selecta* out of Greek into Latin and English verses, and some of Aesop's fables or Tully's sentences into Latin and afterwards into Greek verses.

You need not alway let your scholars have these Greek books but sometimes dictate to them what you would have them write, and afterwards let them compare their own doings with their author, to espy their own failings, and this will be a means to help them to write Greek truly of themselves; you may sometimes dictate a colloquy, or epistle, or a sentence, or a short history in English, and let them write it in Latin or Greek as you spake it, and by this you may try their strength at any time and ready them for extemporary exercises.

(9) Now forasmuch as this form is to be employed weekly in making themes and verses, which they can never well do except they be furnished with matter aforehand, I would have them provide a large commonplace book, in which they should write at least those heads which Mr Farnaby hath set down in his *Index rhetoricus*, and then busy themselves, especially, on Tuesdays and Thursdays in the afternoons, after other tasks ended, to collect:

(i) Short histories out of Plutarch, Valerius Maximus, Justin, Caesar, Lucius Florus, Livy, Pliny, Pareus' *Medulla historiae*, Aelian, etc.

(ii) Apologues[18] and fables out of Aesop, Phaedrus, Ovid, Natalis Comes, etc.

(iii) Adages out of *Adagia selecta*, Erasmi *Adagia*, Drax's *Bibliotheca scholastica*, etc.

(iv) Hieroglyphics out of Pierius and Caussinus, etc.

(v) Emblems and symbols out of Alciati, Beza, Quarles, Reusnerus, Cartari, etc.

(vi) Ancient laws and customs out of Diodorus Siculus, Paulus Manutius, Plutarch, etc.

(vii) Witty sentences out of *Golden-grove*, *Moral philosophy*, *Sphinx philosophica*, *Wit's commonwealth*, *Flores doctorum*, Tully's *Sentences*, Demosthenis *Sententiae*, *Enchiridion morale*, Stobaeus, *Ethica Ciceroniana*, Gruteri *Florilegium*, etc.

(viii) Rhetorical exornations[19] out of Vossius, Farnaby, Butler, etc.

(ix) Topical places out of Caussinus, Tesmarus, *Orator extemporaneus*, etc.

(x) Descriptions of things natural and artificial out of *Orbis pictus*,

Caussinus, Pliny, etc. that I may not forget Textor's *Officina*, Lycosthenes, Erasmi *Apophthegmata, Carolina apophthegmata* and *Polyanthea*, which together with all that can be got of this nature should be laid up in the school library for scholars to pick what they can out of, besides what they read in their own authors.

Now the manner I would have them use them is thus:
Having a theme given then[20] to treat of, as suppose this, 'Non aestas semper fuerit, componite nidos,'[21]

(i) Let them first consult what they have read in their own authors concerning *tempus, aetas, occasio*, or *opportunitas* and then
(ii) Let everyone take one of those books forementioned and see what he can find in it for his purpose, and write it down under one of those heads in his commonplace book, but first let the master see whether it will suit with the theme.
(iii) Let them all read what they have written before the master, and everyone transcribe what others have collected into his own book; and thus they may always have store of matter for invention ready at hand which is far beyond what their own wit is able to conceive.

Now to furnish themselves also with copy[22] of good words and phrases, besides what they have collected weekly and what hath been already said of varying them, they should have these and the like books reserved in the school library: *viz. Silva synonymorum, Calliepeia*, Hewes' *Phrases, Winchester's phrases*, Lloyd's *Phrases*, Farnaby's *Phrases, Enchiridion oratorium*, Clarke's *Phraseologia* and his *English adages*, Willis' *Anglicisms*, Baret's *Dictionary*, Huloet or rather Higgins' *Dictionary*, Drax's *Bibliotheca*, Parei *Calligraphia*, Manutii *Phrases, A little English dictionary*, 16°, and Walker's *Particles*; and if at any time they can wittily and pithily invent anything of their own brain, you may help them to express it in good Latin by making use of Cooper's *Dictionary*, either as himself directeth in his preface or Phalerius will more fully show you in his *Supplementa ad grammaticam*.

And to draw their words and matter into the form of a theme with ease, let them have sound patterns to imitate, because they in everything prevail to do it soonest and sureliest.

First therefore let them peruse that in *Merchant Taylors' school probation book*, and then those at the end of *Winchester's phrases* and those in Mr Clarke's *Formulae oratoriae*; and afterwards they may proceed to those in Aphthonius, Rudolphus Agricola, Catanaeus,

Lorichius and the like, and learn how to prosecute the several parts of a theme more at large by intermixing some of those *formulae oratoriae* which Mr Clarke and Mr Farnaby have collected, which are proper to every part, so as to bring their matter into handsome and plain order, and to flourish and adorn it neatly with rhetorical tropes and figures, always regarding the composure of words, as to make them run in a pure and even style, according to the best of their authors, which they must always observe as precedents.

But the best way, as I conceive, to encourage children at the first against any seeming difficulty in this exercise of making themes is this: after you have showed them how to find matter, and where to help themselves with words and phrases, and in what order they are to dispose the parts, and what formulas they are to use in passing from one to another, propound a theme to them in English and Latin, and let them strive who can soonest return you the best exordium in English and then who can render it into the best Latin, and so you may proceed to the narration and quite through every part of a theme, not tying them to the words of any author but giving them liberty to contract or enlarge or alter them as they please, so that they still contend to go beyond them in purity of expression. This being done, you may dismiss them to adventure to make every one his own exercise in English and Latin, and to bring it fair written and be able to pronounce it distinctly *memoriter* at a time appointed. And when once you see they have gained a perfect way of making themes of themselves, you may let them go on to attain the habit by their own constant practice, ever and anon minding them what places in their authors, as they read, are most worthy notice and imitation, and for what purposes they may serve them.

(10) Touching learning to scan and prove and make all sorts of verses I have spoken in the former chapter; now for diligent practice in this kind of exercise, they may constantly comprise the sum of their themes in a distich, tetrastich, hexastich[23] or more verses, as they grow in strength. For invention of further matter upon any occasion or subject they are to treat upon, they may sometimes imitate places out of the purest poets (which Mr Farnaby's *Index poeticus* will point them to, besides what they find in *Flores poetarum*, and Sabinus *De carminibus ad veterum imitationem artificiose componendis* at the beginning of Textor's *Epistles* will further direct them) and sometime paraphrase or, as some term it, metaphrase upon a piece of an historian or orator, endeavouring more lively to express in verse what the author hath written in prose, and for this Mr Horne hath furnished you with two

examples in his excellent *Cheiragōgia de usu authoris*.

For variety and copy of poetical phrases, there are many very good helps: *viz. phrases poeticae*, besides those of Mr Farnaby's, *Aerarium poeticum*, *Enchiridion poeticum*, *Res Virgiliana*, *Artis poeticae compendium*, *Thesaurus poeticus* and others, worthy to be laid up in the school library. Textor will sufficiently supply choice epithets, and Smetii *Prosodia* will afford authorities (which is lately comprised and printed at the end of Lily's grammar). But for gaining a smooth way of versifying and to be able to express much matter in few words and very fully to the life, I conceive it very necessary for scholars to be very frequent in perusing and rehearsing Ovid and Virgil and afterwards such kind of poets as they are themselves delighted withal, either for more variety of verse or the wittiness of conceit sake. And the master, indeed, should cause his scholars to recite a piece of Ovid or Virgil in his hearing now and then, that the very tune of these pleasant verses may be imprinted in their minds, so that whenever they are put to compose a verse, they make it glide as even as those in their authors; Mr Ross his *Virgilius evangelizans* will easily show how a young scholar may imitate Virgil to the life.

From this little that hath been said, they that have a natural aptness and delight in poetry may proceed to more exquisite perfection in that art than any rules of teaching can reach unto; and there are very few so meanly-witted but by diligent use of the directions now given may attain to so much skill as to be able to judge of any verse, and upon a fit occasion or subject to compose a handsome copy, though not so fluently or neatly as they that have a natural sharpness and dexterity in the art of poetry.

(11) When they in this form have gone thrice over *The Assembly's catechism* in Greek and Latin, they may proceed in Nowell's *Catechism* or *The Palatinate catechism* in Greek.

And now to sum up all concerning the fifth form:

(1) Let them read constantly twelve verses at least in the Greek Testament before parts.

(2) Let them repeat the Latin and Greek grammars and *Elementa rhetorices* on Thursday mornings.

(3) Let them pronounce orations on Mondays, Tuesdays and Wednesdays, instead of parts, out of Livy, etc.

(4) Let their forenoons' lessons on Mondays and Wednesdays be in Isocrates, for three-quarters of a year's space, and for the fourth quarter in Theognis.

(5) Let their forenoon lessons on Tuesdays and Thursdays be in Justin's history and afterwards in Caesar's *Commentaries*, Lucius Florus or Erasmus' *Colloquies*.

(6) Let their afternoon parts on Mondays and Tuesdays be in *Janua linguarum Graeca* and

(7) Their afternoons' lessons in Virgil.

(8) Let them on Tuesdays in the afternoons translate out of Greek Aesop's *Fables*, Aelian's *Histories*, Epictetus or Farnaby's *Epigrammata*.

(9) Let them be employed weekly in making a theme and

(10) In a copy of verses.

(11) Let them say Nowell's *Catechism* or *The Palatinate catechism* on Saturdays.

By this means they will become familiarly acquainted with the Latin and Greek tongues, and be able to peruse any orator or poet in either language and to imitate their expressions and apply what matter they find in them to their own occasions. And then they may courageously adventure to the sixth and highest form.

NOTES

1. 'To be both a speaker of words and a doer of deeds', a quotation from Homer, *Iliad*, IX. 443.

2. See above, note 7, p. 74.

3. Cicero's six *Paradoxes of the Stoics* were exercises in turning philosophical doctrines into a rhetorical mode.

4. *Quintus Curtius*: probably first century AD; the author of a romantic history of Alexander the Great.

5. 'Most loudly or clearly', a variation of a Homeric expression.

6. *Isocrates*: 436-338 BC, Athenian orator.

7. From Plutarch.

8. *Theognis*: gnomic poet, probably of the sixth century BC.

9. *Available*: efficacious.

10. *Justin*: probably third century AD; the author of an epitome of the universal history by the Augustan historian, Pompeius Trogus.

11. *Lucius Florus*: probably second century AD; his *Epitome*, an abridgement of Roman history, in particular Roman wars, was a popular school-book.

12. *Memoriter*: from memory.

13. 'On the method of repeating reading'.

14. Ogilby's translation of Virgil appeared in 1649, and the illustrated folio in 1654.

15. *Servius*: fourth century AD; the author of a famous commentary on Virgil.

16. *Aelian*: c. AD 170-235; author of a miscellany in Greek, called *Varia historia*.

17. *Epictetus*: c. AD 55-135; freed slave and Stoic philosopher; his *Discourses* were preserved by his pupil, Arrian.

18. *Apologues*: fables.
19. *Exornations*: decorations, embellishments.
20. *Then*: *them* should perhaps be conjectured.
21. 'It won't always be summer, build your nests.'
22. *Copy*: store, abundance.
23. Units of two, four and six lines respectively.

# 2 CLASSICISM AND IMITATION

### Erasmus: *The antibarbarians*

*The history of the composition of* The antibarbarians *is complex. (For a full account of the various stages, see the introduction to the edition by Kazimierz Kumaniecki in the Amsterdam Erasmus.) In his introductory letter to the printed edition of 1520, Erasmus says that he began working on a defence of humane studies before he was twenty. He planned four books: the first – the one we have – a refutation of 'the objections habitually raised against us by the superstitious', the second a mock attack on eloquence which was to be overturned in the third, and the fourth an apology for poetry. Probably in 1499, he showed a draft of Book II to Colet, who was convinced by the arguments against eloquence. He took the manuscript to Italy in 1506 and revised the first two books in Bologna; when he left for England in 1509, he left them with a friend, and they were subsequently lost. Some years later, probably in 1517, in Louvain, he found that an early version of Book I was circulating in manuscript (a manuscript preserving this version of c. 1494 has survived); he revised it and had it published in 1520. Book II was never recovered.*

*Our* Antibarbarians *then is only a part of a projected defence of humanist studies, and it is a pity that we have lost the discussion of eloquence. The 1520 version of Book I is a hybrid, but the main message of the book seems to have remained constant through the various reworkings. It is a defence of learning in general against pietistic arguments that it has no place in the religious life (the ignorant are identified as the prime target of attack), and in particular of that branch of learning Erasmus wished to foster, scholarship based on classical learning. It was a popular book in Erasmus' lifetime, with at least ten editions, and it is of prime importance for us as a clear statement of some of Erasmus' basic views, which are only implied elsewhere in his work. Later writers, such as Ben Jonson, were able to take up a similar position in regard to making use of classical wisdom, but without the embattled stance.*

*The book is cast as a dialogue which takes place in the country near Bergen op Zoom, in Brabant, between Erasmus and some friends, Willem Hermans, a fellow monk from Steyn, Willem Conrad, the burgomaster of Bergen, Jodocus, the town doctor, and the chief speaker Jacob Batt, town clerk of Bergen, who is characterised as an enthusiast for the new learning. They meet by chance and begin a discussion of the reasons for the decline of learning, which Batt attributes to ignorant schoolteachers; Batt then undertakes a defence of the new learning. Characteristically, Erasmus' views are presented in a rhetorical rather than a philosophical manner. He caricatures the arguments of his opponents, pours scorn on their ignorance and satirises their morals; he sometimes deals rather cavalierly with his authorities, selecting quotations from St Augustine which support his argument and ignoring passages that contradict it, for example; we may feel that he glosses over the genuine difficulties involved in reconciling the classical and Christian philosophies of life. But the piece is lively and entertaining; it is full of common sense and it is instinct with Erasmus' belief in the value of the classical heritage and in the intellect.*

## A justification for studying pagan writers

*In this central passage, Batt takes up the charge that it is unchristian to study pagan writings. In the first section, he points out that it is impossible to avoid the use of pagan inventions in other spheres, thus showing that Christian civilisation is founded on pagan civilisation. In particular, we note that the pagans invented writing and the Latin language. In the next section, in a striking passage, he goes on to say that pagan learning was part of God's providential plan for man's salvation and was established for Christians to build on. Here Erasmus seems to go beyond the traditional Christian apologetic for classical learning, which suggested that if there was anything worth while in pagan literature, it might be appropriated for the service of Christ, used but not enjoyed; two commonly cited biblical texts, Exodus, 12: 35-6 (describing the spoiling of the Egyptians' goods by the Israelites) and Deuteronomy, 21: 11-12 (describing the shaving of the head of the captive woman) make clear the subordinate position of the classics (see Jacobsen, Translation, pp. 58-60; Erasmus discusses both passages, vol. XXIII in the Toronto translation, pp. 97-8, 91). Erasmus views the contribution of the pagans in a much more positive way; he argues that it would be wrong to reject it. He assigns to the Greeks and Romans the role of chief precursors of the Christian era which was traditionally given to the Hebrews. Whereas Augustine saw a radical split between pagan and Christian wisdom, Erasmus suggests a harmonious continuum between the two. (See further Boyle, Christening pagan mysteries, pp. 10-18.) In the next section, Batt goes on to make the startling assertion that there is no such thing as Christian erudition; all learning is pagan learning, i.e. the disciplines invented by the pagans, e.g. grammar and rhetoric, are the basis of all learning, including Christian studies; it is only the mysteries of the faith that Christianity contributes. After this, he turns to a more general defence of learning, which, in defiance of St Paul, he argues makes men less rather than more arrogant.*

*On the absurdity of faulting something merely because it was discovered by pagans*

'When we pour this vinegar over them, it's remarkable what a shout they raise as they charge against us; they say we aren't Christians but pagans, idolaters, more pernicious than the pagans themselves. "Can one really", they say, "count as a Christian anyone who takes so much trouble over profane disciplines, devised by impious men to serve their pride, and so relishes them? — who finds all his relaxation in them, consecrates all his leisure, all his activity to them, relies on them for all his comfort? Isn't it obvious what a sacrilege it is for a man who's once enlisted in Christian service, who's been initiated and enrolled in the name of Christ the general, to desert to the devils, the enemy, and have dealings with the worshippers of idols? Can you deny that a man is having dealings with them if he likes being called a Ciceronian in oratory, a Virgilian or a Horatian in poetry, an Aristotelian, an Academic,[1] a Stoic, an Epicurean in philosophy? You've heard of the Chrysippean enthymeme? You've heard of the horned syllogism?[2] You can see what tricky snares they're trying to net you simple folk in." I can see that we need some of Carneades'[3] hellebore. What are you saying, you anti-Chrysippeans? That anything deriving from pagans is automatically evil and banned to Christians? Does this mean that we can't make use of any of the inventions of the gentiles without immediately ceasing to be Christians? Well, I do suggest then that a public warning ought to be issued to your carpenters not to venture to use their saws, axes, adzes, bores, in future, nor their wedges, rules, plumb-lines and levels. Why so? It was a pagan, Daedalus, who thought up both the craft of carpentry and its tools.[4] Blacksmiths had better stop working; iron-working was invented by those monstrous men, the Cyclopes. No one must fashion things in bronze; tradition says that the Chalybes revealed this technique. Pottery is Coroebus' work; potters will have a holiday. One Boethus is responsible for cobbling; let no Christian stitch a shoe. Niceas discovered fulling; no one must wash dirty clothes. The Egyptians gave us weaving; let's go back to wearing the skins of wild animals. The Lydians are responsible for dyeing; let no one shear a sheep's fleece and stain it with dye. Cadmus, the Phoenician, discovered metal-smelting; smelters' forges will have to go cold. We must try to create a scruple in sailors against using their normal tackle. Let's warn charioteers not to follow Erichthonius' example. Painters, carvers, glass-workers, in short every class of craftsmen had better think up some other source of income if they can, so that they won't go on polluting themselves and their families by pagan crafts; if they can't, they must starve rather than stop being Christians. And what if we were to create a scruple in soldiers too, those pious men, against using shields, breastplates, helmets, swords, greaves, crests, bows, arrows, lances, spears? All these are said to have been discovered by the impious. But how awful that girls should be deprived of their devotion to Minerva and of the tools she gave them, the ball of wool, the distaff, the thread, the shuttle, the loom, none of which was invented by Christians. I can see too that a holiday for farmers will have to be proclaimed even at the risk of our lives; the plough is an invention of Osiris; let no one henceforth venture to plough the soil, to sow after ploughing, to harvest after sowing — Saturn is supposed to have been responsible for all this. No one must cultivate the vine, for Bacchus devised viticulture. No one must drink unmixed wine, nor wine diluted with water; Staphylus introduced this. The sick mustn't summon doctors; medicine is Apollo's invention. And most people believe that these inventors weren't just impious men but actually evil demons. Are you then allowed to use the inventions of demons, while we're not to be allowed to use the writings of studious men? Even people who want to be thought dialecticians and theologians are perfectly prepared to reproach scholars for using pagan inventions, but if they dared to argue the same case in the villages to diggers and harvesters, I'm blowed if the country folk themselves wouldn't do them in with mattocks and pruning-knives! If we're forbidden to use the inventions of the gentiles, what on earth will be left in fields, towns, churches, houses, workshops, in civic life, in warfare, in private or in public? We Christians just don't have anything that we haven't inherited from pagans. We received from the pagans the practice of writing, and of speaking Latin; they discovered the alphabet and the use of formal speech. "Am I", they say, "to hold in my hands the books of damned men, am I to press them to my heart, read them repeatedly, reverence them? Virgil burns in hell, and does a Christian recite his poems?" As if there weren't lots of Christians burning there too, but if good writings by them survive, no one thinks they ought to be rejected for that reason. Who can bear this arbitrariness of judgement that allows them, with Mercury's rod,[5] as it were, to banish anyone they choose to the underworld and bring up anyone they choose from the shades? I'm not going to embark here on that quarrelsome controversy, not fit even for women, about pagans; it's not our job to argue whether the pagans who lived before our Faith are damned. If we wanted to indulge in guessing I could easily show that either the pagans I'm talking about are saved or none at all are; but what matters to us is how good their teachings were, not how well they lived. A magistrate orders actors to be given a hearing, even though he condemns their lives from his own knowledge of them. The Christian Church reads the works of Origen[6] to benefit from his learning, even though they stand condemned of heresy on many points; but we shun the sacred writings of others on whose morals it would be most presumptuous to pass judgement. Indeed, to be more accurate, these are men whom it would be creditable to judge favourably and a great fault to condemn. "Away with you", they say, "Am I to put up with being called a Ciceronian or a Platonist after I've made my decision to be called a Christian?" Why not, you monster of a man? If we're right to call you a Sardanapalian[7] because you imitate the cursed luxury of Sardanapalus, or a Gnathonian[8] because you're a flatterer, or rather, given your thick-headed conceit, a Thrasonian,[9] why should someone else who imitates Cicero's language be ashamed to be called a Ciceronian, or I a Virgilian if I can emulate some of his qualities? You can go on adopting barbarian titles, and delighting in being called an Albertist or Thomist or Scotist or Occamist or Durandist,[10] just as long as you're named after a Christian; I'm happy to be named after any pagan, just as long as he's very learned and very eloquent. I won't be ashamed of this title provided the pagan teaches me something more worth while than a Christian. To bring the matter to a conclusion at last, if our opponents weren't made blinder than moles by their own envy, they'd certainly see what's obvious even to the blind, that there are differences among the discoveries of the pagans: some are useless, doubtful, pernicious, while others are thoroughly useful, wholesome, indeed indispensable. Let's leave them the evil, but why shouldn't we appropriate the good for ourselves? That's what's proper for a Christian, a man of sense and a lover of knowledge. But in fact, incredible though it seems, we act all the wrong way round: we imitate the vices of the ancients everywhere, their lust, ambition, superstition — indeed we outdo them — but their learning, perhaps the only thing we ought to imitate, is the one thing we spurn; whether that shows more folly in us or pride I'm not yet sure. If we've adopted from them things that are only moderately useful and no blame attaches to us for that, what stops us from doing the same with their arts, than which, if we believe

Jerome, there's nothing more useful or more excellent in human affairs?[11]

*How by the divine plan the disciplines were developed by the pagans for us to use, not to despise*

'In fact, when I look closely at the marvellous order and what people call harmony of things, I usually feel (and I'm not alone in this; many weighty authorities have thought the same) that it was part of the divine plan that the task of discovering the disciplines should be given to the gentiles. The immortal controller of the world, who is wisdom itself, establishes everything according to a perfect plan, differentiating things by a lovely principle of variety and organising them in a perfect order, so that somehow everything marvellously balances everything else; nothing amid the whole immense variety of things does he allow to be carried along at random. It was his wish that all past and future ages should serve that golden age in which he had resolved to be born; he decided that everything in nature should be directed to enhancing the blessedness and glory of that one age. He promised that he would accomplish this when he said, "I, if I be lifted up from the earth, will draw all unto me."[12] Here I think he uses the word "draw" most appropriately, to show that all things, even if they are hostile or pagan or alien in some other way and don't follow the service of Christ voluntarily, must none the less be drawn to it against their will. What of that harmony in things which caused St Augustine to think that not even bad things had been created without purpose? What were all those prefigurations and portents and mysteries pointing towards, right from the very first beginnings of the world? The age of Christ, of course. What about the whole Mosaic law, all those rites, ceremonies, forms of worship, promises, oracles? Doesn't Paul bear witness that they were all given to them as "examples"?[13] To say nothing of the transfers of empire, what was the purpose of "establishing the Roman people with such effort",[14] and through all those disasters and all those bloody victories subjecting the whole earth to one city, mistress of the world? Wasn't it part of the divine plan, so that when the Christian religion was born it would find it easier to penetrate the individual regions of the earth, spreading as it were from one head outwards to the limbs? Come now, what was his purpose in allowing almost the whole world to be ensnared by such mad and shameful religions? Obviously so that when the One religion arose it could win great glory by overthrowing all the rest, since nothing can become outstanding without competition. Learned Greece discovered the arts; Latium[15] entered the contest and didn't just surpass Greece in warfare but almost equalled its fame in literature and oratory. Some men chose to probe the hidden causes of things; others, bound in Prometheus' chains, observed the irregular returns of the fires of heaven.[16] There were those who sought a key to the secrets of Divinity; methods of argument were discovered by one, of oratory by another; some described men's characters with great learning, while some were concerned to transmit a record of history to posterity. And how the ancients sweated over laws and philosophy! What was the point of all this? That we, once we were born, should despise it? Or rather that the best religion should acquire both honour and support from these finest of pursuits? All the brave deeds, clever sayings, ingenious inventions and carefully preserved traditions of the pagans were prepared by Christ for his own Republic. He provided the genius and gave them the passion for enquiry, and it was through no agency but his that they found what they sought. Their age bore this crop of arts for our benefit more than for theirs. Just as a single region can't supply every product, and, as Virgil says, "not every land can bear every crop",[17] so I think different gifts have been distributed among the centuries. Most of the philosophers wore out their lives and their talents in seeking the highest good; Christ reserved for his own century what was really highest and best, but without intending the previous ages to have been lived out uselessly and unproductively. We have the evidence of our own eyes, in physical matters, that nature has taken great care that no period of time should slip away unprofitably. Look! Trees (the sight of them here reminds me to take them as an example[18]) send up sap in early spring to feed their leaves. When the blossom comes, you can see now what a joy it is for us to look at. As summer arrives, the little blossoms will gradually swell out into fleshy apples; in autumn, the trees will stand heavy with ripe fruit; once this has dropped, the remaining time from autumn to winter is spent on making new shoots for the next summer. Not even winter is an idle time; it restores the strength of things by letting them rest for a change. (The roving of the heavenly orbs, which is organised with such variety, has the same effect.) There is the greatest discord in things, but nothing could be more harmonious![19] Everything, both individually and collectively, is being carried to the same point, has the same purpose, tends to a single goal. And so the perfect governor, Christ, having marked out know-ledge of the highest good as the particular gift of his own century, thought that he should grant the immediately preceding centuries what came closest to the highest good, namely the highest learning. For after virtue what greater gift can a man have than knowledge? And in this the

God of the Christians made kind provision for our laziness, or if you prefer our ease, by sparing us a good part of the work, since there were other tasks for us to be busied with. For it's far easier to master an art that's already been thoroughly worked out than to discover one. If they hadn't sown the crop of letters, perhaps there wouldn't be anything for us to harvest; what could we have invented on our own, when we've not only added nothing to their discoveries but have actually reduced them considerably and thrown them all out of order? All the more scandalous is our ingratitude, or rather our envious malice, in refusing to accept even as a gift these discoveries that cost them much labour and would have benefited us greatly. And not only do we reject the splendid gift but we subject the author of it to the greatest contempt, instead of the gratitude we should have shown him.'

*That ignorance rather than learning causes men to become arrogant*
At this point I said, 'You've put your case with great learning, and convincingly, Batt; but I can scarcely believe there's anyone so utterly devoid of human reason as to think that religion has to be isolated from every form of literature − provided of course that the literature's Christian.' Batt replied, 'As if there were any Christian learning that wasn't utterly devoid of learning! I'm not talking about the mysteries of our religion but about the disciplines that have been developed. If we're prepared to tell the truth, have we made any new discovery since the time of those pagans that isn't a product of ignorance? How could we make successful discoveries of our own when we're so bad at preserving other people's? So I think there's no learning except what's "secular" (that's their name for "ancient") or at least seasoned and shaped by secular literature; I'm happy for this to be called Christian too if it's free from perverse and impious beliefs − though I find there are a good number of people of such pig-headed piety that they don't have much regard even for this Christian i.e. ecclesiastical learning. "What does it matter", they say, "if we aren't theologians? If you really know Christ that's enough, even if you know nothing else. Eternal life was promised to the innocent, not the learned. I'm not going to be damned, am I, for not having a very lofty understanding of St Paul's writings? What does it matter if I don't understand Jerome's diction? Or if I've never even read Augustine and Ambrose? Or if I don't even understand the Gospel?" You dolt, what does it matter if you don't even know yourself, if you're a camel and not a man at all! Don't worry, even dumb animals will share in the Kingdom of Heaven. Goodness, this breed of men isn't just incredibly stupid, they're impious too.

I wish these people who're so proud of knowing nothing of letters really did know Christ! But if often happens that the men who present themselves as simpletons in letters turn out to be the most cunning rogues in worldly affairs. However, I'm not concerned with them for the moment. I've just brought up the subject so that you won't be surprised if this learning of ours, as I've described it, is abhorred by men who even spurn the Gospels. But as I said, I'm not concerned with them just now; I'm talking about men who want to be thought learned in matters concerning the Church but shy away from all secular disciplines like a Jew from unclean food, forgetting Paul's dictum that "unto the pure all things are pure".[20] I find these people's learning so scant that I really think it doesn't exist at all and is worse than simple ignorance. But they abominate all our learning as evil, pagan, irreligious; as for what they know themselves, they want people to think they haven't learnt it by human effort but straight from heaven, as it were. And I hear that it's even widely said nowadays that the more educated a man is, the more wicked he is. This insult doesn't concern students of rhetoric and poetry any more than theologians, lawyers, dialecticians and all other scholars; and it ought to be exposed as absurd by all of them. If learning is evil, is it evil in itself or because of something else? If because of something else, why should we simply blame learning? If in itself, why then do writers of the highest authority class it among honourable goods? Why do they rank it above wealth, which is not an evil in itself? And since no truth can be bad in itself, and the liberal arts are truths, they are necessarily good. But if knowledge is good in itself, ignorance is evil, and, if evil, therefore to be avoided (though if we just heed nature's voice, who wouldn't prefer being very knowledgeable to very ignorant?). At this point, our dialecticians turn into barbarians. "We don't fault learning simply for itself", they say, "but because it makes men cunning, proud, uncontrollable, arrogant, disdainful. What are you after", they say, "except to shun the herd, to stand out above other people, to be talked about and become famous, to look down on us and those like us as mere sheep?" So you've heard what's biting our scrupulous friends; they don't want to be despised. They want to give orders and lead, not to obey and be led, and they think the best provision that can be made for public peace is that no one should appear who can correct other people's ignorance. I think you can see that the sole source of attacks upon learning is pride. But it would be an outrage for a man with weak eyes to accuse the sun because its light hurt him. "Knowledge puffeth up", they say, "but charity edifieth."[21] But is arrogance therefore knowledge's fault or our own? I don't think they'll dare to say that it's knowledge's; otherwise there could never have been a learned man who wasn't arrogant, and the more learned a man grew the prouder he would become. Apart from being ridiculous, such a claim can also be seen as thoroughly slanderous. Who against? Against Augustine, Jerome and very many others whom it's scandalous to accuse of pride because they were exceptionally learned. "But", you'll say, "I'm talking about profane learning." Yes, and that's how I interpret you — the kind of learning we admire and reverence in the leaders of the Christian religion I've just mentioned, quite different from the ecclesiastical learning that you profess. Can there be any doubt? If it's a fault in ourselves and not in things outside us that causes us to grow arrogant, should we discipline our own characters or launch groundless attacks on these external things? Wouldn't you be behaving more modestly, you preacher of modesty, if you admitted your ignorance honestly and stopped slandering good things as a way of shielding your own failings? As it is, the one thing you're eloquent about is spreading this slander. "But", you say, "secular learning provides fuel for arrogance." Who denies it? But such fuel can be got from any source, even from what's best and most sacred. Does it follow that these good things should be blamed? Shouldn't it be the individual who villainously abuses what's excellent? A mind that's naturally arrogant can find an opportunity to display its arrogance in anything. Money is a servant to innumerable forms of vice, but no one attacks it as evil; rather we criticise the character of those who misuse it. What is there so good as never to provide an opportunity for evildoing? Not fasting, not alms, not chastity, not virtue itself. "Philosophers are proud, poets are pleased with themselves." Come now, are there no proud theologians? Is there in fact any more arrogant and contemptuous breed? But who would venture to accuse most sacred theology? It leads to pride in very many, but through their own fault not theology's. Is no uncultured man proud? And what increases their arrogance? Their very ignorance. How would they behave then if they had acquired some culture?

*That ignorance is the mother of pride, while learning begets modesty*
'But what falser claim can be made than that literature makes men cunning, proud and disdainful? If "cunning" is their name for prudence, I don't object, since advice in the Gospel itself tells us to imitate the cunning of serpents.[22] But as for disdain, isn't it obvious how absurd that is? How were those stony, rustic men brought to a more humane way of life, a gentler disposition, more civilised ways? Wasn't it by literature?[23] — which fashions the human mind, softens the passions,

breaks down our violent impulses, makes us gentle and stops our temper from being savage. Or do they describe as disdain the fact that we don't admire their own barbarity, that we can't take pleasure in the trifling of thoroughly ignorant men, that we don't treasure dung as though it were a heap of jewels? Does that show disdain, or good sense and the power of distinguishing good and bad? As for modesty, I see that my feeling is the same as St Jerome's; who said truly and elegantly (following a certain Greek thinker) that ignorance brings confidence with it but fear is the companion of knowledge.[24] It's clear that Quintilian understood this well from his saying "The less talented a man is the more he tries to inflate and magnify himself."[25] We often see people who think they are men of consummate learning before they're even really sure what they do know and what they don't. Once they've convinced themselves of their own powers and by their folly have acquired some reputation with the vulgar herd for learning, they necessarily become very pleased with themselves and contemptuous of others. They boldly teach what they don't know, they write, make speeches, interpret; there's nothing they don't try, nothing they wouldn't dare do, relying on their own supporters and despising men of learning both for their opinions and their scarcity – a pestilential breed of men, well deserving their own minds and their own folly.'

NOTES

1. *Academic*: Sceptic. The Academy, founded by Plato, turned to a brand of Scepticism in the third century BC. Cicero called himself an Academic.

2. Logical puzzles, alluded to by St Jerome, *Letters*, LXIX. ii, cited here by the barbarians as pagan wiles. Chrysippus was a Stoic philosopher, third century BC.

3. Carneades, an Academic Sceptic, second century BC, is said to have taken a purge of hellebore before composing a refutation of Zeno the Stoic, see *Adages*, I. viii. 51, *Opera omnia*, vol. II, col. 318A-B. Batt is about to start a refutation of the barbarians.

4. The names of the ancient inventors in this section come from Pliny, *Natural History*, VII. lvi. 191ff.

5. *Mercury's rod*: with which he conducted the shades in his role as Psychopompus.

6. *Origen*: controversial theologian (*c*. AD 185-254), admired by Erasmus; many of his ideas about doctrine were condemned by Councils at Constantinople in 543 and 553.

7. *Sardanapalian*: Sardanapalus, King of Assyria, was a type of luxury.

8. *Gnathonian*: Gnatho is the parasite in Terence's *Eunuchus*.

9. *Thrasonian*: Thraso is the braggart soldier from the same play.

10. Followers of the scholastic theologians Albertus Magnus, Thomas Aquinas, Duns Scotus, William of Occam, Durandus.

11. *Letters*, LIII. vi.

12. John, 12: 32.
13. I Corinthians, 10: 11.
14. Virgil, *Aeneid*, I. 33.
15. *Latium*: i.e. Rome.
16. Aeschylus in the *Prometheus bound* tells how Prometheus was enchained to a rock in the Caucasus as a punishment for stealing fire from heaven to give to man. In later antiquity, the myth was interpreted as an allegory; Prometheus becomes the first astronomer, who taught the art to the Assyrians (see Servius, Commentary on Virgil, *Eclogue* VI. 42).
17. Conflates *Georgics*, II. 109 with *Eclogues*, IV. 39.
18. At this point in the dialogue, the friends are gathered in an orchard.
19. An allusion to the doctrine of *discordia concors*, which originated in classical philosophy and was developed by the Stoics; its Renaissance expounders included the Neo-Platonist Pico della Mirandola.
20. Titus, 1: 15.
21. I Corinthians, 8: 1.
22. Matthew, 10: 16.
23. On the civilising of early man by letters, see Horace, *Art of poetry*, 391-6; Cicero, *On invention*, I. ii. 2; *On the orator*, I. viii. 33.
24. Jerome, *Letters*, LXXIII. x; Thucydides, *History of the Peloponnesian war*, II. xl. 3, although the context gives a different meaning to the words.
25. Quintilian, II. iii. 8.

## Erasmus: *The pious feast*

### 'Saint Socrates, pray for us!'

The pious feast *(*Convivium religiosum*) is one of the* Colloquies, *a work which began as a collection of dialogues to teach Latin to Erasmus' pupils and ended as a lively vehicle for expressing his views on contemporary issues and as one of the most popular of his works. The pious feast presents a sketch of model Christian behaviour; the guests eat and drink pleasantly but moderately, observing a mean between excess and abstinence, and discuss biblical texts the while courteously and learnedly. In this famous passage, the conversation turns to some passages from classical literature and gives expression to Erasmus' conviction of the closeness of classical ethics to Christian ideals. The colloquy first appeared in a collection of 1522, and is given here in the translation of Sir Roger L'Estrange (1680).*

*Chrysoglottus*. If I were not afraid of talking ye out of your dinners, and if I did not make a conscience[1] of mingling things profane with sacred, there is something that I would venture to propound to you — I read it this day with singular delight.

*Eusebius*. Whatsoever is pious and conducing to good manners should not be called profane. The first place must be granted to the authority of the Holy Scriptures, and yet after that I find among the ancients, nay the ethnics,[2] and, which is yet more, among the poets, certain precepts and sentences, so clean, so sincere, so divine that I cannot persuade myself but they wrote them by holy inspiration. And perhaps the spirit of Christ diffuses itself further than we imagine. There are more saints than we find in our catalogue. To confess myself now, among my friends, I cannot read Tully[3] *Of old age*, *Of friendship*, his *Offices*[4] or his *Tusculan questions*[5] without kissing the book, without a veneration for the soul of that divine heathen; and then, on the contrary, when I read some of our modern authors, their politics, economies[6] and ethics — Good God, how jejune and cold they are! And so insensible compared with the other that I had rather lose all Scotus[7] and twenty more such as he than one Cicero or Plutarch. Not that I am wholly against them neither; but from the reading of the one I find myself to become honester and better, whereas I rise from the other extremely dull and indifferent in the point of virtue, but most violently bent upon cavil and contention. Wherefore never fear to make your proposition, whatever it is.

*Chrysoglottus.* Though all Tully's philosophy carries upon it the stamp of something that is divine, yet that treatise *Of old age*, which in his old age he wrote — that piece, I say, do I look upon, according to the Greek proverb, to be the song of the dying swan. I read it this day, and these words I remember in it that pleased me above the rest:

'Should God now put it into my power to begin my life again from my very cradle and once more to run the course over of the years I have lived, I should not upon any terms agree to't. For what's the benefit of life? Or rather, how great is the pain! Or if there were none of this, there would be yet undoubtedly in it satiety and trouble. There are many, I know, and learned men that have taken up the humour of deploring their past lives. This is a thing which I can never consent to, or to be troubled that my life is spent, because I have so lived as to persuade myself that I was not born in vain. And when I leave this body, 'tis but as an inn, not as a place of abode. For Nature has given us our bodies only to lodge in, not to dwell in. Oh, how glorious will that day be when I shall leave the rabble and the trash of this world behind me, to join in council and society with those illustrious spirits that are gone before![8] '

Thus far Cato.[9] What could a Christian have said more? The dialogue of this aged pagan with the youth of his times will rise up in judgement against many of our monks, with their holy virgins.

*Eusebius*. It will be objected that this colloquy of Tully's was but a fiction.

*Chrysoglottus*. 'Tis all one to me whether the honour be Cato's, for the sense and expression of this rapture, or Cicero's, for the divinity of the contemplation and the excellency of representing his thoughts in words answerable to the matter. Though I'm apt to think that although these very syllables were not Cato's, yet that his familiar conversations were not far from this purpose. Neither had Tully the confidence to draw a Cato fairer than he was, especially in a time when his character was yet fresh in the memories of all men. Beside that such an unlikeness in a dialogue would have been a great indecorum and enough to have blasted the credit of the discourse.

*Theophilus*. That which you say is very likely; but let me tell you what came into my head upon your recital. I have often wondered with myself, considering that long life is the wish and death the terror of all mortals, that there is scarce any man so happy — I do not speak of old but of middle-age men — but if it should be offered him to be young again if he would, upon condition of running the same fortune over again of good and ill, he would make the same answer that Cato did, especially passing a true reflection upon the mixture of his past life. For the remembrance, even of the pleasantest part of it, is commonly attended with shame and sting of conscience, insomuch that the memory of past delights is more painful to us than that of past misfortunes. Wherefore it was wisely done of the ancient poets in the fable of Lethe, to make the dead drink the water of forgetfulness before their souls were affected with any desire of the bodies they had left behind 'em.

*Uranius*. It is a thing that I myself have observed in some cases, and well worthy of our admiration. But that in Cato which takes me the most is his declaration that he did not repent himself of his past life. Where's the Christian that lives to his age and can say as much? 'Tis a common thing for men that have scraped estates together by hook or by crook to value themselves at their death upon the industry and success of their lives. But Cato's saying that he had not lived in vain was grounded upon the conscience of having discharged all the parts of an honest and a resolute citizen and patriot and untainted magistrate, and that he should transmit to posterity the monuments of his integrity and virtue. 'I depart', says he, 'as out of a lodging, not a dwelling place.' What could be more divine? 'I am here upon sufferance till the master of the house says begone.' A man will not easily be forced from his own home, but the fall of a chimney, the spark of a coal and a thousand petty accidents drive us out of this world, or at the best the structure of our bodies falls to pieces with old age and moulders to dust, every moment admonishing us that we are to change our quarters.

*Nephalius.* That expression of Socrates in Plato is rather, methinks, the more significant of the two. 'The soul of a man,' says he, 'is in the body as in a garrison. There's no quitting of it without the leave of the captain, nor any longer staying in't than during the pleasure of him that placed it there.'[10] The allusion of a garrison is much more emphatical than that of a house. For in the one is only implied an abode (and that perhaps an idle one, too), whereas in the other we are put upon duty by our governor; and much to this purpose it is that the life of man in Holy Writ is one while called a warfare and another while a race.

*Uranius.* But Cato's speech, methinks, has some affinity with that of St Paul, II Corinthians, chapter 5, where he calls that heavenly station which we look for after this life, in one place, a house, in another, a mansion, and the body he calls '*skēnos*', or a tabernacle. 'For we also', says he, 'in this tabernacle groan, being burdened.'

*Nephalius.* So St Peter, II. 1. 'And I think it meet,' says he, 'as long as I am in this tabernacle, to stir ye up by putting you in mind; being assured that I shall shortly put off this my tabernacle.'[11] And what says Christ himself, Matthew, 24, Mark, 13 and Luke, 21? That we should so live and watch as if we were presently to die, and so apply ourselves to honest things as if we were to live for ever. Now who can hear these words of Cato, 'Oh, that glorious day!', without thinking of St Paul's 'I desire to be dissolved and to be with Christ'?[12]

*Chrysoglottus.* How happy are they that wait for death in such a state of mind! But yet in Cato's speech, though it be great, there is more boldness and arrogance in it, methinks, than would become a Christian. No, certainly, never any ethnic came nearer up to us than Socrates to Crito, before he took his poison. 'Whether I shall be approved or not in the sight of God I cannot tell; but this I am certain of, that I have most affectionately endeavoured to please him. And I am in good hope that he will accept the will for the deed.'[13] This great man's diffidence in himself was yet so comforted by the conscience[14] of pious inclinations and an absolute resignation of himself to the divine will that he delivered up himself in a dependence upon God's mercy and goodness, even for the honesty of his intentions.

*Nephalius.* What a wonderful elevation of mind was this in a man that only acted by the light of nature! I can hardly read the story of this worthy without a 'Sancte Socrates, ora pro nobis,' 'Saint Socrates, pray for us.' And I have as much ado sometimes to keep myself from wishing well to the souls of Virgil and Horace. But how distracted and fearful have I seen many Christians upon the last extremity! Some put their trust in things not to be confided in; others breathe out their souls in desperation, either out of a conscience of their lewd lives or some scruples perhaps injected into their thoughts by meddling with indiscreet men at their dying hours.

NOTES

1. *Make a conscience*: scruple.
2. *Ethnics*: pagans.
3. *Tully*: Cicero.
4. *Offices*: *On duties*.
5. These are all philosophical treatises by Cicero.
6. *Economies*: i.e. books on economics, household management.
7. *Scotus*: Johannes Duns Scotus (*c*. 1265-1308), the scholastic theologian.
8. Cicero, *On old age*, xxiii. 83-4.
9. Cato the Censor is the chief speaker in Cicero's dialogue.
10. Plato, *Phaedo*, 62B.
11. II Peter, 1: 13-14.
12. Philippians, 1: 23.
13. Plato, *Phaedo*, 69D.
14. *Conscience*: consciousness.

## Erasmus and More: Three letters on Lucian

*The late Greek author, Lucian of Samosata (born c. AD 120), who wrote a varied collection of satirical, fantastic and rhetorical sketches, came to Italy from Byzantium in the late fourteenth century and became popular in the fifteenth, when translations into Latin were made of some of his pieces, especially those on moral subjects. Then the Latin translations of Erasmus and More, published first in 1506 and then in several enlarged editions, brought him to Northern Europe and made him popular there; Ben Jonson was one of his English imitators. (For a full survey of Lucian's influence, see Robinson, Lucian.)*

*Lucian was a favourite with both Erasmus and More (see Introduction, pp. 23-4). As the following letters show, they enjoyed his witty treatment of realistic subjects – both apply to him Horace's famous line about mixing profit and delight – and they saw the objects of his satire – philosophers, superstitious beliefs, humbug – in contemporary dress.*

## (i) Erasmus to Christopher Urswick

*This letter (Allen no. 193) is a dedication of the translation of* The cock *in the collection of 1506 to Christopher Urswick, an ecclesiastic who enjoyed royal favour.* The cock *is a dialogue in which a cock lectures his master, the cobbler Micyllus, on the blessings of the simple life.*

My attitude has always been, my humane and distinguished Christopher, to abhor ingratitude more than any other vice; I've always thought that people who are capable of ever forgetting others' services to them don't deserve the name of human beings. On the other hand, I think it's a great blessing if an obliging fortune puts one in a position to meet one's debts of gratitude in full; and it's the greatest of all if one can repay a service with interest. Often before now I've reckoned up all the benefits that your kindness has conferred on me spontaneously (I include everything that was offered in such a way that I don't know whether it was chance's fault or my own, but certainly not yours, that I didn't receive it) and I've cast around for a way of giving you at least some indication of my gratitude; but in my very modest circumstances I've not found anything that would in any sense even satisfy my feelings, to say nothing of matching your deserts. Finally, I had the idea of imitating those refined people who send a particularly fine flower or some similar token and so demonstrate their good will and eagerness to oblige (particularly when they are in humble circumstances themselves and are dealing with people whose fortune and whose temperament leave them in no need of gifts from others).

So I stepped into the Greek *mouseia*[1] (in the gardens of the Muses, you see, it's spring even in midwinter) and amid all the flowers that drew my eye with their various charms I was at once attracted by this flower of Lucian most of all. I picked it, not with my hand but by my pen, and am sending it to you now. It's not just attractive because of its novelty, its varied colouring, its charming shape and its rich fragrance; it's also a potent giver of health because of the swift-acting juices it contains.[2] 'Anyone who can combine instruction and delight will win every vote,' says Horace.[3] If anyone has ever managed to achieve that, it was Lucian; he reproduces the satirical wit of Old Comedy[4] without its excessive aggressiveness, and, dear God, how cheekily, how wittily he tackles every subject, what mockery he heaps on everything, what marvellous salty wit he rubs into every theme. He touches nothing, even in passing, without making it the target of some jest. He's a particular foe of the philosophers, and above all the Pythagoreans and Platonists for their charlatanism and the Stoics for their intolerable pride. He goes for them with the dagger-point, with the sword-edge, with every kind of weapon. And very rightly; for what's more odious and insufferable than villainy masked by a pretence of virtue? And so he acquired the epithet *blasphemos*, i.e. slanderer; but he was given it, of course, by the people whose sores he had touched. He mocks and lashes the Gods with the same freedom throughout his works; this is why he has the nickname atheist — an honourable title, given that it was bestowed by irreligious and superstitious men. He's thought to have flourished approximately in the reign of Trajan, but, Heaven be my witness, he doesn't deserve to be counted among the sophists.[5] He has a marvellous charm of style and felicity of invention; his jokes are full of wit and his satire of vinegar; he teases with his playful manner, and blends grave with gay and gay with grave; he speaks truth in jest and he jests while speaking the truth. He portrays men's manners, feelings and pursuits with a painter's brush, as it were, so vividly that we don't just read about them but can see them before our eyes; the result is that no comedy or satire can be compared to his dialogues either for entertainment or for moral value.

In case you want to know the precise subject of this dialogue, he treats his familiar themes in it. He attacks Pythagoras as a fraud and a charlatan; he makes fun of the pride and sagacious beards of the Stoics; he demonstrates the troubles that the lives of the rich and kings are exposed to, and the freedom by contrast of the cheerful poor who are contented with their lot. I strongly urge you to read it carefully, whenever your commitments allow you a moment's relaxation. You'll find in it Gallus the cock conversing with the cobbler more comically than any professional jester could, but with more sense, none the less, than the herd of theologians and philosophers often show when they dispute in the schools with great pomposity about great trivialities.

Farewell, my excellent and humane Christopher, and count Erasmus among your humble servants, one who will prove second to none in love, devotion and service.

NOTES

1. *Mouseia*: haunts of the Muses.
2. The metaphor of picking a flower is maintained throughout these sentences.
3. *Art of poetry*, 343.
4. *Old Comedy*: the fifth-century Greek comedy of Aristophanes.
5. *Sophists*: teachers of rhetoric, who flourished in great numbers in the second century AD.

## (ii) Erasmus to John Eutychius

*This letter (Allen no. 550) is a dedication added to Erasmus' translation of* The banquet *in an edition of the translations published in 1517. Eutychius may probably be identified as Johann Huttich, a correspondent and friend of Erasmus. The banquet tells of the bad behaviour of some philosophers at a wedding feast.*

This dialogue of Lucian, my learned Eutychius,[1] shows great art in the marvellous propriety with which all the many and varied characters are portrayed, but I've none the less encountered some people who said it ought to be suppressed because it attacks every kind of philosopher with great freedom and, as it were, 'from the cart'.[2] But I think it's much more justifiable to be angry at the ways of our own age: we see the schools of philosophers and theologians squabbling among themselves much more childishly and fighting it out with no less savagery than Lucian portrays; while the battles between the professors of religion are just as bloody as the one that according to Lucian (whether fact or fiction) took place at that Banquet. And so, since it turned out that this little book had been left masterless and yet it seemed to need a patron, I've dedicated it to Eutychius. Farewell, and luck be with you (so that you can live up to your name).

### NOTES

1. *Eutychius*: probably a Latinisation of Huttich. Eutychius means lucky, and Erasmus puns on this sense in the closing sentence.
2. *From the cart*: ritual abuse was exchanged 'from the cart' at the Greek Eleusinian mysteries.

## (iii) More to Thomas Ruthall

*More's translations of* The cynic *(which is now thought to be spurious),* Menippus *or* Necromancy *and* The lover of lies *were given this joint dedication to Thomas Ruthall, an ecclesiastic in the service of the Crown. In* The cynic, *a Cynic philosopher defends his simple way of life.* Menippus *is one of Lucian's fantastic pieces, in which Menippus goes to the Underworld to learn how to live, since the philosophers on earth cannot agree on an answer, and is told by Tiresias to abandon philosophical speculation and follow the life of the common sort. The* lover of lies *is an attack on superstition, in which Tychiades recounts the lying stories of a group of philosophers. On More, see Introduction, pp. 23-4.*

I think, learned sir, that if a writer has ever fulfilled Horace's advice to combine pleasure with profit,[1] Lucian has done so as much as anybody. He avoids both the arrogant dogmas of philosophers and poets' careless play, and throughout his work he points out and attacks men's failings with a humour that's both responsible and very funny. He does this so wittily and with such a good moral effect that though no one strikes deeper, no one can resent his barbs. He's always excellent at this, but I think that he's particularly successful in these three dialogues; that's why I've picked them out to translate from all his many delightful works, but I know that other people may well prefer others. Men don't all choose the same girl, but each a different one according to his taste – an individual doesn't fall in love with the girl he can confidently state is the most beautiful, but the one who seems so to him; so too among Lucian's charming dialogues different people have different preferences, and I like these most, but I hope that I've got good reason for my choice and that I'm not alone in it. I shall start with the shortest, *The cynic*. It's so short indeed that it could seem negligible, but Horace reminds us that a small body often conceals outstanding strength,[2] and we can see for ourselves that even the tiniest gems are precious. My choice of it is supported by the tribute paid to it by St John Chrysostom, a man of outstanding judgement, the most Christian of virtually all men of learning, and, in my view at least, the most learned of Christians. He so relished this dialogue that he included a good part of it in a homily that he wrote on John's Gospel.[3] And with good reason; for what work should have pleased a serious man and a true Christian more than a dialogue which defends the Cynics' life, rough and contented with little, and attacks the effete luxury of voluptuaries? The same arguments also serve to praise the simplicity of the Christian life, its temperance, its frugality, in short the strait and narrow way that leads to eternal life. The second dialogue, *Necromancy* (an inauspicious title, but the contents are splendid) shows marvellous wit in attacking the frauds of sorcerers, the idle fictions of poets and the speculative gladiatorial contests that philosophers engage in on any subject under the sun. There remains *The lover of lies*, which, as the title shows, is entirely devoted to mocking and exposing, not without Socratic irony, the passion for lying; it's hard to say whether the wit of this dialogue is more remarkable or its moral value. I'm not greatly perturbed by the fact that his attitude in it seems to be one of doubt about his own immortality, which means that he shared the error of Democritus, Lucretius, Pliny and very many others.[4] What does it matter to me what a pagan believes on this issue, which is among the chief mysteries of the Christian faith? We can certainly derive benefit from the dialogue; we can learn not to be convinced by the frauds of magic, to be free from superstition, which everywhere creeps upon men under the guise of religion, and to lead a less troubled life, less frightened by miserable and superstitious impostures. These impostures are often recounted with such a show of reliability and authority that even a man of the stature of the blessed St Augustine, a ferocious foe of lies, was deceived by some trickster into telling as a true occurrence of his own day a story about two Spurinnae — one coming back to life, one dying — which Lucian had ridiculed in this dialogue, with a difference of name only, so many years before Augustine was born.[5] So you shouldn't be surprised if the uneducated populace are taken in by the fictions of these people, who think they've done something really worth while and secured Christ's favour for themselves for ever, if they can just invent a pious story about a saint or a tale of horror about the Underworld, to make some old woman shed a few crazed tears or tremble in horror. As a result, there's scarcely a life of a martyr or a virgin that they've left without inserting some lying story of this kind — an act of piety, of course; for wasn't there a danger that truth might prove too weak to sustain itself without the support of lies? They didn't hold back from polluting with their fictions the very religion that truth itself established and intended to consist of unadorned truth; they didn't realise that, so far from helping, nothing does more pernicious harm than fables of that kind. For, as St Augustine, whom I mentioned, bears witness,[6] if one catches a whiff of a lie that's been added, at once the authority of what's true is reduced and subverted. And so I often suspect that a large proportion of such stories were invented by cunning and unprincipled rogues and heretics, whose aim was partly to amuse themselves with the credulousness of simple people (not of the wise, of course) and partly to discredit Christianity's true stories by putting these fabrications on the market; their inventions are often so similar to accounts contained in Holy Scripture that it's clear they are making fun of them by parody. And so we should have unquestioning faith only in the stories which are guaranteed for us by divinely inspired Scripture. As for the others, we should test them, cautiously and judiciously, by Christ's teaching (as if we were applying Critolaus' rule[7]) and so accept or reject them. That is the way to avoid both groundless hopes and superstitious fears. But I'm getting carried away.

My letter's almost grown longer than the book, and I've still not said a single word in praise of you, although another writer might have concentrated on nothing but this. And yet the scope for praise, and praise without any suspicion of flattery, is enormous; to say nothing of your other qualities, there's your remarkable learning and your great skill in practical affairs (witness your successful missions to many different countries on most difficult business); then too there's your outstanding loyalty and seriousness — without complete confidence in these qualities of yours our wise monarch would never have chosen you as his secretary. But your singular modesty resists all proclamation of your other qualities; you're delighted to act with distinction, but you don't like hearing it said that you have done so. I shall respect your modesty as long as I can make this one request: please accept these first fruits of my studies in Greek literature with favour, and treat them, such as they are, as a token of my affection for you and willingness to serve you. I am emboldened to entrust them to you with greater confidence by the thought that, though no one will see any errors in them more clearly than you (so penetrating is your judgement), so generous is your nature that no one will be happier to turn a blind eye. Farewell.

NOTES

1. *Art of poetry*, 343.
2. I.e. Horace, though small (*Epistles*, I.xx. 24), had outstanding gifts.
3. St John Chrysostom, *c*. AD 347-407, a doctor of the Church, was a good orator and delivered homilies on books of the Bible; there seem to be no grounds for More's assertion that he borrowed from *The cynic*.
4. Democritus, the Greek philosopher (fifth century BC), and Lucretius, the Roman poet, believed that the soul was made of atoms and perished with the body; Pliny the Elder denies the possibility of life after death in his *Natural history*, VII. lv. 188-90.
5. Augustine, *On the proper care for the dead*, xii. 15.
6. Augustine, *On lying*, x. 17.
7. Critolaus' rule was that the goods of the soul outweighed the goods of the body, see Cicero, *Tusculan disputations*, V. xvii. 51 (Critolaus was a Peripatetic philosopher of the second century BC).

**Erasmus: Two letters on Plutarch**

*The late Greek author, Plutarch (c. AD 50-120) was another writer to enjoy a resurgence of popularity in the Renaissance. His* Lives *came into prominence in the fifteenth century, when numerous translations* into Latin were made; their influence, through the medium of North's English translation from the French version of Jacques Amyot, is immortalised in Shakespeare's Roman plays. The Moralia, a collection of essays on moral and other topics, were also very influential (I have suggested some reasons for their appeal in the Introduction, see pp. 37-9); translations into Latin appeared in the first half of the sixteenth century, and the work was drawn on by Castiglione, Elyot, Sidney, Montaigne and Ben Jonson.

Plutarch – and particularly the Moralia – was a special favourite with Erasmus, who praises him highly in The pious feast, The education of a Christian prince and On abundance. He helped to prepare the editio princeps in Greek of the Moralia (Aldine, 1509), he translated various essays into Latin, and he drew on Plutarch for the Adages, the Parallels and the Apophthegms, those collections of the wise sayings of the ancients. As the following letters show, he valued Plutarch for his wisdom about everyday life and his knowledge of human nature, and he also had a true appreciation of Plutarch's style, imitating its learned allusiveness in his own writings.

## (i) To Thomas Wolsey

This letter (Allen no. 284) was written in January 1514, as the dedication to a manuscript copy of a translation of Plutarch's How to profit by one's enemies; when the translation was printed by Froben in July 1514 in Plutarchi opuscula (Little works by Plutarch), it had a new dedication to Wolsey. Plutarch's essay contained useful advice for a rising statesman.

For long I've been afraid to approach so important a man with so small a present; as I hesitated, I was encouraged by your goodness but deterred by your eminence, and now the dignity of a bishop[1] has been added to all your other distinctions. But I reflected that the humanity of your character has not been reduced just because your honours have increased, and so I've ventured to testify to my respect for you and to seek your favour by this little gift, such as it is. It's a very short book, but one can praise it very briefly by saying it's by Plutarch. Greece, the fertile mother of so many remarkable talents, never produced one more learned or more elegant than Plutarch. I don't know if anyone has ever matched him in his combination of outstanding eloquence and very exact knowledge. Everything he says is a pure gem. If anything doesn't please you in it, blame it on me. Farewell, and please give Erasmus a place if only in the outermost circle of your humble servants.

NOTE

1. Wolsey had just been nominated Bishop of Lincoln.


*(ii) To Alexius Turzo*

*This letter (Allen no. 1572) is the dedication to a Hungarian nobleman of a translation of two treatises from the* Moralia, On the control of anger *and* On curiosity, *published by Froben in 1525. Only the part of the letter which concerns Plutarch is given here.*


I've been caused no little difficulty by the very subtlety of Plutarch's style and the unfamiliar ideas which he brings out from the inner stores of every author and discipline, and fits together in such a way that the result seems less an essay than a cento or, better, a mosaic, carefully constructed from the choicest inlaid pieces. His mind was so richly furnished with literature that this was easy for him, but that makes it all the more difficult for the translator to spot what he culled from where (particularly as many of the authors from whose meadows he plucked the flowers with which he wove these garlands don't survive). As well as this difficulty, he has a certain concision and abruptness, and will suddenly turn the train of thought in quite a new direction; so careful attention is needed in reading him as well as wide learning. In fact, though Plutarch is a Boeotian,[1] he demands a taste and an intelligence that aren't Boeotian in his readers. I'll say nothing here about the errors of copyists, though they've often delayed my progress, like stretches of broken road. I've resolved many of them; some, though not many, I've evaded rather than removed.

But the value of the argument more than makes up for all these difficulties. Socrates drew philosophy down from heaven to earth;[2] Plutarch brought it into men's chambers and private apartments and bedrooms. I'm particularly glad to be busy with this kind of work at the moment because I see that Christian affairs have reached a pitch of controversy where it's not safe to speak about Christ at all, whether you speak well or ill; there's a scorpion under every stone. But in these books Plutarch is treating subject-matter that anybody could find practically useful at any time. I'm amazed that all his writings on ethics aren't in everybody's hands and aren't given to children to learn by heart. Certainly, though I'd read these books with some care in the past, I feel that I've been much improved now by studying them more thoroughly and going into them in more depth.

Some faults are removed or are at least moderated by old age. But anger, which the young are subject to through the heat of their blood and their ignorance of affairs, revives in the old, doubtless because of their physical weakness, unless experience and philosophy provide a rapid antidote. Curiosity, too, is a fault characteristic of both these ages, childhood and the approach to second childhood, except that in the young it's called levity and in the old suspicion. According to the Peripatetics,[3] for children it serves as a kind of stimulus to learning and for the old as a remedy against the lethargy of age, or perhaps rather as a counsellor against being taken in. I've always been so free from inquisitiveness about other people's affairs that I've taken less interest even in my own than I should have done. But I'm 'quick to anger, though ready to be soothed'.[4] This emotion can outrun one's fixed intentions and bring them to nothing, particularly when the offence that provokes it involves shamelessness and malice. None the less, I think that I'm one of the rare people who hate to renounce a friendship and who even when grossly wronged, and that more than once, can forgive and forget. Perhaps you with your wisdom and gentle temperament have no need of such remedies, but it must be hard for one with such a burden of affairs not to be aroused sometimes. Certainly no one is so perfect that he couldn't improve further, though there may be no one who can teach him. Farewell, my eminent friend.

NOTES

1. *Boeotian*: Boeotians were proverbial for their stupidity.
2. Cicero, *Tusculan disputations*, V. iv. 10-11.
3. *Peripatetics*: the Aristotelian school of philosophy.
4. Horace, *Epistles*, I. xx. 25.

## Erasmus: Two letters on Cicero

*Cicero was, of course, the Renaissance hero and paradigm. Petrarch salutes him thus:*

> *O great father of Roman eloquence! I am not alone in offering you my gratitude; with me are all those who deck themselves with the flowers of Latin speech. We sprinkle our meadows with water from your fountains; you are our guide; it is you who sustain and enlighten us. (Quoted Seigel,* Rhetoric and philosophy in Renaissance humanism, *p. 3)*

*In these two letters, Erasmus lays less emphasis on Cicero's golden eloquence than on the moral value of his philosophical works. These are not very highly regarded today because of their lack of originality, but they were very popular in the Renaissance and were the medium through which most men gained their knowledge of ancient philosophy.*

## (i) To James Tutor

*This letter (Allen no. 1013), dated 1519, is the dedication of a new edition of* On duties *to an old friend, Jacob Voogd ('voogd' is the Dutch for 'guardian', hence the latinisation 'Tutor'), chief magistrate of Antwerp.*

Just as people who are bitten by scorpions turn to scorpions for a cure, so too it seems to me appropriate for those of us who are dedicated to literature, my dear James, most learned of lawyers, that if hard study cause us any mental exhaustion or physical weakness, we should use studies, but of a pleasanter kind, to revive ourselves. Truly studious men do nothing else but study throughout their lives, for as long as the course of their lives is under their own control; they don't interrupt their studies so much as lighten them, and though they occasionally give their minds some relaxation, they're never idle. They're off duty sometimes, but they're busy with something all the while; occasionally they have a holiday, but they can always give a good account of this leisure time. If you like, they are even idle at times, but in such a way that their idleness bears more useful fruit than some people's most hectic activity. It's the same (I'll choose a closer parallel this time) with a brave and energetic soldier. Even when he's in summer or winter quarters, or when there's a truce and he doesn't have to stand in the battle-line or sleep out under skins, in order to relax and recover his strength he still chooses games that have a flavour of soldiering about them. He duels against a stake, throws javelins at a target, whirls a sling, hurls spears, competes in the wrestling-ring, jousts with lances, swims across raging torrents, leaps on horseback armed. In short, his holiday from military duties sends him back to them all the fitter. A roué has one idea of play, a good prince another; the jests of a good and upright man are very different from those of a buffoon.

And so recently, when an excess of scholarly labour over a long period had exhausted me both in mind and body, and illness forced me to try to revive and consolidate my strength, I left Louvain and travelled round through several towns of Brabant and Flanders; my idea was to escape from my books for a while and to enjoy the company and the stories of some learned young friends. But I couldn't bear to abandon my beloved library so utterly as not to carry one or two books with me as travelling-companions, so that even when there happened to be no one very suitable to chat to on the cart, I would still have someone whose conversation would help me cheat the tedium of the journey. Among them were Cicero's *Of duties*, *Laelius*[1] and *Cato*,[2] along with the *Stoic paradoxes*. I was attracted by the smallness of the book, which wouldn't add much to the weight of my luggage. I derived a double benefit from reading it, my dear Tutor. On the one hand, it reminded me so strongly of our intimacy long ago, than which nothing could have been more delightful, that I experienced extraordinary pleasure. On the other, it fired me with a passion for right and virtue such as I haven't felt for many years, as I read these 'modern' writers of ours, who, Christians teaching the mysteries of Christian philosophy, discourse on these same topics with, as it seems to me, great subtlety but equal frigidity.

I don't know what other people feel, but what I felt myself I confess freely (whether the fault for this is theirs or my own). As I read I kept thinking to myself: was this written by a pagan for pagans, by a profane writer for the profane? But what equity there is in his rules for living, what probity, integrity, truth! Everything is in accordance with nature, nothing is artificial or drowsy. What qualities of character he requires in those who control a nation's affairs! How vividly he puts the wonderful and lovable form of virtue before our eyes! How much he teaches, and how nobly, nay divinely! – about helping everybody even without reward, about preserving friendships, about the immortality of souls and about despising things for the sake of which the vast majority today, not just of Christians but even of theologians and monks, will stop at absolutely nothing. Sometimes I felt ashamed of the way we are today; we have sacred books to teach us and innumerable models and rewards to inspire us, and yet though we preach the doctrine of the Gospels we don't practise it! Describe to our satraps a prince or magistrate such as Cicero describes, and hang me if he won't be laughed at as though he were mad along with his model. Who enters public life today except in hope of gain or for the sake of glory? What public figure doesn't behave as if he were conducting a business, and doesn't treat as an enemy the very people whose interests he ought to be protecting even at the cost of his own life? Where among Christians could you find a pair of friends to match the model that Cicero proposes? Where old men who bear the discomforts of old age with such fortitude? And where such dignified discussions between old and young?

Never before have I so strongly felt the truth of Augustine's saying that the good deeds of pagans are a sharper spur to virtue than those of our own people; one thinks what a disgrace it is for a mind over which the light of the Gospel has been cast not to appreciate something that was appreciated by men who had only the light of nature to guide them, and what a disgrace it is for us, who are fighting for religion beneath the standard of Christ and expect immortal life from him as our wages, not to achieve what was achieved by men who either suspected or firmly believed that nothing of man survives the funeral pyre. And despite this, there are still some dimwits who warn students off books of this kind as being in their words 'poetical' and morally harmful. But I think they should be studied in every school by teachers with their classes, and read and re-read by those of mature years on their own account; and so I'm now dedicating to you once again a new edition of the work that I long ago corrected and dedicated to you.[3] The new edition is not merely more accurate but increased in scope: I've added the treatises *On friendship*, *On old age* and on paradoxes, and some notes on all the works, short, but, if I'm not mistaken, by no means useless; my main aim in these is to trounce the joyless pedantry of certain people in matters of language, the type who exclaim at almost every word, 'It's not Latin,' 'It doesn't occur in good writers.' I've also drawn attention to certain corruptions which as far as I know no one had noticed before.

It merely remains that, just as Tutor was constantly before my eyes while I was engaged on this work, so too the image of Erasmus should enter your mind as you read it, Erasmus your most devoted friend. Farewell.

NOTES

1. *Laelius*: i.e. *On friendship*.
2. *Cato*: i.e. *On old age*.
3. Probably in 1501, though the dedication was never printed (see Allen no. 152).

*(ii) To John Vlatten*

*This letter (Allen no. 1390) is the dedication of an edition (Froben, 1523) of Cicero's* Tusculan disputations *to John Vlatten, who was to become counsellor to the Duke of Cleves and a lasting friend of Erasmus;* Ciceronianus *was dedicated to him in 1528.*

When, my distinguished friend, John Froben was preparing to print Cicero's *Tusculan disputations* at his press, he asked me to make some modest addition of my own, so that the book could appear with some useful new material to recommend it. I was happy to undertake the task, all the more so because for several years now I've had few or no dealings with the gentler Muses. So I delegated the job of collating texts to my young assistants and took the task of judgement upon myself. I read through the whole work with care, and I arranged properly the quotations which Cicero collects from Greek and Latin poets. (In this he's following a practice of Plato and Aristotle, but he takes it almost to the point of tediousness.) When the texts offered variant readings, I either adopted what was generally accepted or, if it seemed to be a genuine case for doubt, I preserved both readings, one in the text and one in the margin. I made some restorations without manuscript authority, but not very many, and only where the truth would be perfectly clear to an experienced scholar; and I added a certain number of scholia. While engaged on this, I've had to pause for two or three days in my other projects, in which I'm doing what I can to advance evangelism.

So far am I from regretting this interruption that I'd dearly love to have the chance to return to these old friends of mine and enjoy their company for a few months. I feel that I've profited enormously from re-reading this book; it's not just that it's rubbed some of the rust from my style (though that's certainly valuable, in my view) but also, more importantly, that it helps to control and restrain the desires. As I read, I kept feeling fresh contempt for those fools who constantly repeat that there's nothing remarkable in Cicero except verbal tinsel. His work shows wide acquaintance with the writings of the most learned Greeks on the art of living well and happily; it abounds in valuable and admirable precepts, and his knowledge and recollection of both past and recent history are remarkable. What is more, the profundity of his reflections on man's true happiness shows very clearly that he put his precepts into practice in his own life. And in explaining topics that are far removed from everyday ideas and language, so that many people thought they couldn't be treated in Latin at all, he shows extraordinary clarity, lucidity, fluency, abundance and even gaiety.

Philosophy was originally busy with contemplation of the natural world and so was far removed from everyday life. Socrates is said to have been the first to bring it down to earth and even into men's houses.[1] Plato and Aristotle then tried to introduce it to the courts of kings, to senates and even to popular tribunals. But I think that Cicero actually managed to put it on the stage; it was through him that it learnt a style that even an uneducated audience could applaud. And all his many books of this kind were written in a period of intense difficulty and disorder in the state, some of them even when the situation was utterly desperate.[2] Doesn't it make us ashamed of our gossiping and guzzling to see that a pagan devoted even the free time caused by a national disaster to such admirable writings? And that he didn't seek mere distraction in empty pleasures, but turned to philosophy's sacred precepts for a true cure for affliction?

I don't know what other people feel but the effect Cicero has on me, particularly when he talks about the good life, is so strong that I can't doubt that some divine spirit possessed the mind that produced such thoughts. I'm particularly convinced by this idea of mine whenever I reflect how incalculably vast is the generosity of the eternal godhead. (Some people restrict this all too narrowly, judging it from what they're like themselves, I suppose.) The question of where Cicero's soul is now may be one on which no human judgement is competent to pronounce. But I certainly wouldn't myself be at all hostile, in casting my vote, to the people who hope that he is living in peace in the world above. No one can doubt that he believed in a godhead of surpassing greatness and goodness. And as for his views on the immortality of the soul and on the different destinies or rewards that await men in the afterlife, these are perfectly clear (if his many other writings aren't sufficient proof) from the one letter that he wrote to Octavian when already, as it seems, condemned to death;[3] so too is the confidence that he felt because his conscience was clear.

If a kind of crude and confused credulity in religious matters was enough to ensure salvation for the Jews before the revelation of the Gospel, why shouldn't an even cruder understanding of the divine have helped a pagan, who didn't even know the Law of Moses, towards salvation (especially as he was a man whose life was not just upright but saintly)? Before the light of the Gospel arose, very few Jews had exact knowledge of the Son and the Holy Spirit, and many didn't believe in the Resurrection of the body, but our ancestors didn't abandon hope of their salvation. What then if a pagan merely believed that a God, who he was convinced was omnipotent, utterly wise and utterly good, would reward the good and punish the evil in some way which he himself found most appropriate? Should anyone lay certain taints of his life against him, I don't myself think that Job or Melchisadec were entirely free from every failing throughout their lives. And there's no need to excuse him for sacrificing to idols. He may have done so, but in obedience to the national custom and not to his own judgement; he couldn't abolish the custom as it was enshrined in law. The point that the stories about the Gods were fabrications he could certainly gather from Ennius' *Sacred history*[4] for instance. You may say that he should have exposed the people's folly even at the price of his own life. But even the Apostles lacked such courage as that before they received the Holy Spirit, so that it's unreasonable to expect it of Cicero.

But on this subject everyone should make his own mind up freely. I return now to the fools who think that Cicero's writings contain nothing of value except for a meaningless tinkling of words. How could he have explained all those learned topics so clearly, so abundantly and with such emotional power unless he had a thorough understanding of what he was writing about? Who has ever sat down to read a book of this kind and not arisen from it in a calmer mood? Who has ever been so distressed when he started it that he wasn't happier when he finished? You seem to see what you're reading about actually being done, and the infectious enthusiasm of his speech seizes you just as if you were actually hearing it flow direct from the living man's own most divinely eloquent lips. This is why I often think that, of all the useful discoveries that we owe to men's industry, the most useful is that of letters, and that there's no more valuable art than the printer's. What can be more splendid than to be free whenever one wants to talk with men who combined great eloquence and great sanctity? And to be just as well acquainted with the talents, character, thoughts, interests and doings of men who lived centuries ago as if you had lived on familiar terms with them for many years?

I've never approved more of Quintilian's saying that 'You can know that you have made progress when you begin to like Cicero.'[5] As a boy I preferred Seneca, and it wasn't till I was twenty that I could bear reading Cicero for long, even though I liked almost all the other Latin writers. I don't know if I've improved with age but certainly even in the days when I passionately loved that kind of study I never liked Cicero more than I do now in old age; and not just for the almost divine felicity of his style but also for the sanctity of that learned mind. He has really inspired me and made me better than I was. And so I wouldn't hesitate to urge the young to spend valuable time on reading Cicero's works and even learning them, rather than on the quarrelsome and aggressive pamphlets that one finds on all sides nowadays. As for myself, despite my age, as soon as I'm free from the work I've got in hand, I won't be unwilling or ashamed to be reconciled with my Cicero and renew for a few months our old friendship that's been for too many years interrupted.

I've decided to dedicate my work, such as it is, to you, my most gifted Vlatten; this is partly to show that I've not yet forgotten the delightful time when we shared one another's company in Freiburg and I first got to know fully your great humanity and remarkably winning character; and partly so that you can have this book of Cicero in a more correct form to put on the syllabus for reading with young students of literature. (You said that you were also particularly involved with looking after the school.) I'm afraid it's no surprise that you suffer from a chorus of frogs raising a clamour against good literature there too; there are always some of them here, croaking out their familiar ditty from Old Comedy, 'Brekekekex koax koax'.[6] But we must ignore them firmly and do whatever best serves the interests of the pupils. The most important point is to put in charge of the school someone who is as sound in character as he is well versed in literature, and to increase his salary in proportion to his merits. After laying the foundations of a knowledge of both languages, he should read the best authors with the class, i.e. Cicero and whoever else most resembles him. From the poets, he should choose the pure; as for those who are worth reading for their learning but are dangerously obscene (such as Martial) I think excerpts should be made that can safely be read with pupils.

More about this perhaps on another occasion (though you couldn't find a better adviser than Leonard Pricard, a man admirably qualified by his wide learning, upright character and great experience of affairs). I would be sorry that Conrad Heresbach has been snatched away from us — I'll swear I've never seen anyone more perfect than that young man, whether in knowledge of both languages, intellectual gifts or the blend of charm and integrity in his character — if I didn't know the dunces he's got away from and the prince he's acquired as patron. Farewell.

NOTES

1. Cicero, *Tusculan disputations*, V. iv. 10-11; *Academica*, I. iv. 15.
2. Cicero, an ardent Republican, was on the losing side in the Roman political struggle; his philosophical works were mostly written in 45 to 44 BC, that is, in the year before Caesar's assassination, when Cicero was unable to take part in politics, and the year after it, when the future of the state was uncertain; in 43, when Antony came to power, Cicero was murdered.
3. Presumably an allusion to a letter which is found in manuscripts of Cicero's letters but which is now regarded as spurious; in the last paragraph, Cicero says that if he cannot avoid seeing Rome submit to political servitude he has resolved to join the noble dead. (A text will be found in the Oxford Classical Text of

Cicero's letters, vol. III.)

4. Ennius, the Roman epic poet, wrote a prose work based on the lost novel by Euhemerus (311-298 BC) in which he suggested that the Gods were great men deified by their peoples.

5. *The education of an orator*, X. i. 112.

6. The chant of the frogs in Aristophanes' comedy, *The frogs*.

## Erasmus on Homer, from *On abundance*

*This account, from the 1534 edition of* On abundance, *of a famous episode from* Iliad, *Book VI (lines 392-502), is introduced into a discussion of various ways of expanding a speech, one of which is to give vivid details from everyday life which evoke the gentler emotions and so bring pleasure to the listener or reader. It is included here to show that Erasmus was able to take honest pleasure in narrative for its own sake and 'to respond to the central, obvious appeal of a great work', something which C. S. Lewis says the humanists lost (*English literature in the sixteenth century, p. 26).

Pleasure derived from the gentle emotions is particularly appropriate in the narrative section of a speech, whether because a scene is very vividly presented through these emotions or because everybody recognises them. Who, for instance, could read without pleasure Homer's description of Andromache meeting the armed Hector at the city gate through which he was about to go out to battle? Andromache isn't alone, which would be inappropriate for a modest matron, but accompanied by her maids; in her arms she holds the baby Astyanax, Hector's son and his father's darling. Homer adds that he is 'like a beautiful star', so that the wife can appeal to her husband's feelings through the child. Hector smiles without speaking when he sees his son. Andromache comes up to him, reaches out her right hand and addresses him by name. Then, after an appropriate speech composed for both of them, Hector reaches out to kiss his son, but the child, terrified by the gleam of his armour and the crest waving threateningly from the helmet-top, cries and shrinks back into his mother's arms. At this point both his father and mother laugh. Hector now takes his helmet off, puts it on the ground, and then takes his child and kisses him. Then he prays for the child's success and hands him over to his mother; she takes him in her fragrant bosom, 'laughing tearfully'. Hector is moved by this to pity and, supporting his wife with his hand, consoles her, speaking to her by name; then he replaces his helmet. She obeys her husband and returns home. And there the whole house becomes filled with the weeping of women, because they think he will not come back from that battle. And so they weep for him as though he were dead, while he is still breathing. The epithets with which the scene is interspersed add no little charm: 'Hector of the sparkling helm', 'glorious Hector reached out for his child', 'the fair-girdled nurse', 'the horse-hair crest', 'his dear father and lady mother', 'all-gleaming helm', 'dear son', 'dear wife', the one referred to above, 'fragrant bosom', and 'horsehair-crested helmet'. This gift is above all the reason why no one ever tires of reading Homer but is led onwards by constant delight.

## Ascham: *The schoolmaster*

*Roger Ascham's career mingled the college and the court. Born in Yorkshire in 1515/16, the son of a steward, in 1530 he went up to St John's College, Cambridge, then a flourishing centre of humanist studies. He became a pupil and life-long admirer of Sir John Cheke (1514-57), the promoter of Greek studies, who was to become first Regius professor of Greek in 1540. Ascham could have pursued an academic career; he was elected to a fellowship in 1534 and became public orator in 1546. But, like so many English humanists, he felt the lure of public life, and was tempted by various royal appointments, first as tutor to Princess Elizabeth in 1548-9, then as secretary to the ambassador to Charles V in 1550; he ended his career as Latin secretary first to Mary and then to Elizabeth (1553-68).*

*Ascham's published writings continue the popularising tradition of Sir Thomas Elyot; he develops the vernacular in a rather more personal and anecdotal direction than his predecessor. The schoolmaster, published in 1570 after his death by his widow, is a treatise on education which helped to spread humanist ideas; it was a popular work, which went through several editions. Ascham follows Quintilian, he praises Erasmus and Castiglione, and he leans heavily on the views of his friends, Cheke and Johann Sturm, rector of the gymnasium at Strasburg, with whom he had a long and friendly correspondence. Like Elyot, he laments the attitude of the aristocracy to education and stresses the value of learning to the state (see below, pp. 179-82). He sketches a programme of studies based on close analysis of classical authors rather than on rules of grammar, and emphasises the importance of good expression (see below, pp. 182-4).*

*The sentence quoted here is probably aimed at Peter Ramus (Pierre*

*de la Ramée, 1515-72), who in 1536 had defended the thesis that
everything written by Aristotle was false, and who had criticised Cicero
in some lectures on* The orator *published in 1547. It is a striking
example of humanist conservatism; contrast the approach of Vives and
Ben Jonson (see below, p. 155).*

### Aristotle and Cicero (from Book II)

For he that can neither like Aristotle in logic and philosophy nor Tully
in rhetoric and eloquence will from these steps, likely enough, presume
by like pride to mount higher to the misliking of greater matters —
that is, either in religion to have a dissentious head or in the commonwealth to have a factious heart.

## Ben Jonson on Homer and Virgil

### (i) From Discoveries

Timber, *or discoveries made upon men and matter is a fascinating
humanist source-book. It is a sort of commonplace book which Jonson
seems to have been compiling until his death, from passages in classical
and modern writers that appealed to him. (It may have originated as
lecture notes for a possible period as deputy lecturer in rhetoric at
Gresham College; see Herford and Simpson's edition of Ben Jonson,
vol. XI, pp. 582-5.) Quintilian and Seneca are the two main sources;
others include Cicero, Pliny, Suetonius, the elder Seneca, Aulus Gellius,
Plutarch and Apuleius among the ancients, and Erasmus, Machiavelli,
Bacon, the Spanish humanist Juan Luis Vives, the Neo-Stoic Lipsius
and the scholars J. J. Scaliger and Daniel Heinsius among the moderns.
The themes are literary, political and moral. The passages are all translated into superb English prose, and Jonson assembles paragraphs by
working together sentences drawn from different places in his sources
and adding some of his own; the end product is very much an expression of himself and his own views. He probably had publication in
mind, but the work was not in a finished state when he died;
Sir Kenelm Digby, his literary executor, gathered up his loose papers
and gave them to the publisher of the Folio of 1640.*

The reading of Homer and Virgil is counselled by Quintilian[1] as the best
way of informing youth and confirming man. For besides that the mind
is raised with the height and sublimity of such a verse, it takes spirit
from the greatness of the matter and is tincted with the best things.

NOTE

1. *The education of an orator*, I. viii. 5.


*(ii) From* The New Inn

*This speech of Lovel's from* The New Inn *(I. vi. 119-38) is an interesting expression of humanist ideas. Ben Jonson has the humanist scorn for romance (see also* An execration upon Vulcan, *29-32, 59-70); Erasmus in* The education of a Christian prince *warns princes against reading romances, 'which are not only about tyrants but are also very poorly done, stupid, and fit to be "old wives' tales" ' (Born's translation, p. 200), while Ascham in* The schoolmaster *says that the whole pleasure of* Le morte d'Arthur *stands 'in open man's slaughter and bold bawdry', and makes the same connection as Lovel with monasticism and corrupt learning. In contrast to romance is set the classical epic; Homer and Virgil are viewed as teachers of civilised learning about arms and arts. Such a view of Homer forms a striking contrast to eighteenth-century notions of Homer as the primitive artist* par excellence *(see Hugh Honour,* Neo-classicism, *(Style and civilisation, Penguin, 1977), pp. 62-7; Kirsti Simonsuuri,* Homer's original genius: eighteenth-century notions of the early Greek epic 1688-1798 *(Cambridge University Press, 1979), chapter 10 and* passim*).*


> Did you ever know or hear of the Lord Beaufort,
> Who served so bravely in France? I was his page,
> And, ere he died, his friend! I followed him
> First i'the wars, and i'the times of peace
> I waited on his studies, which were right.
> He had no Arthurs, nor no Rosicleers,
> No Knights o'the Sun nor Amadis de Gauls,
> Primalions and Pantagruels,[1] public nothings,
> Abortives of the fabulous, dark cloister,
> Sent out to poison courts and infest manners;
> But great Achilles, Agamemnon's acts,
> Sage Nestor's counsels and Ulysses' sleights,
> Tydides'[2] fortitude, as Homer wrought them
> In his immortal fancy, for examples
> Of the heroic virtue. Or as Virgil,
> That master of the epic poem, limned
> Pious Aeneas, his religious prince,

Bearing his aged parent on his shoulders,
Rapt from the flames of Troy, with his young son!
And these he brought to practice and to use.

NOTES

1. These are all characters from romances.
2. *Tydides*: Diomedes.

## Erasmus: *Ciceronianus*

### Three passages on imitation

*The correct way to imitate had been a frequent topic of debate before Erasmus wrote his dialogue in 1527. (For a full account, see Scott, Controversies over the imitation of Cicero, pp. 10-23.) There were those who favoured eclectic imitation of a wide range of classical authors, employing the vocabulary of many periods, and those who thought that Cicero was the supreme model for prose and who strove to write correct Ciceronian Latin. The former generally stressed the importance of originality and individuality in writing; while even the latter advocated assimilating the spirit of Cicero and not just copying his words, and agreed that it was foolish to imitate faults. In an exchange of letters with Paolo Cortesi in c. 1490, Politian had said that one should read a wide range of authors and then learn to swim without a float; and he asserted that the aim of his writing was to express himself, not Cicero. In an exchange of letters in 1512-13 with the most famous of the Ciceronian purists, Pietro Bembo, Gianfrancesco Pico, the nephew of Pico della Mirandola, had put in a plea for variety: people have different temperaments and standards of judgement and hence choose different models; the ancients themselves did not imitate slavishly or follow the same model.*

*Erasmus' contribution to the debate is cast as a dialogue; Bulephorus ('Counsel-bearer') attempts to cure Nosoponus ('Disease-sufferer') of his excessive passion for Cicero. Nosoponus is a caricature of a Ciceronian; he banishes all other authors from his library, employs no grammatical forms which are not found in Cicero, and starts imitating at night, sustained only by ten currants and three coriander seeds coated with sugar. As the following passages show, Bulephorus recapitulates many of the arguments of the eclectic imitators; in particular we may note his strong insistence that writing must bear the imprint of the* writer, and that whatever has been borrowed must be thoroughly assimilated (*Erasmus employs the digestion and bee metaphors from Seneca, Moral letters, lxxxiv, to express this idea, and adds some more of his own*). *Erasmus' chief new argument against the Ciceronians is the charge of paganism; always concerned to show the harmony between classical and Christian, he was naturally opposed to the attitude of Bembo, who warned Sadoleto against letting St Paul corrupt his style. Erasmus argues that, just as Cicero's great virtue was the ability to adapt his speech to different circumstances ('decorum'), so moderns must take account of changed circumstances and speak as Christians.*

*The controversy continued after Erasmus' book. J. C. Scaliger and Etienne Dolet wrote violent pamphlets defending Cicero and Ciceronian imitation. Two proponents of eclectic imitation who were influential in England were the Spanish humanist Juan Luis Vives and Peter Ramus. Vives (1492-1540) was a friend and admirer of Erasmus; he lived in England in the 1520s, under the patronage of Katherine of Aragon. He gives an Erasmian liberal account of imitation in* On the transmission of knowledge *(1531) (Book IV, chapter 4, pp. 189-200, in Foster Watson's translation), a book which Ben Jonson drew on for* Discoveries. *Peter Ramus, who revolutionised the study of rhetoric and dialectic, had a strong following in the University of Cambridge. His* Ciceronianus *(1557) picks up many of Erasmus' arguments, and was in turn utilised by Gabriel Harvey for his* Ciceronianus *(1577), where he says that he was converted from extreme Ciceronianism by reading Ramus.*

### (i)

*Nosoponus*. How then can it be brought about that one day we become true Ciceronians? I won't refuse to follow your plan, if you've one that's better than mine.

*Bulephorus*. Here then are the gifts I can wish us to have and the advice I can give you; there isn't much besides. I can wish for us Cicero's ability and nature, but I can't bestow it. Men's individual abilities have something distinctive of their own, which is so powerful that it's useless for a man composed by nature for a particular kind of speaking to strive for a different one. Fighting against the gods brings success to no one, as the Greeks say.

*No*. I know that Quintilian[1] gives the same advice with some emphasis.

*Bu*. So this would be my first piece of advice, that no one whose genius is radically different from Cicero's dedicates himself to copying Cicero; otherwise he'll turn out a kind of monster, as he'll have left his natural shape and yet not got another's. One ought, therefore, to consider above all what kind of speaking nature has moulded one for. If there's any truth in astrology, it's hard for anyone to be successful in anything at odds with his horoscope. A man born for the Muses will never be successful in war. A man born for war will never write successful poems. A man born for marriage will never be a good monk. A man born for agriculture will never prosper at court, and vice versa.

*No*. And yet there's nothing that 'relentless work'[2] can't overcome. We see stone turn to water, lead into silver, bronze into gold, by human skill, and plants shedding their wild nature through cultivation. Why shouldn't human ability be transformed by skill and practice, too?

*Bu*. Cultivation improves an adaptable nature, wins over a mildly uncooperative one and corrects a depraved one; but you'd be wasting your time, Nosoponus, in harrying one that's wholly uncooperative and fitted for different ends. A horse learns to be ridden round in a circle, he learns how to walk steadily, but it's useless to lead an ox to the ring, to call a dog to the plough or an antelope to a contest for horses. Water perhaps turns to air, and air to fire (if there really is such a thing as elemental fire), but earth never turns to fire, or fire to water.

*No*. But what prevents us adapting Cicero's diction to every subject?

*Bu*. I allow that there are certain general qualities in Marcus Tullius which are relevant to any topic, for example purity, lucidity, linguistic elegance, proper layout and anything of this kind. But this isn't enough for those apes of Cicero who demand the entire form of his diction – an ideal which could be achieved to some extent in treating certain subjects akin to his, but which is utterly impossible with topics which are quite different. You'll admit, I imagine, that Virgil holds the first place among poets as Marcus Tullius does among orators.

*No*. Yes.

*Bu*. Well, if you were preparing to write a lyric poem, would you model yourself on Horace or Virgil?

*No*. Horace, as supreme in this genre.

*Bu*. What about satire?

*No*. Horace still more.

*Bu*. What if you were planning a comedy?

*No*. I would go to Terence as a model.

*Bu*. Because of the complete dissimilarity of subject, of course.

*No*. But Cicero's diction has a *je ne sais quoi*, an aptness all its own.

*Bu*. I too can use the same words, 'a *je ne sais quoi*'. Many people are misled by their inordinate love of Cicero. To use Marcus Tullius' diction for totally different subjects is to become different from him.

And there's no need to aim at similarity, if one can succeed in being equal or at least close to him, although dissimilar. What are more dissimilar than emerald and carbuncle, and yet they're equal in value and esteem. A rose is unlike a lily, the smell's different, and yet each flower is a match for the other. Haven't you often seen two girls of dissimilar appearance but both of such remarkable beauty that it would be hard to choose between them, if one were given the choice? What comes nearer to the likeness of Cicero isn't automatically better. As I began to say, no animal resembles a man's shape more closely in all its limbs than an ape; if nature had given it a voice, you could really take it for a man; nothing's more unlike a man than a peacock or a swan, and yet you'd prefer to be a swan or a peacock, I think, than an ape.

*No.* I'd even prefer to be a camel or an antelope than the fairest of apes.

*Bu.* Tell me, Nosoponus, would you rather be given a nightingale's voice or a cuckoo's?

*No.* A nightingale's.

*Bu.* And yet a cuckoo sounds more like a man. Would you rather sing with the larks or caw with the crows?

*No.* Sing with the larks.

*Bu.* And yet a crow's voice is more like a man's. Would you rather bray with the asses or whinny with the horses?

*No.* Whinny with the horses, if fate really made me choose one of the two.

*Bu.* And yet an ass as it were tries to speak in a human way.

*No.* But I think that my natural capacity isn't totally at odds with the genius of Cicero. And what nature lacks, practice will make perfect. So finish off the advice you think needs to be given.

*Bu.* You're right to call me back on course; I was about to be side-tracked. The sum total is that we should really do what we want, that is express the whole of Cicero; and the whole of Cicero isn't in words or formulae, in rhythms or in his writings – no, he is scarcely half there, as has been sufficiently stated earlier.[3]

*No.* So where is the whole of Cicero?

*Bu.* Nowhere, except in himself. But if you want to express the whole of Cicero, you can't express yourself. If you don't express yourself, your discourse will be a lying mirror, and the result will seem no less absurd than if you were to daub your face with pigment and pretend to be Petronius rather than Nosoponus.

*No.* You speak in riddles.

*Bu.* I'll speak more bluntly. People who torture themselves to express the whole of Cicero in those ways are fools; it can't be done even if it were worth while, and it isn't worth while even if it could be done. But the whole of Cicero can be expressed, if we don't strive to reproduce his virtues, but to express their equal in imitation of him, or, if we can, even to surpass them. For it may be the case that the best Ciceronian is the man who's most unlike Cicero, the man, that is, who speaks best and most fittingly, although he speaks differently — obviously so, since circumstances are now entirely altered. In the same way, if someone wanted to paint as an old man a subject Apelles[4] had painted as a youth, and tried to paint him in the same way as Apelles had done, although he was now different, he would be unlike Apelles for this very reason.

*No.* A riddle worthy of the Sphinx, that someone's different in the very way he's like.

*Bu.* But wouldn't this be the case, if someone sang at a funeral in the same way as Hermogenes[5] used to sing at a wedding, or were to plead a case among the Areopagites[6] with the same gestures that Roscius[7] used when dancing in the theatre? But we can make likeness to Cicero a goal to this extent: in our quest for the palm of eloquence we can follow the same path that led Cicero to it.

*No.* What was that?

*Bu.* Did he devote himself to the imitation of one model? Certainly not. Instead, he tried to express from the best authors what was most appropriate in each. Demosthenes was his main but not his only model; and he didn't take Demosthenes as a pattern to be expressed whole, but he selected what was appropriate to himself; he wasn't content to follow him, but carefully avoided some features by selection and corrected others, and what he approved of he imitated with the intention of surpassing it. In addition, he filled the store-room of his mind to bursting with knowledge of every discipline, every author, of things old and new; he carefully learnt the families, rites, customs, laws, edicts, plebiscites of his state. Not only did he frequent the shrines of the philosophers devotedly but he also withdrew repeatedly into the retreats of the Muses; from one model he learned pronunciation, from another, gesture. Anyone who acts in just the same way will emerge very unlike Marcus Tullius; anyone who behaves in an equivalent or comparable way will be the one to merit the name Ciceronian.

*No.* Speak a bit more clearly.

*Bu.* The man who exerts himself with as much diligence in learning Christian philosophy as Cicero did in profane philosophy; who imbibes the Psalms and the Prophets with the same feeling with which he drank in the books of the poets; who is prepared to apply himself as hard to learning the decrees of the Apostles, the rites of the Church, the beginnings, development and eclipse of the Christian republic, as did Cicero when he laboured to master the rights and laws of the provinces, boroughs and allies of the city of Rome; and the man who adapts the knowledge provided by all these studies to contemporary affairs – he'll be entitled to canvass for the name of Ciceronian with some justice.

*No*. I don't see the direction of your remarks, unless it's that we should speak in a Christian, not a Ciceronian, manner.

*Bu*. What? Is anyone a Ciceronian in your eyes who doesn't speak appropriately and doesn't understand the subjects he's making his speeches about?

*No*. Certainly not.

*Bu*. But this is the direction of the studies of the people today who want to be considered Ciceronians. We're making our enquiry so that this won't happen to us. Nothing prevents the same person speaking both in a Christian and in a Ciceronian manner, if only you allow that the true Ciceronian is the man who speaks clearly, with a wealth of material, with force and appropriateness, in accordance with the nature of the subject and the circumstances of the times and persons involved. Now certain people have it that the ability to speak well isn't an art, but part of wisdom. Marcus Tullius himself, in the *Partitions*, defines eloquence elegantly as 'wisdom speaking with abundance'.[8] And it can't be doubted that he himself aimed at this sort of eloquence. But, good Lord, how far removed from this principle are people who want to speak in the manner of Cicero on subjects that are completely different, subjects that they neither understand nor love. The feeling that whatever differs from Cicero is mean and a solecism is a false, pernicious delusion in our minds, and one we must put far from us, if we want to win among Christians the distinction that Cicero won among his own people. 'The beginning and source of writing well is wisdom,' says that most acute of critics.[9] What then is the source of Ciceronian eloquence? A mind richly imbued with varied knowledge of all subjects, especially those you propose to speak about; a mind prepared by the precepts of art, much practice in writing and speaking, and long rehearsal; and – this is the heart of the whole business – a mind which loves what it recommends and feels real hatred for what it attacks. Allied to all this, there ought to be natural judiciousness, prudence and sense, things which can't be conveyed through any precepts. From where, I ask you, can these qualities come to people who read nothing except Cicero, who are keen 'to turn with nocturnal hand, to turn with diurnal hand'[10] his pages alone?

*No*. And yet it's been said sensibly that those who spend long in the sun are coloured by it, and those who sit long in a perfumery take with them the smell of the place when they leave.

*Bu*. I like your comparison very much. They take with them only a tincture of the skin and a whiff of odour that quickly disappears. Let those who're content with this glory sit as much as they like in the spice-boxes or rose-gardens of Cicero, let them warm themselves in his sun. I'd prefer to send down whatever good spices are available into my stomach, to transfer them to the veins, so that not only do I spread a mild perfume among my neighbours but also grow warm myself all through and become more vigorous; so that, whenever the situation demands, a voice issues forth which really seems the voice of a healthy and well-fed mind. The speech which keeps the attention of a listener, which moves him and draws him into whatever mental state you like, is born deep within the veins, not on the surface of the skin. I don't say this because I think that only a small and inadequate knowledge of actual subjects can be gathered from Cicero's books, but because he is not sufficient by himself to provide a rich store of discourse on every topic. What then remains except to learn from Cicero himself how to imitate Cicero? Let's imitate him as he imitated others. If Cicero stuck to reading one author exclusively, if he bound himself to the rule of one model, if he paid more attention to words than things, if he only wrote at bedtime, if he tortured himself for a whole month over one letter, if he thought anything eloquent which was not appropriate to the matter treated, let's do the same in order to be Ciceronians. But if all this is quite at odds with Cicero's example, then let's fill our minds after his example with the furniture of essential knowledge; let our first care be for ideas, only then for words, and let's fit words to things, not vice versa; and let's never turn our eyes in our writing from the principle of decorum. Only if it's born in the heart and doesn't float on the lips will our discourse be alive. We shouldn't ignore the precepts of art; for they contribute much to invention, disposition, handling of subjects and the avoidance of things that are either superfluous or which hinder the case. But when a serious case is to be conducted, sense should hold the first place. (Though even in imaginary cases which are handled for practice it's a good idea for what's said to be very like real cases.) Cicero wrote that the spirit of Laelius breathed in his writings.[11] But it's silly to try to write with someone else's disposition, and to take pains to make the spirit of Marcus Tullius breathe in your writings. You must digest what you devour in your long and varied reading, and by study transmit it into the veins of your mind, not just into your memory or a notebook; so that your mind, stuffed with every kind of food, produces discourse that smells, not of this or that flower, leaf or grass, but of the disposition and feelings of your own heart; so that the reader doesn't recognise fragments culled from Cicero, but the image of a mind filled with every kind of learning. Cicero had read every one of his predecessors; he had weighed carefully what there was to approve of or criticise in each, but you wouldn't recognise any of them in their own voice in Cicero, but rather the force of a mind invigorated by the ideas of all of them. But if the example of your favourite doesn't influence you, let's look at an example from nature. Do bees collect the material for making honey from one shrub? Don't they in fact fly around every kind of flower, plant and bush with amazing diligence, frequently fetching something from far away to store in their hives? And what they bring doesn't become honey at once; actually, they make a fluid with their mouths and internal organs, and bring out again from inside themselves what has been transformed into a part of themselves; you wouldn't recognise in it the taste or smell of any flower or shrub that has been plucked, but instead an apian product blended from all of them.[12] She-goats, too, don't feed on just one kind of foliage and so produce milk that only tastes like them; they fatten themselves on every kind of foliage, and so produce not the juice of plants but milk transformed out of them.

NOTES

1. *The education of an orator*, X. ii. 19-21.
2. A famous expression from Virgil, *Georgics*, I. 145-6.
3. Bulephorus has argued earlier that one should not confine oneself to imitating Cicero's writings, partly because he has not expressed himself on every topic in them, partly because some of his works are lost, while those that remain are textually corrupt or even forgeries, partly because some of his writings are inferior and do not live up to his own standards.
4. *Apelles*: celebrated painter of the fourth century BC.
5. *Hermogenes*: a singer who appears in Horace's *Satires*.
6. *Areopagites*: members of the ancient Athenian court on the Hill of Ares.
7. *Roscius*: famous Roman actor.
8. *On the classification of rhetoric*, xxiii. 79.
9. Horace, *The art of poetry*, 309.
10. Ibid., 269.
11. *Brutus*, xxiv. 94.
12. Compare Seneca, *Moral letters*, lxxxiv. 3-8. Another source for bee imagery is Horace, *Odes*, IV. ii. 27-32.

*(ii)*

*No*. So what is your advice? That I should throw Cicero away?

*Bu*. No, rather that Cicero should always be in the hands of the young aspirant to eloquence; but what we must completely reject is the pedantry and captiousness of certain people who'll reject a piece of writing that's learned and elegant in other respects, and judge it not worth reading, for the sole reason that it hasn't been fashioned as an imitation of Cicero. In the first place, Ciceronian language doesn't suit each and every disposition, so that in these cases the aspiration's bound to turn out badly. Secondly, if the natural strength that's required to achieve that inimitable felicity of speech is lacking, what's more stupid than to torture oneself over something which can't be attained? Further, Ciceronian language doesn't suit every topic or all characters, and even if it did, it's better to neglect some points rather than pay too dear for it. If his eloquence had cost Marcus Tullius as much as it costs us, he would, I suspect, have neglected the rhetorical ornaments of his writing to some extent. We pay too dear for anything which is bought at so great a cost to time, health and even life. We pay too dear for anything for the sake of which we neglect areas of knowledge that we need to know more. Above all, we pay too dear for anything which is bought at the expense of religion. If the aim of learning eloquence is to delight the idle, what point is there in mastering a mere entertainment by so many vigils? But if it's to persuade people to do what's honourable, Phocion the Athenian[1] spoke more effectively than Demosthenes, Cato of Utica[2] persuaded men more often than Marcus Tullius. Again, if eloquence is sought so that our writings will be in everybody's hands, then even if a likeness to Cicero's language could be achieved without effort, we still ought to seek variety by art, to cure the reader's sated stomach. Variety is so important in human affairs that it's a good idea not to use even what's best all the time. The point made familiar by a Greek proverb is universally true: 'In all things change is sweet.' Nothing commends Homer and Horace as much as their ability, through their marvellous variety of subject and figures of speech, to prevent boredom occurring. Furthermore, nature has somehow so fashioned us, giving to each his own nature, that you can scarcely find two people who have the same capacities or tastes. And given that nothing's more delicate or fussy than the human stomach, and we have to devour so many volumes to acquire learning, who could bear to go on reading continually if every author had the same style and similar diction? As at feasts, so too in writings, it's better for some parts to be inferior than for everything to be just the same. What kind of a host would he be who, when he was entertaining a large party of guests, among whom scarcely two shared the same tastes, put before them dishes all seasoned in the same way, even if they were the dainties of Apicius?[3] As it is, since different people are charmed by different ways of writing, the result is that nothing's left unread. I needn't repeat the point that nature herself opposes this affectation, since she intended speech to be the mirror of the mind. But since there's almost more dissimilarity in men's temperaments than in their appearance or their voices, this mirror will be false unless it returns an authentic image of the mind; what gives a reader special pleasure, however, is to learn a writer's feelings, character, judgement and ability from his writings as well as if he'd enjoyed intimacy with him for several years. This is why different people have such different feelings towards the writers of books, according as the genius of each, akin or alien, wins over or repels each reader; just as with the shapes of people's bodies different forms delight or offend different people. I'll tell you what happened to me. As a lad, I loved all the poets. But as soon as I became more familiar with Horace, in comparison with him all the rest began to lose their appeal, excellent though they were in themselves. What do you think was at the root of this, if not a certain secret affinity of dispositions, recognised in those dumb writings? There is no breath of this authentic, personal quality in the discourse of those who express nothing except Cicero. And what of the fact that honest men, even though born ugly, wouldn't want to wear a mask and so usurp the appearance of someone very attractive, and wouldn't even allow themselves to be painted in a different guise from the one nature gave them, on the grounds that it's disgraceful to impose on anyone with disguised looks, and that a lying mirror or a flattering image is a ridiculous thing? But it would be a more disgraceful deception if, though I'm Bulephorus, I wanted to pass myself off as Nosoponus or anyone else. So, aren't the learned right to mock certain wretched individuals, who reject and as it were remove from their libraries learned, eloquent writers, deserving immortal renown, for the sole reason that in their style they preferred to express themselves rather than Cicero, since it's a kind of imposture not to express oneself in one's writing but to present someone else's form fraudulently to men's eyes? In fact, I don't know whether, if it were possible, God so permitting, we should find many who would want to exchange the whole appearance of their body with someone else's, and there would be even fewer, in my opinion, who would change their minds and whole disposition for another's. This is because, first, no one would want to be other than he is, secondly, each of us has by nature's providence such a blend of

peculiar gifts that even if he has some weakness, he can balance things
out with his virtues. The mind has a certain form of its own, which is
reflected in its discourse as in a mirror; to reshape it out of its natural
form into something different is equivalent to going out in public
wearing a mask.

*No*. Take care your argument doesn't, as they say, overleap its
bounds; it seems to me to have reached the point of condemning all
imitation, even though the art of rhetoric consists of three main parts:
rules, imitation and practice — unless somehow those who imitate
Marcus Tullius take on someone else's appearance, while those who
imitate other authors keep their own.

*Bu*. I welcome imitation, provided that it improves and doesn't
spoil nature, corrects and doesn't overwhelm her gifts. I approve of
imitation, but imitation of a model that agrees with your natural
ability, or at least isn't in opposition to it, so that you don't seem to be
joining the giants in 'fighting the gods'. Again, I approve of imitation
that isn't given over to a single rule from whose lines it wouldn't dare to
depart, but that plucks from every author, or at any rate the best,
whatever in each is especially remarkable and suits an individual's
temperament; an imitation that doesn't weave straight into the fabric of
the writing any pretty thing it comes across, but despatches it into the
author's mind, as though into his stomach, so that it's transfused into
the veins and can appear a true product of your own talent, not something begged from somewhere else, and can breathe out the vigour
and character of your own mind and nature; thus, the reader will
recognise not a gem-stone drawn from Cicero, but a child of your own
brain, just as they say Pallas was born from the brain of Jove and
reflected a living image of her father;[4] and your discourse won't seem a
kind of patchwork quilt or mosaic, but the breathing image of your
breast, or a river flowing from the spring of your heart. But your first
and principal care should be to know thoroughly the subject you
undertake to treat. That'll provide you with abundant matter for your
discourse, and with true and authentic feelings. And so the result will
be that your discourse lives, breathes, acts, moves and sways others,
and expresses the whole of you.

NOTES

1. *Phocion*: an Athenian general and contemporary of Demosthenes; he
advised Athens to treat with Philip of Macedon; Plutarch wrote a life of him.
2. *Cato of Utica*: the arch Republican and enemy of Caesar.

3. *Apicius*: name of several Roman gourmets.
4. Compare Seneca, *Moral letters*, lxxxiv. 8.


*(iii)*

*Bu*. I think the only thing that's left is to summarise the points which have so far been discussed in a scattered way.

*No*. What's your opinion of Marcus Tullius?

*Bu*. A supreme artist of speech, and also, as far as may be among pagans, a good man, who, I think, had he learned the Christian philosophy, would have been numbered among those who're now honoured as saints on account of their lives passed in innocence and goodness. I admit that art and practice were of very great value to him, but he owed by far the greatest part of his eloquence to nature, which no one can give himself. And I think that no other Latin writer should be kept more constantly in the hands of boys and youths who're being educated to win distinction in eloquence. However, I want the reading of at least Latin poets to come first, because this branch of art's more suited to tender years. And I don't want anyone to be called to imitate Cicero precisely, until he's learnt the precepts of rhetoric. After this, I want there to be someone available to point out the features of his art, just as painters show their pupils in some famous painting what has been done artistically and what not. And I want Marcus Tullius to be part of their studies, indeed a principal and special part, but not the only one; I think they shouldn't just copy Cicero but should imitate him and even compete with him. Anyone who copies walks in another's footsteps and is a slave to rules. And it's been truly said that no one can walk properly who always puts his feet in another man's tracks; and no one can ever swim properly who doesn't dare to throw away his floats. But the imitator doesn't aim to make the same so much as similar points, or rather not even similar sometimes but equivalent; and a competitor tries to speak better than his model if he can. There's never been an artist so perfect that you can't find something to criticise in his work, something which could be done better. Also, I wouldn't want this imitation to be too meticulous and pedantic; this in itself prevents us from achieving our goal. And I don't think that Marcus Tullius should be worshipped to such an extent that you shrink from all the other writers; no, all the best writers should be read first, and then what's best in these best writers should be culled from each; for it isn't necessary to imitate the whole of any author. And I don't think that writers should be spurned who, admittedly, don't help much over diction but still provide a copious supply of information, such as Aristotle, Theophrastus[1] and Pliny.[2] In addition, I wouldn't want anyone to be so given over to imitating Cicero that he departs from his natural bent, and pursues at cost of health and life what he can't achieve if Minerva[3] resists or what would cost too much if he eventually did achieve it. Further, I don't want the student to be concerned with Cicero alone, and I don't think that the distinction of a Ciceronian style should be pursued to the extent of neglecting the liberal arts, which are absolutely essential. And you must shrink, as from a plague, from those who clamour that it's wrong to use a word which isn't found in Cicero's works. For now that the norms of Latin have ceased to depend on colloquial usage, let's appropriate when necessary any words that are found in suitable writers on our own authority, and if words that have been used by only a few seem rather harsh and outdated, let's bring them out into the light and soften them by continuous and timely use. Given that the old writers borrowed Greek vocabulary whenever Latin words were lacking or were regarded as insufficiently meaningful, what kind of malice is it that prevents us from using expressions that we find in reputable authors, when the occasion demands? And I think we should be just as careful to ignore the people who clamour that anything which isn't designed as an imitation of Cicero in vocabulary, forms of words and rhythm has to be rejected and simply isn't worth reading, even though it's possible to have different virtues and still be, if not similar, at any rate equal to Cicero. Away with that pernickety fussiness; let's show seriously in our reading of authors what Ovid playfully narrates happened to him in his love affairs with girls.[4] He liked a tall girl because she seemed of heroic stature; a short girl pleased him because of her neatness; the bloom of youth commended a youngster, experience in affairs one who was rather older; the simplicity of an uneducated girl delighted him, the talents of a learned one; in a fair girl he loved the charm of her complexion, in a dusky girl he found for himself some hidden charm. If we show equal tolerance in gathering from individual writers everything commendable that they contain, we will spurn none, but take from them all anything which can give flavour to our discourse. But above all we must guard against naïve and untutored youth being taken in by the deception of the Ciceronian name and becoming pagan instead of Ciceronian. For we see plagues of this kind, not yet properly extinguished, repeatedly threatening a recrudescence, under one disguise old heresies, under another Judaism, under yet another paganism. Thus, some years ago, factions of Platonists and Peripatetics[5] began to arise among the Italians. Let's banish these divisive names; and instead let's inculcate ideas which in studies and in religion and in the whole of life will procure and nourish mutual goodwill. So, first, we must absorb the conviction about sacred matters which is truly worthy of a Christian. Once this is achieved, nothing will seem better embellished than the heavenly philosophy, nothing sweeter than the name of Jesus Christ, nothing more elegant than the words with which the luminaries of the Church have treated the religious mysteries. And no one's discourse will seem elegant unless it's appropriate to his character and adapted to the subject-matter; while a discourse which treats religious matters with the words of the irreligious, and which pollutes Christian material with pagan trifles will seem a positive monstrosity. And if some indulgence is shown to youth in this matter, a more advanced age shouldn't be allowed to arrogate the same right. Anyone who is a Ciceronian of such a stamp that he isn't a true Christian isn't even a Ciceronian, because he doesn't speak appropriately, or really understand what he's talking about, and he isn't affected in his heart by the subjects on which he pours out his words; and finally, he doesn't handle the subject-matter of his own belief with the same elegant elaboration with which Cicero treated the subjects of his own day. The one reason for studying the arts, philosophy and rhetoric is to understand Christ and celebrate his glory. This is the target of all learning and eloquence. And we must also learn to imitate what's best in Cicero. This consists not in words or in the surface of the discourse but in things and ideas, in his mind and in his judgement. What does it matter if a son resembles a father in the lineaments of his face, if he is dissimilar in mind and character? And finally, if we don't succeed in being judged Ciceronians by those people's votes, we must bear it with patience, because it's a fate we share with all those excellent men we've enumerated before. It's folly to pursue what you can't achieve. It's self-indulgent to torture ourselves miserably for something so many excellent writers bore with equanimity. It's unseemly to aim at something that doesn't suit us. It's silly to want to speak in a style different from that which the subject demands. It's mad to buy, at the price of so many vigils, what'll scarcely ever be of any use. That physician who brought medicine of roughly this kind freed me from my disease; if you're not reluctant to take it, I hope we'll find that the fever leaves both you, Nosoponus, and you, Hypologus.

*Hypologus*. For some while now I've been free of the disease.

*No*. And so have I, pretty well, except that even now I feel some surviving traces of the long familiar evil.

*Bu*. They'll disappear little by little; and if there's any need we'll again summon as our physician the Word.[6]

NOTES

1. *Theophrastus*: a pupil of Aristotle, who wrote two treatises on plants.
2. *Pliny*: Pliny the Elder, who wrote on natural history.
3. *Minerva*: i.e. his natural bent.
4. Ovid, *Amores*, II. iv. 10-46.
5. *Peripatetics*: Aristotelians.
6. The Logos, the Word of God, should be the true inspirer of human speech. On the healing power of the Word, see Boyle, *Erasmus on language*, pp. 46-8.


## Ascham: *The schoolmaster*

*Three passages on imitation (from Book II)*

The schoolmaster *offers the first discussion of imitation in English. Ascham says that he drew his ideas on the subject from Cheke, his teacher, and from Sturm, his correspondent. Like Sturm, he was less eclectic and more of a Ciceronian than Erasmus; we may note that in his survey of studies of imitation he praises Cortesi and Bembo rather than Politian and Gianfrancesco Pico (see above, p. 134). Although the book breaks off before the description of Cicero, there is little doubt that Cicero, 'whom above all other I like and love best', would have been cited as 'that example to follow which hath a perfect head, a whole body, forward and backward, arms and legs and all'. This does not mean that Ascham advocated mere copying; Sturm in his book on imitation (published in 1574) was to reiterate that one should assimilate and rival one's model, and Ascham emphasises the element of dissimilarity in his definition of imitation, 'similar handling of dissimilar material and dissimilar handling of similar material'. The chief thrust of Ascham's discussion lies in his conviction that examples are more efficacious than abstract precepts and his recommendation of detailed study of ancient methods of imitation; the precise strategy with which, for example, Cicero imitated Demosthenes should be analysed according to a five-point plan. To those who argue that imitation is pedantic slavery, Ascham replies that we should be content to follow Cicero, who imitated Aristotle and Plato in* On the orator, *and that though men 'do sometimes stumble upon doing well by chance and benefit of good wit', he would have his pupils 'always able to do well by order of learning and right skill of judgement' – a characteristic expression of the humanist belief that art is based on knowledge and rational ordering (compare Jonson, below, pp. 207-8).*

*(i)*

But to return to imitation again, there be three kinds of it in matters of learning.

The whole doctrine of comedies and tragedies is a perfect imitation or fair lively painted picture of the life of every degree of man. Of this imitation writeth Plato at large in 3 *De republica*, but it doth not much belong at this time to our purpose.

The second kind of imitation is to follow for learning of tongues and sciences the best authors. Here riseth amongst proud and envious wits a great controversy whether one or many are to be followed, and, if one, who is that one, Seneca or Cicero, Sallust or Caesar, and so forth, in Greek and Latin.

The third kind of imitation belongeth to the second: as, when you be determined whether ye will follow one or more, to know perfectly and which way to follow that one, in what place, by what mean and order, by what tools and instruments ye shall do it, by what skill and judgement ye shall truly discern whether ye follow rightly or no.

This *imitatio* is 'dissimilis materiei similis tractatio', and also 'similis materiei dissimilis tractatio',[1] as Virgil followed Homer, but the argument to the one was Ulysses, to the other Aeneas. Tully[2] persecuted Antony[3] with the same weapons of eloquence that Demosthenes used before against Philip.

Horace followeth Pindar,[4] but either of them his own argument and person, as the one, Hieron, King of Sicily, the other, Augustus, the Emperor, and yet both for like respects: that is, for their courageous stoutness in war and just government in peace.

One of the best examples for right imitation we lack, and that is Menander,[5] whom our Terence, as the matter required, in like argument, in the same persons, with equal eloquence, foot by foot did follow.

Some pieces remain, like broken jewels, whereby men may rightly esteem and justly lament the loss of the whole.

Erasmus, the ornament of learning in our time, doth wish[6] that some man of learning and diligence would take the like pains in Demosthenes and Tully that Macrobius[7] hath done in Homer and Virgil, that is, to write out and join together where the one doth imitate the other. Erasmus' wish is good, but surely it is not good enough; for Macrobius' gatherings for the *Aeneid* out of Homer and Eobanus Hessus'[8] more diligent gatherings for the *Bucolics* out of Theocritus,[9] as they be not fully taken out of the whole heap as they should be, but even as though they had not sought for them of purpose but found them scattered here and there by chance in their way, even so only to point out and nakedly to join together their sentences, with no further declaring the manner and way how the one doth follow the other, were but a cold help to the increase of learning.

But if a man would take this pain also, when he hath laid two places of Homer and Virgil or of Demosthenes and Tully together, to teach plainly withal, after this sort:

(i) Tully retaineth thus much of the matter, these sentences, these words.

(ii) This and that he leaveth out, which he doth wittily to this end and purpose.

(iii) This he addeth here.

(iv) This he diminisheth there.

(v) This he ordereth thus, with placing that here not there.

(vi) This he altereth and changeth either in property of words, in form of sentence, in substance of the matter or in one or other convenient[10] circumstance of the author's present purpose.

In these few rude English words are wrapped up all the necessary tools and instruments wherewith true imitation is rightly wrought withal in any tongue. Which tools, I openly confess, be not of mine own forging, but partly left unto me by the cunningest master and one of the worthiest gentlemen that ever England bred, Sir John Cheke, partly borrowed by me out of the shop of the dearest friend I have out of England, Johann Sturmius. And therefore I am the bolder to borrow of him and here to leave them to other, and namely[11] to my children; which tools, if it please God that another day they may be able to use rightly, as I do wish and daily pray they may do, I shall be more glad than if I were able to leave them a great quantity of land.

This foresaid order and doctrine of imitation would bring forth more learning and breed up truer judgement than any other exercise that can be used, but not for young beginners, because they shall not be able to consider duly thereof. And truly, it may be a shame to good students, who, having so fair examples to follow as Plato and Tully, do not use so wise ways in following them for the obtaining of wisdom and learning as rude ignorant artificers do for gaining a small commodity. For surely the meanest painter useth more wit, better art, greater diligence in his shop in following the picture of any mean man's face than commonly the best students do, even in the university, for the attaining of learning itself.

NOTES

1. Similar handling of dissimilar material and also dissimilar handling of similar material.

2. *Tully*: Cicero.

3. In the *Philippics*.

4. *Pindar*: Greek choral lyric poet of the fifth century BC, who wrote victory odes for the Games.

5. *Menander*: (fourth century BC) the leading writer of New Comedy.

6. In a letter to John Paungartner, Allen no. 2695.

7. *Macrobius*: the *Saturnalia* of Macrobius (fourth century AD), a scholarly work about Virgil cast in dramatic form, includes a detailed illustration of Virgil's borrowings from Homer and others.

8. *Eobanus Hessus*: Helius Eobanus Hessus (1488-1540) taught at the universities of Erfurt, Nuremberg and Marburg, and translated Homer and Theocritus. His *Notes on the Bucolics and Georgics of Virgil* (Hagenau, 1529) gives parallels between Virgil and Theocritus.

9. *Theocritus*: Greek poet of the third century BC, whose *Idylls* on pastoral and other themes were the model for Virgil's *Eclogues* (or *Bucolics*).

10. *Convenient*: according with his purpose.

11. *Namely*: especially.


*(ii)*

Therefore, in perusing thus so many diverse books for imitation, it came into my head that a very profitable book might be made *de imitatione* after another sort than ever yet was attempted of that matter, containing a certain few fit precepts, unto the which should be gathered and applied plenty of examples out of the choicest authors of both the tongues. This work would stand rather in good diligence for the gathering and right judgement for the apt applying of those examples than any great learning or utterance at all.

The doing thereof would be more pleasant than painful, and would bring also much profit to all that should read it and great praise to him would take it in hand, with just desert of thanks.

Erasmus, giving himself to read over all authors Greek and Latin, seemeth to have prescribed to himself this order of reading: that is, to note out by the way three special points — all adages, all similitudes and all witty sayings of most notable personages — and so, by one labour, he left to posterity three notable books and namely two his *Chiliades*, *Apophthegmata* and *Similia*.[1] Likewise, if a good student would bend himself to read diligently over Tully and with him also at the same time as diligently Plato and Xenophon with his[2] books of philosophy, Isocrates and Demosthenes with his orations and Aristotle with his rhetorics — which five of all other be those whom Tully best loved and specially followed — and would mark diligently in Tully where he doth *exprimere* or *effingere*[3] (which be the very proper words of imitation) either *copiam Platonis* or *venustatem Xenophontis, suavitatem Isocratis* or *vim Demosthenis, propriam et puram subtilitatem Aristotelis*,[4] and not only write out the places diligently and lay them together orderly but also to confer[5] them with skilful judgement by those few rules which I have expressed now twice before — if that diligence were taken, if that order were used, what perfect knowledge of both the tongues, what ready and pithy utterance in all matters, what right and deep judgement in all kind of learning would follow is scarce credible to be believed.

These books be not many, nor long, nor rude in speech, nor mean in matter, but next the majesty of God's holy word most worthy for a man, the lover of learning and honesty, to spend his life in. Yea, I have heard worthy Master Cheke many times say, 'I would have a good student pass and journey through all authors both Greek and Latin, but he that will dwell in these few books only — first in God's holy Bible, and then join with it Tully in Latin, Plato, Aristotle, Xenophon, Isocrates and Demosthenes in Greek — must needs prove an excellent man.'

NOTES

1. Puzzling: there were three, not two, books of *Chiliades*. *Chiliades:* the *Adages*; *Apophthegmata:* the *Apophthegms*; *Similia:* the *Parallels*.
2. *His*: i.e. Cicero's.
3. *Exprimere or effingere*: both these words can mean 'copy' or 'reproduce'.
4. 'The abundance of Plato or the grace of Xenophon, the fluency of Isocrates or the power of Demosthenes, the exact and pure subtlety of Aristotle'. Cicero, *On the orator*, III. vii. 28, uses some of the same nouns.
5. *Confer*: compare.

*(iii)*

Now to return to that question whether one, a few, many or all are to be followed, my answer shall be short: all, for him that is desirous to know all (yea, the worst of all, as questionists[1] and all the barbarous nation of schoolmen, help for one or other consideration), but in every separate kind of learning and study by itself ye must follow choicely[2] a few and chiefly some one, and that namely[3] in our school of eloquence, either for pen or talk. And as in portraiture and painting wise men choose not that workman that can only make a fair hand or a well-fashioned leg but such one as can furnish up fully all the features of the whole body of a man, woman and child, and withal is able, too, by good skill, to give to every one of these three, in their proper kind, the right form, the true figure, the natural colour that is fit and due to the dignity of a man, to the beauty of a woman, to the sweetness of a young babe, even likewise do we seek such one in our school to follow, who is able always, in all matters, to teach plainly, to delight pleasantly and to carry away by force of wise talk all that shall hear or read him, and is so excellent indeed as wit is able or wish can hope to attain unto; and this not only to serve in the Latin or Greek tongue but also in our own English language. But yet, because the providence of God[4] hath left unto us in no other tongue save only in the Greek and Latin tongue the true precepts and perfect examples of eloquence, therefore must we seek in the authors only of those two tongues the true pattern of eloquence, if in any other mother tongue we look to attain either to perfect utterance of it ourselves or skilful judgement of it in others.

NOTES

1. *Questionists*: theological questioners, scholastic theologians.
2. *Choicely*: with careful choice, discriminatingly.
3. *Namely*: especially.
4. *The providence of God*: compare Erasmus, *The antibarbarians*, above, pp. 103-4.

## Ben Jonson: *Discoveries*

### Three passages on imitation

*Jonson inherits the liberal approach to imitation of Erasmus and Vives (see further Richard S. Peterson,* Imitation and praise in the poems of Ben Jonson, *Yale University Press, 1981, chapter 1). In the first passage, adapting Büchler and Pontanus, he makes use of the digestion and bee metaphors which derive from Seneca (*Moral letters, lxxxiv) *and which Erasmus, too, had employed in* Ciceronianus *to express the personal element in imitation. In the second, adapting Quintilian, he reminds us that imitation may be an unconscious process (something it is worth bearing in mind when reading English poetry of the period). In the third passage, following Vives, he adopts an independent stance towards classical authority, a stance which itself had good ancient precedent; Quintilian had said (*The education of an orator, X. ii. 4-10) *that imitation was not enough and that the achievements of our predecessors must be added to, and Seneca, in the letter quoted by Vives and Jonson,* *also condemns lack of independent thought and over-reliance on the past. Compare Daniel, below, p. 260.*

## (i) 'Imitatio'[1]

The third requisite in our poet or maker is imitation, to be able to convert the substance or riches of another poet to his own use. To make choice of one excellent man above the rest and so to follow him till he grow very he, or so like him as the copy may be mistaken for the principal. Not as a creature that swallows what it takes in crude, raw or indigested, but that feeds with an appetite and hath a stomach to concoct,[2] divide and turn all into nourishment. Not to imitate servilely, as Horace saith,[3] and catch at vices for virtue, but to draw forth out of the best and choicest flowers with the bee and turn all into honey, work it into one relish and savour, make our imitation sweet, observe how the best writers have imitated and follow them. How Virgil and Statius[4] have imitated Homer, how Horace Archilochus,[5] how Alcaeus[6] and the other lyrics,[7] and so of the rest.

### NOTES

1. 'Imitation'. Adapted from Joannes Buchlerus, *A new training in poetry* (1633), abridging J. Pontanus, *Poetic education* (1594), which Jonson probably used as well.
2. *Concoct*: digest.
3. *Epistles*, I. xix. 10-20; *Art of poetry*, 134-5.
4. *Statius*: (first century AD), Roman epic poet, author of the *Thebaid*.
5. *Archilochus*: Greek iambic poet, imitated by Horace in his *Epodes*.
6. *Alcaeus*: Greek lyric poet, imitated by Horace in the *Odes*.
7. *Lyrics*: lyric poets.

## (ii) 'De stylo et optimo scribendi genere'[1]

Besides, as it is fit for grown and able writers to stand of themselves and work with their own strength, to trust and endeavour by their own faculties, so it is fit for the beginner and learner to study others and the best. For the mind and memory are more sharply exercised in comprehending another man's things than our own; and such as accustom themselves and are familiar with the best authors shall ever and anon find somewhat of them in themselves, and in the expression of their minds, even when they feel it not, be able to utter something like theirs, which hath an authority above their own. Nay, sometimes it is the reward of a man's study, the praise of quoting another man fitly, and, though a man be more prone and able for one kind of writing than another, yet he must exercise all.

NOTE

1. 'On style and the best way of writing'. Adapted from Quintilian, *The education of an orator*, II. vii. 2-4.

*(iii) 'Non nimium credendum antiquitati'*[1]

I know nothing can conduce more to letters than to examine the writings of the ancients, and not to rest in their sole authority or take all upon trust from them, provided the plagues of judging and pronouncing against them be away, such as are envy, bitterness, precipitation, impudence and scurrile scoffing. For to all the observations of the ancients we have our own experience, which, if we will use and apply, we have better means to pronounce. It is true they opened the gates and made the way that went before us, but as guides, not commanders; 'non domini nostri sed duces fuere'.[2] Truth lies open to all; it is no man's several.[3] 'Patet omnibus veritas; nondum est occupata. Multum ex illa, etiam futuris relictum est.'[4]

If in some things I dissent from others whose wit, industry, diligence and judgement I look up at and admire, let me not therefore hear presently of ingratitude and rashness. For I thank those that have taught me and will ever, but yet dare not think the scope of their labour and enquiry was to envy their posterity what they also could add and find out.

If I err, pardon me; 'nulla ars simul et inventa est et absoluta'.[5] I do not desire to be equal to those that went before, but to have my reason examined with theirs and so much faith to be given them or me as those shall evict.[6] I am neither author or fautor[7] of any sect.[8] I will have no man addict[9] himself to me, but if I have anything right, defend it as truth's not mine (save as it conduceth to a common good). It profits not me to have any man fence or fight for me, to flourish or take a side. Stand for truth, and 'tis enough.

NOTES

1. 'Not too much trust should be put in antiquity.' Adapted from Vives, the preface to *On the transmission of knowledge*.
2. A quotation from Seneca, *Moral letters*, xxxiii. 11, translated in the previous phrase.

3. *Several*: private property.

4. Also from the letter by Seneca. Jonson translates the first Latin sentence beforehand; the second means 'Much of it [i.e. truth] has been left even for posterity.' (The Folio reads 'relictam'.)

5. 'No art was complete at its invention.'

6. *Evict*: show to be justified, prove, establish.

7. *Fautor*: partisan.

8. Compare Quintilian, *The education of an orator*, III. i. 22.

9. *Addict*: bind, devote.

# 3  WISDOM AND ELOQUENCE

**Erasmus: *The antibarbarians***

*Two passages on the value of learning to the Christian*

*Erasmus believed in the value of developing the intellect and of properly directed knowledge; he thought that learning had a more important role to play in Christian renewal than monasticism or pilgrimages. In these two passages from* The antibarbarians, *Batt vigorously defends learning as part of the Christian life. In the first passage, he argues that a man who is learned as well as good is superior to one who is ignorant and good, and that the doctors were more useful to the Church than the martyrs. In the second, he pours scorn on those who, citing certain biblical texts, hold that wisdom can be acquired through inspiration rather than study; goodness and learning are only acquired through hard work.*

*(i)*

[*Batt*] 'But to analyse the matter more fully, let's postulate four classes of men. I'm taking you, doctor, as a kind of advocate for the ignorant; please go on defending your clients' cause. So, as I said, let's postulate two pairs: the first a learned but wicked man and an unlearned but equally wicked man; which do you think is the better?'

'Obviously the first of the two will be much the worse,' said the doctor. 'And that's a clear enough proof in itself that literature can't be a good thing, if it can make a man worse. I'm using your own sword to cut your throat with.'

'I wouldn't care myself to lay down which of the two was worse,' said Batt. 'Certainly I think they're both at fault: the one for misusing something that's excellent, the other — and much more so, perhaps — for not even troubling to acquire it. The first falls under the prophet's charge, "They are wise to do evil, but to do good they have no knowledge,"[1] the other under David's "He hath left off to be wise, and to do good."[2] From uneducated wickedness nothing good can be looked for; educated wickedness is a bane to the man possessed of it, but it may bring some benefit to others. Wherever an evil disposition's joined to ignorance, there's more confidence and less shame about doing wrong. Anything an ignorant man really wants he thinks is justified. Learning

157

may not prevent base desires altogether but it can't help moderating them. It's impossible for anyone who really understands the difference between right and wrong not to recoil before vice at times and admire the beauty of virtue. The learned man at least puts on a show of decency — which is the next thing to true virtue — while the man without learning even expects to win credit by his faults. The one knows very well that he's ill, which makes him easier to cure; the other is beyond treatment because he thinks he's well. The one has tools all ready to win virtue with but the other has nothing to help him. But that's not relevant to our argument. Let's grant that uneducated wickedness is less damaging than educated wickedness; does it follow that the study of letters is a bad thing? No, this very point proves what a good thing it is (to turn back against you the weapon you planned to cut my throat with). First, the study of letters doesn't cause wickedness; when it's combined with it, it merely makes the wickedness all the more conspicuous, like a torch held over it. Consider a parallel: I might see two adulterers, one single and one married. There's no difference in their crime but there is in their guilt, because adultery's much more shameful on the part of a married man. Why so? Is it because marriage is a bad thing? Of course not! It's because marriage is a more sacred condition and so it's a worse offence to violate it by adultery. Anyone who lays hands on sacred property is guilty of a worse crime than mere theft, because it's sacrilege; does it follow that profane property is superior? Fornication is a worse sin in a priest than in a layman; does it follow that priesthood is a bad thing? Why not, after all? The offender is wickeder because he's a priest. No! If priesthood weren't a higher condition, the offender wouldn't be wickeder through the fact of being a priest. The more sacred a thing is, the more shameful is its abuse. And now let's compare another pair of men. Take two men, both good, but one ignorant and one educated; which is preferable? My opponents shuffle and hesitate; "Just find me a man who's learned and good too," they say. I admit that men like that are hard to find — for there are lots of ignorant and wicked men everywhere. But why do they hesitate when Jerome didn't, but freely and, as they say, "with his cheeks blown out" placed holy learning ahead of holy simplicity. "Daniel", he writes, "says at the end of his most sacred vision that the righteous shine like stars, and that the wise, that is the learned, like the firmament. Do you see what a huge difference there is between righteous simplicity and learned righteousness? The one is compared to the stars, the other to the heavens."[3] A little before that, he said, "Sacred simplicity benefits itself alone; by as much as it builds up the Church by the excellence of its life, by so much does it harm it, should it fail to resist those who seek its overthrow."[4] Of course, Jerome was right here, as always; the broader the influence of any good thing, the more valuable it is. A righteous life is a great achievement, but it only benefits the righteous man himself or at most the small circle of his associates. But add learning to his righteousness and his virtue will shine out fairly, far and wide, as though a torch had been held to it! And if further he's capable of expressing his splendid thoughts in literary form, that's to say if he's eloquent as well as learned, then the good this man can do will have the widest possible scope: it will reach not just his associates, not just his peers, not just his neighbours, but foreigners too, men still to be born, earth's most distant inhabitants. Unless it's commended to posterity in writing, goodness without learning dies along with its author. But as for learning, lands, seas and the long succession of ages can't prevent it from spreading to mankind at large. I don't want to set up here an invidious comparison as to whether the blood of the martyrs or the pens of men of learning contributed more good to our religion. I don't detract from the glory of the martyrs; no one could match it even by the richest of writings. But as far as advantage to us is concerned, we almost owe more to some heretics[5] even than to certain martyrs. And there were an enormous number of martyrs but very few doctors of the Church. By their deaths the martyrs reduced the number of Christians, while men of learning increased it by their persuasiveness. In short, it would have been useless for the one group to pour forth their blood for Christ's teachings so bravely, had not the other protected it from heretics by their writings. And so the Christian religion won't be so ungrateful as to drive into exile now, in a time of peace and prosperity, those literary pursuits that it found such a protection in times of affliction, the pursuits that allowed it to achieve peace and fortune. Which is why I can't help being amazed at certain people who say that they deliberately shun learning (for as for their assertion that they make no use of things discovered by pagans, I've already shown that it's more than ridiculous).[6] Or is there something in their claim that they want to avoid pride? But I suspect that this may be less the unease of a mind unsure of itself than a disguise for sloth — just pretending that there's guilt in something where there isn't any in fact. I could only be sure that they had simply made a mistake on this point, if they put it right when advised and corrected. If they won't, what kind of scruple is this, to fall into a really disastrous state out of fear of a trifling evil? In their folly, they're as timid as women and, obsessed with escaping the vice of curiosity, they stumble into a different vice that's far more destructive.

"There's no point in your avoiding that vice," says Horace, "if you twist yourself round into a fault on another side."[7] You'll do ill to escape Scylla if you fall foul of Charybdis, or to turn away from a storm if you break your ship on the rocks of the shore. These are the people whose childish, not to say perverse, timidity was criticised by David, the holiest of kings and prophets: "They were afraid where no fear was."[8] Anyone who watches the wind too scrupulously will never trust himself to the sea; anyone who scans the clouds anxiously won't ever get the harvest in. But what could be more pernicious than to pretend to be frightened where there's noble work to be done, but where there's great and certain danger to lie on one's back, snoring? Stupidly fussy, they want to take the mote of curiosity out of our eyes but they don't notice the beam of sloth in their own. Against us they bring the charge that, though we already know more than we need to, we always want to learn more; but they aren't interested themselves in acquiring even that knowledge without which we aren't men or living beings at all. But grant that we have no sense of moderation, in a good activity, is it better to go beyond the bounds or not to reach them? Is it preferable to go too far or to fall short? They're afraid that here and there in pagan literature something a little less than proper may strike their prudish ears, but they aren't afraid of our Lord's terrifying words, "Thou wicked servant, wherefore gavest not thou my money into the bank, that at my coming I might have required mine own with usury."[9] So true is it that God abhors nothing so much as sloth! He welcomes back with delight the prodigal son, who had squandered his whole substance on whores and pimps and taverns, but he heaps these savage reproaches on the servant who actually handed back the talent untouched. Those seeds of fair arts that God our father placed in us — understanding, intellectual powers, memory and the other gifts of the mind — are talents entrusted to us to lend out; if we, as it were, double them by practice and effort, the Lord will praise us on his return as hard-working servants, and will allow us to keep what we have earned; but if we bury the talent we have been given, how will we feel, confronted with our Lord's eyes and face and voice at his return, when others count out the profit from the share they received but we through our idleness merely hand back the useless talent? This is what those punctilious men ought really to be anxious about, not about something that offers enormous benefit and very little danger.'

NOTES

1. Jeremiah, 4: 22.
2. Psalms, 36: 3.
3. Jerome, *Letters*, LIII, iii.
4. Ibid.
5. Erasmus is perhaps thinking of Origen (see above, p. 108, note 6).
6. See above, pp. 100-3.
7. *Satires*, II. ii. 54-5.
8. Psalms, 53: 5.
9. Luke, 19: 23.


*(ii)*

Then the burgomaster said, 'I feel like quibbling with you over objections of detail in the true scholastic way. So how do you explain the fact that Christ himself told his disciples not to worry what they would say before kings and governors: "For it shall be given you in that same hour what ye shall speak. For it is not ye that speak but the Spirit of your Father which speaketh in you"?[1] What of Peter's saying that men of God speak moved by the Holy Ghost?[2] And what of James' "If any of you lack wisdom, let him ask of God, that giveth to all men liberally, and upbraideth not"?[3] If I'm not mistaken, the implications of all these sayings are very different from what you are arguing.'

*Batt.* 'Thank you for that timely reminder. But these points can be dealt with very easily. Surely you don't suppose that in the remark you've just quoted Christ was discouraging his disciples from thinking in advance what they would say when they were to speak before princes; no one in his senses ever did that, and even Christ didn't speak without preparation in so far as he was a man. He wasn't concerned to spare the Apostles the precautions any reasonable man would take, but to stop them being frightened; otherwise, lowly and inexpert as they were, they might have been afraid to speak out before princes and men of learning and eloquence, an audience that can cause the best and most experienced speaker to turn pale; but he promised that he wouldn't desert his advocates, so long as they were of good heart. He wanted to give them courage, not to lay a ban on conscientiousness and effort. I'm prepared to say that all the Apostles and particularly Paul sometimes made speeches that they'd prepared and perhaps even written in advance (this can be confidently conjectured from his defences in the Acts of the Apostles); and the Epistles of Peter, James and John aren't such that one can suppose they were written without care. But you'll now object that "Men of God spoke moved by the Holy Ghost." How then do you think they spoke? Like possessed prophets or Apollo's priestesses, seized by a kind of frenzy and not understanding themselves what they were saying? Surely not. But it will be more convenient to treat this point a bit later. As for James' saying about asking for wisdom from God, their interpretation of it is thoroughly stupid. Wisdom must be asked for from God, I grant it, but asked for in what sense? Just like food, clothing and the other necessities of human life. We are told to ask God for our daily bread each day, and it's granted each day, but not if we just yawn idly! We ask for clothing and it's provided, but only if we work for it. In just the same way, we ask for wisdom, but without being entitled to relax one jot of our human efforts. Is it likely that, though physical goods can only be secured by effort, you'll be given goods of the mind for nothing? Or that though bread comes only to those who sweat for it wisdom will be poured over you while you sleep? The man who preferred to die of hunger while waiting for bounty from heaven, rather than seek bread by his own labour and so save himself, is felt to be a rogue guilty of self-slaughter; can we then regard as a person of high principle the man who chooses to persist in shameful ignorance rather than receive life-giving teachings from another human? "But", you say, "wisdom was poured into the Apostles without any human effort." Granted, and we also read that food rained down from heaven upon the Israelites in the desert. But it's impious to expect such manna from heaven, and it would be no less impious, perhaps even more, to stand idle and wait for wisdom from the clouds, like the Apostles; for in the Gospels we are forbidden to worry about food or clothing for the morrow, but we aren't told anywhere not to seek wisdom. It isn't a reproach to us that we save, seek, sow and build, not just for the morrow but for many years ahead, with posterity in mind as well as our own lifetime; is a man to be reproached if he does the same in cultivating a much finer crop, wisdom? In that case we accept the sensible interpretation, that a ban isn't being placed on working to earn our bread but on pointless, neurotic worry; why don't we do the same in this case? The heavenly oracle promised wisdom to Solomon and rule over Israel to his father,[4] but neither put absolute trust in the oracle; the one didn't spare himself any human efforts to deserve the kingship and the other didn't slacken off in his pursuit of wisdom; they obviously understood the profound point one writer has made, that the Gods sell us everything at the price of toil.[5] They will give you food, but only if you work for it; they will equip you with wisdom, but only if you strive for it; they will grant continence, but only if you make an effort to achieve it; they will teach you, but only if you study, and they will help you in battle, but only if you fight yourself. They'll not abandon anybody, provided only that he doesn't give himself up first. Otherwise, why did the Aposties themselves write? Or the Evangelists? Or Jerome? Or Augustine? Why did others, too, leave us memorials of their talents? Valuable works, if it's by effort that wisdom is to be acquired, but quite idle if we can idly wait for it to come to us as we sleep. I've already granted that wisdom was poured into the Apostles (I'm not insisting on the point that both before and after the Resurrection they were prepared by constant instruction from the best of teachers, Christ; nor do I insist that they read constantly by themselves and compared their views on the Scriptures with one another), but why did God not instil equal wisdom in them all? Why was Paul wiser and James more eloquent than Peter? Why are John's writings more inspired than those of the other Evangelists? Why do the other holy doctors vary in learning and eloquence? It was certainly the same divine force that moved them all as they wrote. The reason must be that the most Holy Spirit did not find the same learning ready in all of them. The Spirit improves what we've created by our own efforts; he promotes our studies, favours our endeavours. If it's not wrong to bring in poets' fables here, we should imitate Prometheus: he ventured to seek life from the stars for the image he'd made from mud, but only after he'd equipped it with everything human skill could provide.[6] Do we think that if we just offer an unshaped lump, the Spirit will do it all for us while we sleep? Have we forgotten that Paul himself, who was favoured by being carried up to the third heaven,[7] asked by letter for the books that were written on parchment,[8] and later consulted with Peter and the other Apostles on the doctrine of the Faith? That the Apostles themselves communicated with one another more than once about the new religion? That Peter was reproached by the voice of Paul?[9] Where was the Holy Spirit idling then? Why did he let Paul read, Peter go wrong and all of them be at a loss? You can see that the gift of this Spirit didn't exclude human effort but assisted it. He did sometimes help in a kind of miraculous way, but only when the situation required a miracle or human efforts were powerless. We read that many studious men became learned with the aid of the Spirit. But who's ever read or heard of an ass being suddenly transformed into a theologian? I'm not at all swayed by the cases people tell of a dove seen by someone's ear as he spoke or wrote, or a book handed to him in a dream. They may be stories invented by people who were well disposed to enhance their authority, or they may be true; others may want to dispute the point, but I don't. On any view, we find that each individual's learning was proportionate to the force of his mind and his own efforts in study. Talent and natural ability come to many men without effort, for they are gifts of nature; but no one acquires goodness or learning like that.'

NOTES

1. Matthew, 10: 19-20.
2. II Peter, 1: 21.
3. James, 1: 5.
4. I Kings, 3: 12; II Samuel, 7: 8-9.
5. Xenophon, *Memorabilia*, II. i. 20, quotes a line to this effect by Epicharmus.
6. There are various versions of the story of how Prometheus made man from clay; see e.g. Ovid, *Metamorphoses*, I. 76ff; Horace, *Odes*, I. xvi. 13-16.
7. II Corinthians, 12: 2.
8. II Timothy, 4: 13.
9. Galatians, 2: 11-14.

## Castiglione: *The courtier*

Il libro del cortegiano *(*The book of the courtier*), which celebrates life at the court of Urbino in the opening years of the sixteenth century, was the most popular and influential of all the many Italian humanist treatises dealing with education, ethics and social behaviour and drawing on the wisdom of Plato, Aristotle, Cicero and Plutarch. Its adaptation of humanist ideals to the particular social role of the courtier made a strong appeal to non-Italian Europe, where the court was the centre of life; its idealisation of courtly service proved more palatable than the republican values of fifteenth-century Florence (see Hay, *The Italian Renaissance, pp. 203-4) — Ottaviano Fregoso's defence of monarchy in Book IV was echoed by Elyot in the opening chapters of* The governor. *Men who were themselves courtiers were able to savour the combination of the practical and the ideal which is characteristic of Castiglione's book. For* The courtier *should not be seen as a flight of fancy, describing a dream of unattainable refinement and culminating in a Neo-Platonic fantasy of sublimated sex. Rather, it is rooted in the actualities of the dangerous life of the courtier of the period; J. H. Woodhouse has described it as a handbook for survival (*Baldesar Castiglione, p. 3). *Its author (1478-1529) had need of all the diplomatic skills which he details in the book in the course of a life spent in the service of various Italian courts — Milan, Mantua, Urbino and the Papacy. The courtier, published in 1528, records his period of service to Guidobaldo da*

*Montefeltro, at the court of Urbino, which is presented nostalgically as a lost oasis of cultivation in the unstable and brutal world of Italian politics (Guidobaldo's successor, Francesco Maria della Rovere, was driven from the duchy by Pope Leo X while Castiglione was writing his book; Rome was sacked by the Imperial troops the year before it was published). The book is cast in the form of a conversation, which takes place over four evenings in March 1507, during the reign of Guidobaldo and his wife Elisabetta Gonzaga, when some members of Pope Julius II's entourage had stayed on after a visit by their master. The participants are Castiglione's friends and acquaintances (he is not present), and the conversation ranges over many topics: the fine arts, the vernacular, jokes, the role of women, love, good government. The dialogue form allows the topics to be presented obliquely and the conclusions to be suggested rather than laid down; it is handled with great charm and skill. These qualities, together with its mellow and moderate philosophy, make the book of more than merely representa-tive interest, and must have contributed to its popularity.*

*The extracts given here are in the translation published in 1561 by Sir Thomas Hoby (1530-66), himself a courtier and diplomat, who had been educated at St John's College, Cambridge, in its golden period, and was a friend of Ascham and Cheke.*

## (i) A defence of letters (from Book I)

*In this important passage, Castiglione defends the new humanist ideal of the gentleman, who adds to the old chivalric qualities of courage and martial prowess, cultivation and learning. This passage may be felt behind the similar defences of education and cultivation by Elyot and Ascham against those noblemen who say learning is a waste of time, and also behind Daniel's defence of letters in* Musophilus. *Alexander's love of Homer and his training in philosophy by Aristotle, attested by Plutarch, are cited again and again in defences of learning (see Introduction, above, p. 26, and Sir Philip Sidney,* An apology for poetry, *ed. Geoffrey Shepherd, Manchester University Press, 1973, p. 206). An important ancient source for defences of letters is Cicero's speech* In defence of the poet Archias, *where he expatiates on the social utility of literature, giving examples of public figures who have cultivated letters (vii. 15-16) and, like Castiglione, emphasising the importance of literary fame as a spur to virtue (x, xi, vi. 14). Jonson takes several passages from the speech for* Discoveries, *see below, pp. 202, 205.*

*The main speaker is Lodovico Canossa (1476-1532), a friend and relative of Castiglione, who has been given the task of describing the perfect courtier. The Lord Julian is Giuliano de' Medici, youngest son of Lorenzo de' Medici, in exile from Florence.*

'But, beside goodness, the true and principal ornament of the mind in every man, I believe, are letters; although the Frenchmen know only the nobleness of arms and pass for[1] nothing beside, so that they do not only set by[2] letters but they rather abhor them, and all learned men they count very rascals, and they think it a great villainy[3] when any one of them is called a clerk.'[4] Then answered the Lord Julian, 'You say very true; this error indeed hath long reigned among the Frenchmen. But if Monseigneur d'Angoulême[5] have so good luck that he may, as men hope, succeed in the crown, the glory of arms in France doth not so flourish nor is had in such estimation as letters will be, I believe. For it is not long since I was in France and saw this prince in the court there, who seemed unto me, beside the handsomeness of person and beauty of visage, to have in his countenance so great a majesty, accompanied nevertheless with a certain lovely courtesy, that the realm of France should ever seem unto him a small matter. I understood afterward by many gentlemen both French and Italian very much of the most noble conditions,[6] of the greatness of courage, prowess and liberality that was in him; and, among other things, it was told me that he highly loved and esteemed letters, and had in very great reputation all learned men, and blamed the Frenchmen themselves that their minds were so far wide from this profession, especially having at their doors so noble an university as Paris is, where all the world resorteth.' Then spake the Count, 'It is great wonder that, in these tender years, only by the provocation of nature, contrary to the manner of the country, he hath given himself to so good a way. And because subjects follow always the conditions of the higher powers, it is possible that it may come to pass, as you say, that the Frenchmen will yet esteem letters to be of that dignity that they are indeed. The which, if they will give ear thereto, they may soon be persuaded; forsomuch as men ought to covet of nature nothing so much and that is more proper for them than knowledge, which thing it were a great folly to say or to hold opinion that it is not always good.[7] And in case[8] I might commune with them or with other that were of a contrary opinion to me, I would do my diligence to show them how much letters, which undoubtedly have been granted of God unto men for a sovereign gift, are profitable and necessary for our life and estimation. Neither should I want the examples of so many excellent captains of old time which all joined the ornament of letters with the prowess of arms. For, as you know, Alexander had Homer in such reverence that he laid his *Iliad* always under his bed's head;[9] and he applied diligently not these studies only but also the speculations of philosophy under the discipline of Aristotle.[10] Alcibiades increased his good conditions and made them greater with letters and with the instructions of Socrates.[11] Also, what diligence Caesar used in study, those things which he hath so divinely written himself make trial. It is said[12] that Scipio Africanus carried always in his hand the books of Xenophon wherein under the name of Cyrus he instructeth a perfect king.[13] I could recite unto you Lucullus, Sulla, Pompey, Brutus and many other Romans and Grecians, but I will do no more but make mention of Hannibal, which, being so excellent a captain (yet, for all that, of a fierce nature and void of all humanity, an untrue dealer and a despiser of men and of the Gods) had also understanding in letters and the knowledge of the Greek tongue. And if I be not deceived, I trow, I have read in my time that he left a book behind him of his own making in the Greek tongue.[14] But this kind of talk is more than needeth; for I know all you understand how much the Frenchmen be deceived in holding opinion letters to do any hurt to arms. You know in great matters and adventures in wars the true provocation is glory; and whoso for lucre's sake or for any other consideration taketh it in hand, beside that he never doth anything worthy praise, deserveth not the name of a gentleman, but is a most vile merchant. And every man may conceive it to be the true glory that is stored up in the holy treasure of letters, except such unlucky creatures as have had no taste thereof. What mind is so faint, so bashful and of so base a courage that, in reading the acts and greatness of Caesar, Alexander, Scipio, Hannibal and so many other, is not incensed[15] with a most fervent longing to be like them, and doth not prefer the getting of that perpetual fame before this rotten life, that lasteth two days? Which, in despite of death, maketh him live a great deal more famous than before. But he that savoureth not the sweetness of letters cannot know how much is the greatness of glory which is a long while preserved by them, and only measureth it with the age of one or two men; for further he beareth not in mind. Therefore can he not esteem this short glory so much as he would do that which, in a manner, is everlasting, if by his ill hap he were not barred from the knowledge of it. And not passing upon it so much, reason persuadeth and a man may well believe he will never hazard himself so much to come by it as he that knoweth it. I would not now someone of the contrary part should allege unto me the contrary effects, to confute mine opinion withal, and tell me how the Italians with their knowledge of letters have showed small prowess in arms from a certain time hitherto, the which nevertheless is too true. But in very deed, a man may well say that the offence of a few hath brought, beside the great damage, an everlasting reproach unto all other. And the very cause of our confusion and of the neglecting of virtue in our minds (if it be not clean dead) proceeded of them. But it were a more shameful matter unto us to publish it than unto the Frenchmen the ignorance in letters. Therefore it is better to pass that over with silence that cannot be rehearsed without sorrow, and leaving this purpose, into the which I am entered against my will, return again unto our courtier, whom in letters I will have to be more than indifferently well seen, at the least in those studies which they call humanity, and to have not only the understanding of the Latin tongue but also of the Greek, because of the many and sundry things that with great excellency are written in it. Let him much exercise himself in poets and no less in orators and historiographers, and also in writing both rhyme and prose, and especially in this our vulgar tongue. For beside the contentation[16] that he shall receive thereby himself, he shall by this means never want pleasant entertainments with women, which ordinarily love such matters.'

NOTES

1. *Pass for*: care for.
2. *Set by*: disregard. (I have omitted a superfluous 'not' after 'not only'.)
3. *Villainy*: insult.
4. *Clerk*: scholar. In the Middle Ages, learning was largely restricted to the clergy, hence 'clericus' came to mean 'learned man'.
5. *Monseigneur d'Angoulême*: the future Francis I.
6. *Conditions*: personal qualities, morals, behaviour.
7. Compare Cicero, *On duties*, II. ii. 5.
8. *In case*: if.
9. Plutarch, *Lives*, *Alexander*, viii. 2.
10. Ibid., vii. 2-9.
11. Plutarch, *Lives*, *Alcibiades*, iv. 1-4, vi.
12. Cicero, *Tusculan disputations*, II. xxvi. 62; *Letters to his brother Quintus*, I. i. 23.
13. The *Cyropaedia* or *The education of Cyrus*, a popular book in the Renaissance.
14. See Cornelius Nepos, *On famous men*, *Hannibal*, xiii. 2.
15. *Incensed*: inflamed, kindled.
16. *Contentation*: contentment.

*(ii) The necessity of knowledge (from Book IV)*

*In this passage, Ottaviano Fregoso, following Plutarch, who in* Can virtue be taught? *said that virtue must be learned like the other arts, argues for the Platonic identification of knowledge and virtue against Bembo's Aristotelian objection that there exists* akrasia, *weakness of will. Fregoso makes the Platonic distinction between* doxa *and* epistêmê, *opinion and knowledge; the man who has true knowledge can never do wrong. The passage is instinct with the humanist faith in the educability of man and in his innate capacity for virtue.*

*Ottaviano Fregoso (1470-1524) was a Genoese exile; it is his task in Book IV to expound the true end of the courtier. His interlocutors are Gaspare Pallavicino (1486-1511) and Pietro Bembo (1470-1547); the latter, later a cardinal, was the purist imitator of Cicero and the champion of Florentine as the norm for the vernacular.*

The Lord Octavian held his peace as though he would have said no more, but the Lord Gaspar, 'I cannot see, my Lord Octavian', said he, 'that this goodness of mind and continency and the other virtues which you will have the courtier to show his lord may be learned, but I suppose that they are given the men that have them by nature and of God. And that it is so, you may see that there is no man so wicked and of so ill conditions in the world, nor so untemperate and unjust, which if he be asked the question will confess himself such a one. But every man, be he never so wicked, is glad to be counted just, continent and good – which should not be so in case[1] these virtues might be learned, because it is no shame not to know the thing that a man hath not studied, but a rebuke it is not to have that which we ought to be endowed withal of nature. Therefore doth each man seek to cover the defaults of nature as well in the mind as also in the body, the which is to be seen in the blind, lame, crooked and other maimed and deformed creatures. For although these imperfections may be laid to nature, yet doth it grieve each man to have them in himself, because it seemeth, by the testimony of the selfsame nature, that a man hath that default or blemish, as it were, for a patent and token of his ill inclination. The fable that is reported of Epimetheus[2] doth also confirm mine opinion, which was so unskilful in dividing the gifts of nature unto men that he left them much more needy of everything than all other living creatures. Whereupon Prometheus stole the politic wisdom from Minerva and Vulcan that men have to get their living withal. Yet had they not, for all that, civil wisdom to gather themselves together into cities and the

knowledge to live with civility, because it was kept in the castle of
Jupiter by most circumspect overseers, which put Prometheus in such
fear that he durst not approach nigh them. Whereupon Jupiter taking
pity upon the misery of men, that could not fellowship[3] together for
lack of civil virtue, but were torn in pieces by wild beasts, he sent
Mercury to the earth to carry justice and shame, that these two things
might furnish cities and gather citizens together; and willed that they
should be given them not as other arts were, wherein one cunning[4] man
sufficeth for many ignorant, as physic, but that they should be imprinted
in every man. And ordained a law that all such as were without justice
and shame should be banished and put to death as contagious to the
city. Behold then, my Lord Octavian, God hath granted these virtues to
men, and are not to be learned but be natural.' Then the Lord Octavian,
somewhat smiling, 'Will you then, my Lord Gaspar', quoth he, 'have
men to be so unfortunate and of so peevish a judgement that with
policy they have found out an art to tame the natures of wild beasts,
as bears, wolves, lions, and may, with the same, teach a pretty bird to
fly as a man list, and return back from the wood and from his natural
liberty of his own accord to snares and bondage – and with the same
policy cannot or will not find out arts whereby they may profit themselves, and with study and diligence make their mind more perfect?
This, in mine opinion, were like as if physicians should study with all
diligence to have the art only to heal felons[5] in fingers and the red
gum[6] in young children, and lay aside the cure of fevers, pleurisy and
other sore diseases, the which how out of reason it were every man may
consider.[7] I believe, therefore, that the moral virtues are not in us
altogether by nature, because nothing can at any time be accustomed
unto it that is naturally his contrary; as it is seen in a stone, the which,
though it be cast upward ten thousand times, yet will he never accustom
to go up of himself. Therefore, in case virtues were as natural to us as
heaviness to the stone, we should never accustom ourselves to vice. Nor
yet are vices natural in this sort; for then should we never be virtuous,
and a great wickedness and folly it were to punish men for the faults
that came of nature without our offence; and this error should the laws
commit, which appoint not punishment to the offenders for the tres-
pass that is past, because it cannot be brought to pass that the thing
that is done may not be done, but they have a respect to the time to
come, that whoso hath offended may offend no more, or else with ill
precedent give not a cause for others to offend. And thus yet they are
in opinion that virtues may be learned, which is most true, because we
are born apt to receive them and in like manner vices; and therefore,

there groweth a custom in us of both the one and the other through long use, so that first we practise virtue or vice, after that we are virtuous or vicious. The contrary is known in the things that be given us of nature; for first we have the power to practise them, after that we do practise, as it is in the senses – for first we can see, hear, feel, after that, we do see, hear and feel; although notwithstanding many of these doings be also set out more sightly with teaching. Whereupon good schoolmasters do not only instruct their children in letters but also in good nurture[8] in eating, drinking, talking and going,[9] with certain gestures meet for the purpose. Therefore, even as in the other arts, so also in the virtues, it is behoveful to have a teacher that with lessons and good exhortations may stir up and quicken in us those moral virtues whereof we have the seed enclosed and buried in the soul, and, like the good husbandman, till them and open the way for them, weeding from about them the briars and darnel of appetites, which many times so shadow and choke our minds that they suffer them not to bud nor to bring forth the happy fruits which alone ought to be wished to grow in the hearts of men. In this sort, then, is naturally in every one of us justice and shame, which, you say, Jupiter sent to the earth for all men. But, even as a body without eyes how sturdy ever he be, if he remove to any certain place, oftentimes faileth, so the root of these virtues that be potentially engendered in our minds, if it be not aided with teaching, doth often come to naught. Because, if it should be brought into doing and to his perfect custom, it is not satisfied, as is said, with nature alone, but hath need of a politic[10] usage and of reason, which may cleanse and scour that soul, taking away the dim veil of ignorance, whereof arise, in a manner, all the errors in men. For, in case good and ill were well known and perceived, every man would always choose the good and shun the ill. Therefore may virtue be said to be, as it were, a wisdom and an understanding to choose the good, and vice a lack of foresight and an ignorance that leadeth to judge falsely. Because men never choose the ill with opinion that it is ill, but they are deceived through a certain likeness of good.' Then answered the Lord Gaspar, 'Yet are there many that know plainly they do ill and do it notwithstanding, and that because they more esteem the present pleasure which they feel than the punishment that they doubt shall fall upon them, as thieves, murderers and such other.' The Lord Octavian said, 'True pleasure is always good, and true sorrow evil; therefore, these be deceived in taking false pleasure for true and true sorrow for false, whereupon many times through false pleasures they run into true displeasures. The art, therefore, that teacheth to discern this truth from falsehood may in like case be learned; and the virtue by the which we choose this good indeed, and not that which falsely appeareth to be, may be called true knowledge, and more available[11] for man's life than any other, because it expelleth ignorance, of the which, as I have said, spring all evils.' Then Master Peter Bembo, 'I wot not, my Lord Octavian', quoth he, 'how the Lord Gaspar should grant you that of ignorance should spring all evils, and that there be not many which, in offending, know for certainty that they do offend, neither are they any deal[12] deceived in the true pleasure nor yet in the true sorrow; because it is sure that such as be incontinent judge with reason and uprightly, and know it whereunto they are provoked by lust, contrary to due, to be ill; and therefore they make resistance and set reason to match greedy desire, whereupon ariseth the battle of pleasure and sorrow against judgement. Finally, reason, overcome by greedy desire far the mightier, is clean without succour, like a ship that for a time defendeth herself from the tempestuous sea storms, at the end beaten with the too raging violence of winds, her gables and tacklings broken, yieldeth up to be driven at the will of fortune, without occupying helm or any manner help of pilot for her safeguard. Forthwith, therefore, commit they the offences with a certain doubtful remorse of conscience and, in a manner, whether they will or no, the which they would not do unless they knew the thing that they do to be ill, but, without striving of reason, would run wholly headlong after greedy desire; and then should they not be incontinent, but untemperate, which is much worse.[13] Therefore is incontinency said to be a diminished vice, because it hath in it a part of reason, and, likewise, continency an unperfect virtue, because it hath in it part of affection;[14] therefore, methink that it cannot be said that the offences of the incontinent come of ignorance, or that they be deceived and offend not, when they know for a truth that they do offend.' The Lord Octavian answered, 'Certes, Master Peter, your argument is good; yet, in my mind, it is more apparent than true. For, although the incontinent offend with that doubtfulness, and reason in their mind striveth against greedy desire, and that that is ill seemeth unto them to be ill indeed, yet have they no perfect knowledge of it, nor understand it so thoroughly as need requireth. Therefore, of this, it is rather a feeble opinion in them than certain knowledge whereby they agree to have reason overcome by affection; but if they had in them true knowledge, there is no doubt but they would not offend, because evermore the thing whereby greedy desire overcometh reason is ignorance; neither can true knowledge be ever overcome by affection, that proceedeth from the body and not from the mind, and in case it be well ruled and governed by reason, it becometh a virtue, if not, it becometh a vice. But such force reason hath that she maketh the sense always to obey and, by wondrous means and ways, pierceth, lest ignorance should possess that which she ought to have; so that, although the spirits and the sinews and the bones have no reason in them, yet, when there springeth in us that motion of mind that the imagination, as it were, pricketh forward and shaketh the bridle to the spirits, all the members are in a readiness – the feet to run, the hands to take or to do that which the mind thinketh upon; and this is also manifestly known in many which unwittingly otherwhile eat some loathsome and abhorring[15] meat, but so well dressed that to their taste it appeareth most delicate; afterward understanding what manner thing it was, it doth not only grieve them and loathe them in their mind, but the body also agreeth with the judgement of the mind, that of force[16] they cast that meat up again.'

NOTES

    1. *In case*: if.
    2. Plato, *Protagoras*, 320D-322D.
    3. *Fellowship*: here a verb.
    4. *Cunning*: knowledgeable.
    5. *Felons*: small abscesses, boils.
    6. *Red gum*: a rash common to young children.
    7. Compare Plutarch, *Can virtue be taught?*, *Moralia*, 440A.
    8. *Nurture*: breeding.
    9. *Going*: walking.
  10. *Politic*: judicious, skilful.
  11. *Available*: serviceable, beneficial.
  12. *Any deal*: any whit.
  13. On the difference between incontinence and intemperance, see Plutarch, *On moral virtue*, *Moralia*, 445B-446C.
  14. *Affection*: emotion.
  15. *Abhorring*: abhorrent.
  16. *Of force*: perforce, unavoidably.

**Elyot: *The governor***

*(i) 'Why gentlemen in this present time be not equal in doctrine to the ancient noblemen' (from Book I)*

*In this passage, in reply to those who consider knowledge unnecessary for a nobleman, Elyot argues that knowledge is useful for statesmen and is that which distinguishes man from beast. Compare the first part of the piece with the first passage from* The courtier *given above in this chapter. To the standard exempla employed by Castiglione – Alexander and Aristotle, Julius Caesar – Elyot adds some exempla from English history. Elyot had almost certainly read Castiglione's book, published three years before his own; we know that Thomas Cromwell, his patron and friend, owned a copy (Caspari,* Humanism and the social order, *p. 85 and note, p. 241), and there are many correspondences between the two works, the defence of monarchy, the discussion of the cardinal virtues, the advocacy of painting and music. Compare the second half of the passage with the second passage from Erasmus'* On giving children an early and a liberal education *given above in chapter 1; both cite the anecdote about Aristippus and the two stones given by Diogenes Laertius, and speak of a man without learning as a piece of unformed flesh.*

*That there was hostility at this period among noblemen to having their sons educated is suggested by a possibly apocryphal anecdote told by Richard Pace, Dean of St Paul's, who wrote a humanist treatise on education; over the dinner table, a horn-carrying nobleman said that 'gentlemen's sons ought to be able to blow their horn skilfully, to hunt well, and to carry and train a hawk elegantly; but the study of letters is to be left to the sons of peasants', to which Pace replied that the king needed educated servants for, say, receiving embassies, and that such attitudes would result in the sons of peasants obtaining all the positions of power (Caspari, pp. 136-7). By the end of the century humanist attitudes had helped to bring about a change; education became requisite for the aristocracy (see further Introduction, p. 26).*

Now will I somewhat declare of the chief causes why in our time noblemen be not as excellent in learning as they were in old time among the Romans and Greeks. Surely, as I have diligently marked in daily experience, the principal causes be these. The pride, avarice and negligence of parents, and the lack or fewness of sufficient masters or teachers.

As I said, pride is the first cause of this inconvenience.[1] For of those persons be some which, without shame, dare affirm that to a great gentleman it is a notable reproach to be well learned and to be called a great clerk,[2] which name they account to be of so base estimation that they never have it in their mouths but when they speak anything in derision; which, perchance, they would not do if they had once leisure to read our own chronicle of England, where they shall find that King Henry the First, son of William Conqueror and one of the most noble princes that ever reigned in this realm, was openly called Henry

Beauclerc, which is in English fair clerk, and is yet at this day so named. And whether that name be to his honour or to his reproach, let them judge that do read and compare his life with his two brethren, William called Rouse[3] and Robert le Courtoise,[4] they both not having semblable[5] learning with the said Henry; the one for his dissolute living and tyranny being hated of all his nobles and people, finally was suddenly slain by the shot of an arrow as he was hunting in a forest, which to make larger and to give his deer more liberty he did cause the houses of fifty-two parishes to be pulled down, the people to be expelled, and all being desolate to be turned into desert and made only pasture for beasts savage, which he would never have done if he had as much delighted in good learning as did his brother. The other brother, Robert le Courtoise, being Duke of Normandy and the eldest son of William Conqueror, albeit that he was a man of much prowess, and right expert in martial affairs, wherefore he was elect before Godfrey of Boulogne to have been King of Jerusalem, yet notwithstanding, when he invaded this realm with sundry puissant armies, also divers noblemen aiding him, yet his noble brother, Henry Beauclerc, more by wisdom than power, also by learning adding policy to virtue and courage, oftentimes vanquished him and did put him to flight. And after sundry victories, finally took him and kept him in prison, having none other means to keep his realm in tranquillity.

It was for no rebuke but for an excellent honour that the Emperor Antoninus[6] was surnamed philosopher; for, by his most noble example of living and industry incomparable, he during all the time of his reign kept the public weal of the Romans in such a perfect estate that by his acts he confirmed the saying of Plato that blessed is that public weal wherein either philosophers do reign or else kings be in philosophy studious.[7] These persons that so much contemn[8] learning that they would that gentlemen's children should have no part or very little thereof, but rather should spend their youth alway, I say not only in hunting and hawking, which moderately used, as solaces ought to be, I intend not to dispraise, but in those idle pastimes which, for the vice that is therein, the commandment of the prince and the universal consent of the people, expressed in statutes and laws, do prohibit, I mean playing at dice and other games named unleeful.[9] These persons, I say, I would should remember or else now learn, if they never else heard it, that the noble Philip, King of Macedonia, who subdued all Greece, above all the good fortunes that ever he had, most rejoiced that his son Alexander was born in the time that Aristotle the philosopher flourished, by whose instruction he might attain to most excellent learning.[10] Also, the same Alexander oftentimes said that he was equally as much bound to Aristotle as to his father, King Philip; for of his father he received life, but of Aristotle he received the way to live nobly.[11] Who dispraised Epaminondas, the most valiant captain of Thebans, for that he was excellently learned and a great philosopher?[12] Who ever discommended Julius Caesar for that he was a noble orator and, next to Tully,[13] in the eloquence of the Latin tongue excelled all other? Who ever reproved the Emperor Hadrian for that he was so exquisitely learned not only in Greek and Latin but also in all sciences liberal that openly at Athens, in the universal assembly of the greatest clerks of the world, he by a long time disputed with philosophers and rhetoricians which were esteemed most excellent, and by the judgement of them that were present had the palm or reward of victory? And yet by the governance of that noble emperor not only the public weal flourished but also divers rebellions were suppressed and the majesty of the empire hugely increased. Was it any reproach to the noble Germanicus (who by the assignment of Augustus should have succeeded Tiberius in the empire, if traitorous envy had not in his flourishing youth bereft him his life) that he was equal to the most noble poets of his time, and, to the increase of his honour and most worthy commendation, his image was set up at Rome in the habit that poets at those days used? Finally, how much excellent learning commendeth and not dispraiseth nobility it shall plainly appear unto them that do read the lives of Alexander called Severus, Tacitus, Probus Aurelius, Constantine, Theodosius and Charles the Great, surnamed Charlemagne, all being emperors, and do compare them with other which lacked or had not so much of doctrine.[14] Verily, they be far from good reason, in mine opinion, which covet to have their children goodly in stature, strong, deliver,[15] well singing, wherein trees, beasts, fishes and birds be not only with them equal but also far do exceed them; and cunning,[16] whereby only man excelleth all other creatures in earth, they reject and account unworthy to be in their children. What unkind[17] appetite were it to desire to be father rather of a piece of flesh, that can only move and feel, than of a child, that should have the perfect form of a man? What so perfectly expresseth a man as doctrine? Diogenes, the philosopher, seeing one without learning sit on a stone, said to them that were with him, 'Behold where one stone sitteth on another.'[18] Which words well considered and tried shall appear to contain in it wonderful matter for the approbation of doctrine, whereof a wise man may accumulate inevitable arguments, which I of necessity, to avoid tediousness, must needs pass over at this time.

NOTES

1. *Inconvenience*: harm, misfortune.
2. *Clerk*: scholar, see above, p. 168 note 4.
3. *Rouse*: red-haired, i.e. William Rufus.
4. *Courtoise*: Elyot's rendering of 'Curt-hose', short boot, the nickname given to Robert from the shortness of his legs.
5. *Semblable*: like, similar.
6. *Antoninus*: Marcus Aurelius Antoninus, the Stoic philosopher.
7. Plato, *The republic*, 473C-D.
8. *Contemn*: despise.
9. *Unleeful*: not permissible or allowable (leave + ful).
10. Aulus Gellius, *Attic nights*, IX. iii. 5-6.
11. Plutarch, *Lives*, *Alexander*, viii. 4.
12. See Cornelius Nepos, *On famous men, Epaminondas*, ii. 1-2, v. 1. (Epaminondas was a Theban general who defeated the Spartans in the fourth century BC.)
13. *Tully*: Cicero.
14. *Doctrine*: learning, erudition, knowledge.
15. *Deliver*: active, agile.
16. *Cunning*: knowledge, wisdom, intelligence.
17. *Unkind*: unnatural.
18. Actually Aristippus, Diogenes Laertius, *Lives of eminent philosophers*, II. 72.

## (ii) The true orator (from Book I)

*Here, Elyot adopts the standard humanist position that eloquence by itself is not enough, and that it must be paired by wisdom. He supports his argument with often quoted passages from Cicero's* On the orator *and* On invention.

Now some man will require me to show mine opinion if it be necessary that gentlemen should after the age of fourteen years continue in study. And to be plain and true therein, I dare affirm that if the elegant speaking of Latin be not added to other doctrine,[1] little fruit may come of the tongue, since Latin is but a natural speech and the fruit of speech is wise sentence,[2] which is gathered and made of sundry learnings.

And who that hath nothing but language only may be no more praised than a popinjay,[3] a pie[4] or a stare,[5] when they speak featly.[6] There be many nowadays in famous schools and universities which be so much given to the study of tongues only that when they write epistles they seem to the reader that, like to a trumpet, they make a sound without any purpose, whereunto men do hearken more for the noise than for any delectation that thereby is moved. Wherefore they be much abused that suppose eloquence to be only in words or colours of rhetoric; for, as Tully[7] saith, what is so furious or mad a thing as a vain sound of words of the best sort and most ornate containing neither cunning[8] nor sentence?[9] Undoubtedly, very eloquence is in every tongue where any matter or act done or to be done is expressed in words clean, propice,[10] ornate and comely, whereof sentences be so aptly compact[11] that they, by a virtue inexplicable, do draw unto them the minds and consent of the hearers, they being therewith either persuaded, moved or to delectation induced. Also, every man is not an orator that can write an epistle or a flattering oration in Latin, whereof the last, as God help me, is too much used. For a right orator may not be, without a much better furniture. Tully saying that to him belongeth the explicating or unfolding of sentence with a great estimation, in giving counsel concerning matters of great importance; also to him appertaineth the stirring and quickening of people languishing or despairing, and to moderate them that be rash and unbridled.[12] Wherefore noble authors do affirm that, in the first infancy of the world, men, wandering like beasts in woods and on mountains, regarding neither the religion due unto God, nor the office[13] pertaining unto man, ordered all thing by bodily strength, until Mercury, as Plato supposeth, or some other man helped by sapience and eloquence, by some apt or proper oration, assembled them together and persuaded to them what commodity[14] was in mutual conversation and honest manners.[15] But yet Cornelius Tacitus describeth an orator to be of more excellent qualities, saying that an orator is he that can or may speak or reason in every question sufficiently elegantly and to persuade properly, according to the dignity of the thing that is spoken of, the opportunity of time, and pleasure of them that be hearers.[16] Tully before him affirmed that a man may not be an orator heaped with praise but if he have gotten the knowledge of all things and arts of greatest importance.[17] And how shall an orator speak of that thing that he hath not learned? And because there may be nothing but it may happen to come in praise or dispraise, in consultation or judgement, in accusation or defence, therefore an orator by others' instruction perfectly furnished may in every matter and learning commend or dispraise, exhort or dissuade, accuse or defend eloquently as occasion happeneth; wherefore, inasmuch as in an orator is required to be a heap of all manner of learning, which of some is called the world of science, of other the circle of doctrine, which is in one word of Greek *encyclopedia*,[18] therefore at this day may be found but a very few orators. For they that come in message from princes be for honour named now orators if they be in any degree of worship, only poor men, having equal or more of learning, being called messengers. Also they which do only teach rhetoric, which is the science whereby is taught an artificial form of speaking, wherein is the power to persuade, move and delight, or by that science only do speak or write without any adminiculation[19] of other sciences ought to be named rhetoricians, declamators, artificial speakers, named in Greek *logodaidali*,[20] or any other name than orators.

NOTES

1. *Doctrine*: learning.
2. *Sentence*: meaning, sense.
3. *Popinjay*: parrot.
4. *Pie*: magpie.
5. *Stare*: starling.
6. *Featly*: aptly, neatly, cleverly.
7. *Tully*: Cicero.
8. *Cunning*: knowledge, intelligence.
9. *On the orator*, I. xii. 51 (also quoted by Jonson, see p. 203).
10. *Propice*: suitable.
11. *Compact*: made up.
12. *On the orator*, II. ix. 35.
13. *Office*: duty, function, part.
14. *Commodity*: convenience, benefit.
15. Plato, *Protagoras*, 322B-D; Cicero, *On invention*, I. ii. 2.
16. Tacitus, *A dialogue on oratory*, xxx. 5.
17. *On the orator*, I. vi. 20.
18. Quintilian, *The education of an orator*, I. x. i., speaks of 'the circle of learning (*orbis doctrinae*) called by the Greeks *enkuklios paideia*'.
19. *Adminiculation*: help, support.
20. *Logodaidalos*: a word used by Plato, *Phaedrus*, 266E, cited by Cicero, *The orator*, xii. 39, and Quintilian, III. i. 11.

## Ascham: *The schoolmaster*

### (i) The importance of knowledge (from Book I)

*In this passage, Ascham begins, like Elyot before him, by deploring the attitude of the nobility to learning; he says that it cannot be blamed on French influence (contrast Castiglione, above, p. 166). He goes on to argue, leaning heavily on the passage from Erasmus' On giving children an early and a liberal education given above (see pp. 57-8), from which he borrows sentences and images, that experience is only profitable if it is backed with good precepts. The final paragraph expresses his (and Elyot's) ideal of state service; properly educated gentlemen will be able to use their knowledge to serve the state.*

And whether there be any such or no I cannot well tell, yet I hear say some young gentlemen of ours count it their shame to be counted learned, and perchance they count it their shame to be counted honest also; for I hear say they meddle as little with the one as with the other. A marvellous case that gentlemen should so be ashamed of good learning and never a whit ashamed of ill manners; such do lay[1] for them that the gentlemen of France do so, which is a lie, as God will have it. Langaeus and Bellaeus,[2] that be dead, and the noble Vidame of Chartres,[3] that is alive, and infinite more in France which I hear tell of prove this to be most false. And though some in France which will needs be gentlemen whether men will or no, and have more gentleship in their hat than in their head, be at deadly feud with both learning and honesty, yet I believe if that noble prince, King Francis the First, were alive, they should have neither place in his court nor pension[4] in his wars, if he had knowledge of them. This opinion is not French, but plain Turkish; from whence some French fetch more faults than this, which I pray God keep out of England, and send also those of ours better minds which bend themselves against virtue and learning, to the contempt of God, dishonour of their country, to the hurt of many others, and at length to the greatest harm and utter destruction of themselves.

Some other, having better nature but less wit (for ill commonly have over-much wit) do not utterly dispraise learning, but they say that, without learning, common experience, knowledge of all fashions and haunting all companies shall work in youth both wisdom and ability to execute any weighty affair. Surely long experience doth profit much, but most and almost only to him (if we mean honest affairs) that is diligently before instructed with precepts of well-doing. For good precepts of learning be the eyes of the mind, to look wisely before a man which way to go right and which not.

Learning teacheth more in one year than experience in twenty, and learning teacheth safely when experience maketh more miserable than wise. He hazardeth sore that waxeth wise by experience. An unhappy master he is that is made cunning[5] by many shipwrecks, a miserable merchant that is neither rich nor wise but after some bankrupts.[6] It is costly wisdom that is bought by experience. We know by experience itself that it is a marvellous pain to find out but a short way by long wandering. And surely, he that would prove wise by experience, he may be witty[7] indeed, but even like a swift runner that runneth fast out of his way and upon the night, he knoweth not whither. And verily they be fewest of number that be happy or wise by unlearned experience. And look well upon the former life of those few, whether your example be old or young, who without learning have gathered by long experience a little wisdom and some happiness, and when you do consider what mischief they have committed, what dangers they have escaped (and yet twenty for one do perish in the adventure), then think well with yourself whether ye would that your own son should come to wisdom and happiness by the way of such experience or no.

It is a notable tale that old Sir Roger Cholmley,[8] sometime chief justice, would tell of himself. When he was ancient[9] in Inn of Court, certain young gentlemen were brought before him to be corrected for certain misorders, and one of the lustiest said, 'Sir, we be young gentlemen, and wise men before us have proved[10] all fashions, and yet those have done full well'; this they said because it was well known that Sir Roger had been a good fellow in his youth. But he answered them very wisely. 'Indeed', saith he, 'in youth I was as you are now, and I had twelve fellows like unto myself, but not one of them came to a good end. And therefore, follow not my example in youth, but follow my counsel in age, if ever ye think to come to this place or to these years that I am come unto, lest ye meet either with poverty or Tyburn[11] in the way.'

Thus experience of all fashions in youth, being in proof always dangerous, in issue seldom lucky, is a way indeed to over-much knowledge, yet used commonly of such men which be either carried by some curious affection of mind or driven by some hard necessity of life to hazard the trial of over-many perilous adventures.

Erasmus, the honour of learning of all our time, said wisely that experience is the common schoolhouse of fools[12] and ill men; men of wit and honesty be otherwise instructed. For there be that keep them out of fire and yet was never burnt, that beware of water and yet was never nigh drowning, that hate harlots and was never at the stews,[13] that abhor falsehood and never broke promise themselves.

But will ye see a fit similitude of this adventured experience? A father that doth let loose his son to all experiences is most like a fond hunter that letteth slip a whelp to the whole herd. Twenty to one, he shall fall upon a rascal,[14] and let go the fair game. Men that hunt so be either ignorant persons, privy stealers or night walkers.[15]

Learning therefore, ye wise fathers, and good bringing up, and not blind and dangerous experience, is the next[16] and readiest way that must lead your children first to wisdom and then to worthiness, if ever ye purpose they shall come there.

And to say all in short, though I lack authority to give counsel, yet I lack not good will to wish that the youth in England, specially gentlemen and namely[17] nobility, should be by good bringing up so grounded in judgement of learning, so founded in love of honesty, as when they should be called forth to the execution of great affairs in service of their prince and country, they might be able to use and to order all experiences, were they good, were they bad, and that according to the square, rule and line of wisdom, learning and virtue.

## NOTES

1. *Lay*: allege.
2. *Langaeus*: Guillaume du Bellay, Seigneur de Langey (1491-1543); *Bellaeus*: Cardinal Jean du Bellay (1498-1560). Patrons of the arts at the time of Francis I.
3. Jean de Ferrières (*c*. 1521-86), a Huguenot, who paid several visits to the English court in the 1560s to negotiate with Queen Elizabeth. *Vidame*: a title; one who holds lands from a bishop or ecclesiastic as his secular representative.
4. *Pension*: salary, regular payment.
5. *Cunning*: expert.
6. *Bankrupts*: bankruptcies.
7. *Witty*: clever.
8. Sir Roger Cholmley, d. 1565, of Lincoln's Inn.
9. *Ancient*: one of the senior members forming the governing body of the Inns of Court.
10. *Proved*: tried.
11. *Tyburn*: where the gallows stood.
12. In *On the utility of colloquies*, *Opera omnia*, vol. I, col. 901E. And see the adages 'When a thing is done, a fool can see it' and 'Trouble experienced makes a fool wise' in the Toronto translation of Erasmus, vol. XXXI, pp. 78-80.
13. *The stews*: brothels.
14. *Rascal*: a young or inferior deer.
15. *Night walkers*: i.e. thieves.
16. *Next*: shortest, most direct.
17. *Namely*: particularly, above all.

## (ii) The importance of words (from Book II)

*In this famous passage, which Bacon was to trounce in* The advancement of learning, *Ascham, digressing from the theme of imitation, voices the humanist conviction of the intimate and necessary connection between eloquence and wisdom, words and things: bad writing is a sign of bad thinking, and neglect of style leads to corruption in learning and life. Such ideas are in harmony with those of Erasmus and of Sturm, Ascham's correspondent:*

But knowledge of things without grace in speech is wont to be barbarous and vile, and likewise with the corruption of speech we observe that a kind of captious conviction of their own wisdom

*steals into men. Whence it may be seen, that the first tender age of*
*children ought to be given over to instruction in proper speaking.*
*(Sturm,* On the right way of beginning schools for literary education,
*quoted Ryan,* Roger Ascham, *pp. 334-5)*

*The notion of pagan learning as forming part of God's providential plan*
*may remind us of* The antibarbarians *(see above, pp. 103f); Ascham had*
*read Erasmus' book in a manuscript in Cambridge (see vol. XXIII of the*
*Toronto Erasmus, p. lvii, note 139).*

Imitation is a faculty to express lively and perfectly that example
which ye go about to follow. And, of itself, it is large and wide; for all
the works of nature, in a manner, be examples for art to follow.

But, to our purpose, all languages, both learned and mother tongues,
be gotten, and gotten only, by imitation. For, as ye use to hear, so ye
learn to speak; if ye hear no other, ye speak not yourself; and whom ye
only hear, of them ye only learn.

And therefore, if ye would speak as the best and wisest do, ye must
be conversant[1] where the best and wisest are; but if you be born or
brought up in a rude country, ye shall not choose but speak rudely —
the rudest man of all knoweth this to be true.

Yet nevertheless, the rudeness of common and mother tongues is no
bar for wise speaking. For in the rudest country and most barbarous
mother language, many be found can speak very wisely; but in the
Greek and Latin tongue, the two only learned tongues, which be kept
not in common talk but in private books, we find always wisdom and
eloquence, good matter and good utterance, never or seldom asunder.
For all such authors as be fullest of good matter and right judgement in
doctrine be likewise always most proper in words, most apt in sentence, most plain and pure in uttering the same.

And contrariwise, in those two tongues, all writers, either in religion
or any sect of philosophy, whosoever be found fond in judgement of
matter be commonly found as rude in uttering their mind. For Stoics,
Anabaptists and friars, with Epicures, libertines and monks, being most
like in learning and life, are no fonder and pernicious in their opinions
than they be rude and barbarous in their writings.[2] They be not wise,
therefore, that say, 'What care I for a man's words and utterance, if his
matter and reasons be good.' Such men say so not so much of ignorance
as either of some singular pride in themselves, or some special malice of
other, or for some private and partial matter, either in religion or other
kind of learning. For good and choice meats be no more requisite for

healthy bodies than proper and apt words be for good matters, and also plain and sensible utterance for the best and deepest reasons; in which two points standeth perfect eloquence, one of the fairest and rarest gifts that God doth give to man.

Ye know not what hurt ye do to learning that care not for words but for matter, and so make a divorce betwixt the tongue and the heart.[3] For, mark all ages, look upon the whole course of both the Greek and Latin tongue, and ye shall surely find that, when apt and good words began to be neglected and properties of those two tongues to be confounded, then also began ill deeds to spring, strange manners to oppress good orders, new and fond opinions to strive with old and true doctrine, first in philosophy and after in religion, right judgement of all things to be perverted — and so virtue with learning is contemned[4] and study left off, of ill thoughts cometh perverse judgement, of ill deeds springeth lewd talk. Which four misorders, as they mar man's life, so destroy they good learning withal.

But behold the goodness of God's providence for learning; all old authors and sects of philosophy which were fondest in opinion and rudest in utterance, as Stoics and Epicures, first contemned of wise men and after forgotten of all men, be so consumed by times as they be now not only out of use but also out of memory of man; which thing, I surely think, will shortly chance to the whole doctrine and all the books of fantastical Anabaptists and friars, and of the beastly libertines and monks.

Again, behold on the other side how God's wisdom hath wrought that, of *Academici* and *Peripatetici*,[5] those that were wisest in judgement of matters and purest in uttering their minds, the first and chiefest that wrote most and best in either tongue, as Plato and Aristotle in Greek, Tully[6] in Latin, be so either wholly or sufficiently left unto us as I never knew yet scholar that gave himself to like and love and follow chiefly those three authors but he proved both learned, wise and also an honest man, if he joined withal the true doctrine of God's holy Bible, without the which the other three be but fine edge-tools[7] in a fool or madman's hand.

NOTES

1. *Be conversant*: dwell.
2. The intriguing grouping here is an index of Ascham's prejudices. Stoics and Epicureans were the two main Hellenistic schools of philosophy: the former (though in general well thought of in the Renaissance) were sometimes criticised for the self-sufficiency and the lack of realism of their ethics and for their advocacy

of suicide; the latter were believed, falsely, to advocate sensual indulgence. The Catholic monks and friars are disliked by the moderate Protestant, Ascham, as are the opposite extreme, the Anabaptists, a word used loosely to describe, hostilely, any Protestant sectarian. A contrast is also implied between the severity of the Stoics, Anabaptists and friars (an allusion to Savonarola?) and the loose living of the Epicureans and monks; Ascham favoured a mean between the two: see his statement earlier in *The schoolmaster*, 'I was never either Stoic in doctrine or Anabaptist in religion, to mislike a merry, pleasant and playful nature, if no outrage be committed against law, measure and good order.'

3. Compare Cicero, *On the orator*, III. xvi. 61.

4. *Contemned*: despised.

5. *Academici*: followers of Plato; *Peripatetici*: followers of Aristotle.

6. *Tully*: Cicero.

7. *Fine*: sharp; *edge-tools*: sharp implements, proverbial in 'to play with edge-tools'.


## Wilson: *The art of rhetoric*

*Thomas Wilson (1525?-81) was educated at King's College, Cambridge; he became a member of the reforming humanist group there, and a friend of Ascham. A characteristic product of English humanism, he pursued a career in public life, becoming a secretary of state under Elizabeth; as with Elyot and Ascham, his humanist interests found expression in the patriotic task of popularising the classical heritage. He wrote treatises in the vernacular on logic and rhetoric, and published a translation of three of Demosthenes' speeches.* The art of rhetoric *was one of the first manuals of classical rhetoric in English; it was published in 1553 and went through several editions. It is based on Quintilian, Cicero and the pseudo-Ciceronian* To Herennius; *it includes as an example of a deliberative oration a translation of Erasmus'* Praise of marriage *(written for Erasmus' pupil, Lord Mountjoy, and then included in* On *writing letters as an example of a 'suasory epistle'), as well as using anecdotes taken from the English translation of Erasmus'* Apophthegms *by Nicholas Udall.*

*The first extract is the preface to the work, and is a tribute to the power of eloquence. It recasts in a Christian form the opening of* On invention *(I. ii. 2-3), where Cicero, defending eloquence, argues that it was oratory which first brought men together and civilised them; speech is what separates man from the animals. The second extract is from the beginning of the third book, which deals with* elocutio *(or the 'applying of apt words and sentences to the matter' of the speech); it is a short praise of eloquence.*

## (i) *'Eloquence first given by God, after lost by man, and last repaired by God again'*

Man, in whom is poured the breath of life, was made at his first being an everliving creature, unto the likeness of God, endued with reason and appointed lord over all other things living. But after the fall of our first father, sin so crept in that our knowledge was much darkened, and, by corruption of this our flesh, man's reason and intendment[1] were both overwhelmed. At what time, God, being sore grieved with the folly of one man, pitied of his mere goodness the whole state and posterity of mankind. And therefore, whereas through the wicked suggestion of our ghostly enemy[2] the joyful fruition of God's glory was altogether lost, it pleased our heavenly father to repair mankind of his free mercy, and to grant an everliving inheritance unto all such as would by constant faith seek earnestly thereafter. Long it was ere that man knew himself, being destitute of God's grace, so that all things waxed savage, the earth untilled, society neglected, God's will not known, man against man, one against another, and all against order. Some lived by spoil, some like brute beasts grazed upon the ground, some went naked, some roamed like woodwoses;[3] none did anything by reason, but most did what they could by manhood.[4] None almost considered the everliving God, but all lived most commonly after their own lust. By death they thought that all things ended; by life they looked for none other living. None remembered the true observation of wedlock; none tendered[5] the education of their children; laws were not regarded; true dealing was not once used. For virtue, vice bore place; for right and equity, might used authority. And therefore, whereas man through reason might have used order, man through folly fell into error. And thus, for lack of skill and for want of grace, evil so prevailed that the devil was most esteemed, and God either almost unknown among them all or else nothing feared among so many. Therefore, even now when man was thus past all hope of amendment, God, still tendering his own workmanship, stirred up his faithful and elect to persuade with reason all men to society. And gave his appointed ministers knowledge both to see the natures of men and also granted them the gift of utterance, that they might with ease win folk at their will and frame them by reason to all good order.

And therefore, whereas men lived brutishly in open fields, having neither house to shroud them in, nor attire to clothe their backs, nor yet any regard to seek their best avail,[6] these appointed of God called them together by utterance of speech and persuaded with them what was good, what was bad, and what was gainful for mankind. And although at first the rude could hardly learn, and either for strangeness of the thing would not gladly receive the offer or else for lack of knowledge could not perceive the goodness, yet being somewhat drawn and delighted with the pleasantness of reason and the sweetness of utterance, after a certain space, they became, through nurture and good advisement, of wild, sober, of cruel, gentle, of fools, wise, and of beasts, men. Such force hath the tongue, and such is the power of eloquence and reason that most men are forced even to yield in that which most standeth against their will. And therefore the poets do feign that Hercules,[7] being a man of great wisdom, had all men linked together by the ears in a chain to draw them and lead them even as he listed. For his wit was so great, his tongue so eloquent and his experience such that no one man was able to withstand his reason, but everyone was rather driven to do that which he would and to will that which he did, agreeing to his advice both in word and work, in all that ever they were able.

Neither can I see that men could have been brought by any other means to live together in fellowship of life, to maintain cities, to deal truly, and willingly to obey one another, if men at the first had not by art and eloquence persuaded that which they full oft found out by reason. For what man, I pray you, being better able to maintain himself by valiant courage than by living in base subjection, would not rather look to rule like a lord than to live like an underling, if by reason he were not persuaded that it behoveth every man to live in his own vocation[8] and not to seek any higher room than whereunto he was at the first appointed? Who would dig and delve from morn till evening? Who would travail and toil with the sweat of his brows? Yea, who would for his king's pleasure adventure and hazard his life, if wit had not so won men that they thought nothing more needful in this world, nor anything whereunto they were more bound, than here to live in their duty and to train their whole life according to their calling. Therefore, whereas men are in many things weak by nature and subject to much infirmity, I think in this one point they pass all other creatures living, that they have the gift of speech and reason.

And among all other I think him most worthy fame and amongst men to be taken for half a God that therein doth chiefly and above all other excel men wherein men do excel beasts.[9] For he that is among the reasonable of all most reasonable, and among the witty of all most witty, and among the eloquent of all most eloquent, him think I among all men not only to be taken for a singular man but rather to be counted for half a God. For, in seeking the excellency hereof, the sooner he draweth to perfection, the nigher he cometh to God, who is the chief wisdom, and therefore called God because he is most wise, or rather wisdom itself.

Now then, seeing that God giveth his heavenly grace unto all such as call unto him with stretched hands and humble heart, never wanting to those that want not to themselves, I purpose by his grace and especial assistance to set forth precepts of eloquence, and to show what observation the wise have used in handling of their matters, that the unlearned, by seeing the practice of other, may have some knowledge themselves, and learn by their neighbours' device what is necessary for themselves in their own case.

NOTES

1. *Intendment*: understanding.
2. *Ghostly enemy*: the devil. *Ghostly* = spiritual.
3. *Woodwoses*: wild men of the woods, savages.
4. *Manhood*: here, might, strength (Cicero has 'vires corporis').
5. *Tendered*: cherished.
6. *Avail*: advantage, good.
7. This conception of Hercules derives from Lucian, *Heracles: an introduction*, where he describes how the Gauls picture Hercules pulling along a crowd of men tethered to his tongue by golden chains, because they associate him, rather than Hermes (Mercury), with Eloquence, and consider that he achieved his deeds by the power of persuasion. Lucian's account seems to have been influential in the Renaissance; Alciati has an emblem entitled 'Eloquentia fortitudine praestantior', 'Eloquence superior to force', with a picture of the Gallic Hercules after Lucian, and Vincenzo Cartari, in his *Images of the Gods of the ancients*, describes the figure in his entry for Mercury (both these books ran to many editions); Dürer made a drawing on the theme.
8. *Vocation*: calling.
9. Cicero, *On invention*, I. iv. 5.


*(ii) 'Of apt choosing and framing of words and sentences together, called elocution'*

And now we are come to that part of rhetoric the which above all other is most beautiful, whereby not only words are aptly used but also sentences are in right order framed. For whereas invention helpeth to find matter and disposition serveth to place arguments, elocution[1] getteth words to set forth invention, and with such beauty commendeth the matter that reason seemeth to be clad in purple, walking afore both bare and naked. Therefore Tully[2] saith well, to find out reason and aptly to frame it is the part of a wise man, but to commend it by words and with gorgeous talk to tell our conceit — that is only proper to an orator.[3] Many are wise, but few have the gift to set forth their wisdom. Many can tell their mind in English, but few can use meet terms and apt order, such as all men should have and wise men will use, such as needs must be had when matters should be uttered. Now then, what is he at whom all men wonder and stand in amaze at the view of his wit? Whose doings are best esteemed? Whom do we most reverence and count half a God among men? Even such a one, assuredly, that can plainly, distinctly, plentifully and aptly utter both words and matter, and in his talk can use such composition that he may appear to keep an uniformity, and, as I might say, a number[4] in the uttering of his sentence. Now an eloquent man, being smally learned, can do much more good in persuading, by shift of words and meet placing of matter, than a great learned clerk[5] shall be able with great store of learning, wanting words to set forth his meaning. Wherefore I much marvel that so many seek the only knowledge of things without any mind to commend or set forth their intendment,[6] seeing none can know either what they are or what they have without the gift of utterance. Yea, bring them to speak their mind and enter in talk with such as are said to be learned, and you shall find in them such lack of utterance that, if you judge them by their tongue and expressing of their mind, you must needs say they have no learning. Wherein, methinks, they do like some rich snudges[7] that, having great wealth, go with their hose out at heels, their shoes out at toes and their coats out at both elbows. For who can tell if such men are worth a groat, when their apparel is so homely and all their behaviour so base? I can call them by none other name but slovens that may have good gear and neither can nor yet will once wear it cleanly. What is a good thing to a man if he neither know the use of it nor yet, though he know it, is able at all to use it? If we think it comeliness and honesty to set forth the body with handsome apparel, and think them worthy to have money that both can and will use it accordingly, I cannot otherwise see but that this part deserveth praise which standeth wholly in setting forth matter by apt words and sentences together, and beautifieth the tongue with great change of colours[8] and variety of figures.

NOTES

1. *Inventio*, *dispositio* and *elocutio* are the first three requisites of oratory; *memoria* and *pronuntiatio* the last two.
2. *Tully*: Cicero.
3. Most probably a reference to *The orator*, xiv. 44, reported by Quintilian, *The education of an orator*, VIII. Pr. 14-15; see also, *The orator*, xix. 61; xxxii.

113; xxxiii. 117.
   4. *Number*: rhythm, proportion.
   5. *Clerk*: scholar, see above, p. 168, note 4.
   6. *Intendment*: meaning, conception, understanding.
   7. *Snudge*: miser, niggard.
   8. *Colours*: rhetorical ornaments.

## Peacham: *The garden of eloquence*

### *Two praises of eloquence*

*The elder Henry Peacham (1546-1634; his more famous son wrote* The complete gentleman*) was a clergyman.* The garden of eloquence, *first published in 1577, is another of the early vernacular manuals of rhetoric. It is a dictionary of rhetorical terms, with definitions and examples, drawing on compilations by Renaissance scholars, such as* The epitome of tropes *(1540) by Johannes Susenbrotus.*

*The two passages given here are the dedications of the first and second editions of the work. Both celebrate the humanist commonplace of the union of wisdom and eloquence, and pay tribute to the persuasive power of the orator. Cicero is the main inspiration of the ideas, in particular the opening of* On invention *(see p. 185), where he argues that eloquence and wisdom should be combined.*

### *(i) From the dedication of the 1577 edition to the Bishop of London, John Aylmer*

When we consider and call to mind, Right Reverend, the great might and worthiness of wisdom, then do we perfectly perceive and evidently see that God of his goodness hath poured forth his divine virtue into the mind of man far more largely and much more abundantly than in any other creature upon the face of the whole earth. Whereby he hath made man able not only to govern himself and to live after a most goodly order but also to subdue the monstrous beasts to his will. By this divine virtue and intellective power, man doth seek, find out and comprehend the causes of things, he doth meditate and muse upon the wonderful works of God, he searcheth out the secrets of nature and climbeth up to the knowledge of sapience supernatural, he learneth the cunning reasons of numbers, the mathematical demonstrations, the motions of stars, the course and alteration of times, the musical consent of harmonies and diversity of tunes, he conceiveth trim devices and is full of many profitable and pleasant inventions, he seeth what is comely[1] for his dignity and to what end he is created, which no other is able to do.

And to the end that this sovereign rule of reason might spread abroad her beautiful branches, and that wisdom might bring forth most plentifully her sweet and pleasant fruits for the common use and utility of mankind, the Lord God hath joined to the mind of man speech, which he hath made the instrument of our understanding and key of conceptions, whereby we open the secrets of our hearts and declare our thoughts to other, and herein it is that we do so far pass and excel all other creatures, in that we have the gift of speech and reason and not they; for we see what difference there is between those men in whom these two virtues do smally appear and brute beasts, that have no understanding. Therefore, how worthy of high commendations are those men that, perceiving this, do bestow their studies, their travail and their time to obtain wisdom and eloquence, the only ornaments whereby man's life is beautified and a praise most precious purchased. For, by these manner of studies, we see that many have attained to a great excellency in their kind, who have got to themselves and their country many commodities, clothed themselves with ample honours and deserved by their worthy works to be praised for ever of posterity. Of this sort among the Grecians we see was Demosthenes, Plato, Aristotle, among the Latins, Marcus Tullius Cicero, Lucius Crassus,[2] Marcus Antonius,[3] Fabius Quintilianus,[4] most famous and renowned orators, and many other more who by their earnest travails obtained these two most notable treasures; whose excellent wisdom is now wondered at and their singular eloquence had in great admiration, whose worthy praises the injury of time shall never be able to oppress, nor the devouring course of years strong enough to abolish or darken the brightness of their glory — for their honours posterity shall uphold and their noble renown everlasting memory shall maintain — whose worthy works may be sufficient examples how we should apply our studies, which are both fraughted with great wisdom and garnished with goodly eloquence. Many, not perceiving the nigh and necessary conjunction of these two precious jewels, do either affect fineness of speech and neglect the knowledge of things or, contrariwise, covet understanding and contemn[5] the art of eloquence, and therefore it cometh to pass that such take great pains and reap small profits, they ever seek and never find the thing they would fainest have; the one sort of these speak much to small purpose and the other, though they be wise, are not able aptly to express their meaning. From which calamity, they are free that do use a right judgement in applying their studies, so that their knowledge may be joined with apt utterance and their copy[6] of speech with matter of importance, that is to say, that their eloquence may be wise and their wisdom eloquent. And, therefore, right Reverend, when of late I had considered the needful assistance that the one of these do require of the other, that wisdom do require the light of eloquence and eloquence the fertility of wisdom, and saw many good books of philosophy and precepts of wisdom set forth in English and very few of eloquence, I was of a sudden moved to take this little garden in hand, and to set therein such figurative flowers both of grammar and rhetoric as do yield the sweet savour of eloquence and present to the eyes the goodly and beautiful colours of elocution, such as shine in our speech like the glorious stars in firmament, such as beautify it as flowers of sundry colours a gallant garland, such as garnish it as precious pearls a gorgeous garment, such as delight the ears as pleasant reports, repetitions and running points[7] in music, whose utility is so great that I cannot sufficiently praise them and the knowledge of them so necessary that no man can read profitably or understand perfectly either poets, orators or the holy Scriptures without them, nor any orator able by the weight of his words to persuade his hearers, having no help of them; but being well stored with such plausible[8] furniture, how wonderfully shall his persuasions take place in the minds of men and his words pierce into their inward parts! For by figures, as it were by sundry streams, that great and forcible flood of eloquence is most plentifully and pleasantly poured forth; by the great might of figures, which is no other thing than 'wisdom speaking eloquently',[9] the orator may lead his hearers which way he list and draw them to what affection[10] he will: he may make them to be angry, to be pleased, to laugh, to weep and lament; to love, to abhor and loathe; to hope, to fear, to covet, to be satisfied, to envy, to have pity and compassion; to marvel, to believe, to repent; and, briefly, to be moved with any affection that shall serve best for his purpose.

NOTES

1. *Comely*: proper.
2. *Lucius Crassus*: b. 140 BC, Roman orator admired by Cicero, who made him the chief speaker in *On the orator*.
3. *Marcus Antonius*: not the triumvir whose oratory Shakespeare celebrated in *Julius Caesar*, but a contemporary of Crassus and another speaker in *On the orator*.
4. *Fabius Quintilianus*: i.e. Quintilian.
5. *Contemn*: despise.
6. *Copy*: *copia*, abundance.
7. *Reports, repetitions and running points*: musical terms.
8. *Plausible*: pleasing.

9. I think this is an allusion to Cicero, *On the classification of rhetoric*, xxiii. 79, where eloquence is defined as 'wisdom speaking copiously' ('copiose loquens sapientia').

10. *Affection*: emotion.

## (ii) From the dedication of the 1593 edition to Sir John Puckering, Lord Keeper of the Great Seal

Albeit, Right Honourable, it may seem to some men at the first sight a matter importunate to interrupt your lordship's grave, deep and weighty considerations, sitting as you do at the stern of the commonwealth in these days of danger, yet seeing the infirmity of our mortal estate cannot possibly endure to stand continually bent, no, not in the contemplation of the most excellent subject or matter of greatest importance, may it therefore please your good lordship, if for no other cause yet, partly for your own ease, release and recreation, and partly for patronage to poor and painful students, to lend your honourable view to these my simple labours, hoping that as you are not wont either to close your eyes or stop your ears to the meanest or the poorest, so your lordship will not refuse to spare some time, when your leisure may best permit, to cast your eye upon these mean and simple fruits of my studies; the argument whereof, albeit I confess it subject to the exceptions of many, and peradventure to the reprehensions of some which seem to make a divorce between nature and art and a separation between policy and humanity,[1] yet Cicero, being both a most excellent orator and prudent politic,[2] doth mightily support and defend it against all objections, as we may plainly see in one short sentence of his, among many other tending to this purpose, where he saith 'ut hominis decus est ingenium, sic ingenii lumen est eloquentia',[3] that is, 'as wit is man's worship, or wisdom man's honour, so eloquence is the light and brightness of wisdom'; in which sentence he both expresseth the singular praises of two most worthy virtues and also enforceth the necessity and commendeth the utility of their excellent conjunction. And true it is that if we join with this prudent orator in a diligent inquisition and contemplation of wisdom, and in a deliberate consideration of art, we shall see that verified which he hath here affirmed. For if we enquire what wisdom is, we shall find that it is the knowledge of divine and human things,[4] if whose gift it is, we shall be certified that it is the gift of God, if we consider the inventions thereof, they are wonderful, if the works, they are infinite, if the fruits, they are in use sweet, in nature necessary, both for the search of truth and for the direction of human life. Briefly, this virtue is the loving and provident mother of mankind, whom she nourisheth with the sweet milk of prosperity, defendeth against manifold dangers, instructeth with her counsel and preferreth to the imperial dominion over all earthly creatures; and lest, dissenting with himself, he should by his own contention work his own confusion, she deviseth laws to support equity and appointeth punishments to repress injury, she inventeth the art and skill of war to resist violence offending against peace, she maintaineth the one and directeth the other, and is the mighty empress of them both.

Finally, by her the true felicity of man is found out and held up, without her it falleth by a sudden and woeful ruin; by her his honour is highly advanced, without her it sinketh into shame and reproach and is utterly confounded; by her he is endued with a blessed state of life, without her he perisheth in misery and death. Now lest so excellent a gift of the divine goodness as wisdom here appeareth to be and is should lie suppressed by silence, and so remain hid in darkness, almighty God, the deep sea of wisdom and bright sun of majesty, hath opened the mouth of man as the mouth of a plentiful fountain, both to pour forth the inward passions of his heart and also as a heavenly planet to show forth, by the shining beams of speech, the privy thoughts and secret conceits of his mind. By the benefit of this excellent gift, I mean of apt speech given by nature and guided by art, wisdom appeareth in her beauty, showeth her majesty and exerciseth her power, working in the mind of the hearer, partly by a pleasant proportion and, as it were, by a sweet and musical harmony, and partly by the secret and mighty power of persuasion, after a most wonderful manner. This, then, is the virtue which the orator[5] in his praise before mentioned calleth eloquence and the brightness of wisdom, for that by the mean hereof as well the rare inventions and pleasant devices as the deep understanding, the secret counsels and politic considerations[6] of wisdom are most effectually expressed and most comely beautified; for even as by the power of the sunbeams the nature of the root is showed in the blossom, and the goodness of the sap tasted in the sweetness of the fruit, even so the precious nature and wonderful power of wisdom is by the commendable art and use of eloquence produced and brought into open light. So that hereby plainly appeareth both the great necessity and singular utility of their conjunction before commended, for the one without the other do find both great want and show great imperfection; for to possess great knowledge without apt utterance is as to possess great treasure without use; contrariwise, to affect eloquence without the discretion of wisdom is as to handle a sweet instrument of music without skill. But the man which is well furnished with both, I mean with ample knowledge and excellent speech, hath been judged able and esteemed fit to rule the world with counsel, provinces with laws, cities with policy and multitudes with persuasion; such were those men in times past who by their singular wisdom and eloquence made savage nations civil, wild people tame and cruel tyrants not only to become meek but likewise merciful.[7] Hence it was that, in ancient time, men did attribute so great opinion of wisdom to the eloquent orators of those days that they called them sacred, holy, divine and the interpreters of the gods; for so doth Horace, commending Orpheus – his words be these:

> Agrestes homines sacer interpresque deorum,
> Caedibus et foedo victu deterruit Orpheus:
> Dictus ob id lenire tigres rigidosque leones.[8]

The poet here under the name of tigers and lions meant not beasts but men, and such men as by their savage nature and cruel manners might well be compared to fierce tigers and devouring lions, which, notwithstanding, by the mighty power of wisdom and prudent art of persuasion were converted from that most brutish condition of life to the love of humanity and politic government; so mighty is the power of this happy union – I mean of wisdom and eloquence – that by the one the orator forceth and by the other he allureth, and by both so worketh, that what he commendeth is beloved, what he dispraiseth is abhorred, what he persuadeth is obeyed and what he dissuadeth is avoided; so that he is, in a manner, the emperor of men's minds and affections, and next to the omnipotent God in the power of persuasion by grace and divine assistance. The principal instruments of man's help in this wonderful effect are those figures and forms of speech contained in this book, which are the fruitful branches of elocution and the mighty streams of eloquence, whose utility, power and virtue I cannot sufficiently commend; but speaking by similitude, I say they are as stars to give light, as cordials to comfort, as harmony to delight, as pitiful spectacles to move sorrowful passions and as orient colours to beautify reason. Finally, they are as martial instruments both of defence and invasion, and being so, what may be either more necessary or more profitable for us than to hold those weapons always ready in our hands, wherewith we may defend ourselves, invade our enemies, revenge our wrongs, aid the weak, deliver the simple from dangers, conserve true religion and confute idolatry? For look what the sword may do in war, this virtue may perform in peace, yet with great difference: for that with violence, this with persuasion, that with shedding of blood, this with piercing the affections, that with desire of death, this with special regard of life.

## NOTES

1. A difficult passage. Nature and art (*ingenium* and *ars*) are commonly opposed as sources of good writing. Policy and humanity seem here to stand for wisdom and oratory (rhetoric is the staple of the *studia humanitatis*) or art. Like Cicero in *On the orator*, III. xvi. 59-61 (a passage echoed by Ascham; see above, pp. 184-5), Peacham deplores making a division between the two.

2. *Politic*: politician.

3. *Brutus*, xv. 59.

4. Cicero, *On duties*, II. ii. 5; *Tusculan disputations*, IV. xxvi. 57.

5. *The orator*: i.e. Cicero.

6. *Politic*: prudent, sagacious; *considerations*: contemplations, thoughts.

7. For the general idea, see Cicero, *On invention*, I. ii. 2-3; *On the orator*, I. viii. 33.

8. *The art of poetry*, 391-3:

> Orpheus, a priest and speaker for the Gods,
> First frighted men, that wildly lived, at odds,
> From slaughters and foul life; and for the same
> Was tigers said and lions fierce to tame. (Jonson's translation)

## Daniel: *Musophilus*

*In* A defence of rhyme *(1603) Daniel speaks disparagingly of the humanist revival of eloquence:*

> *Eloquence and gay words are not of the substance of wit; it is but the garnish of a nice time, the ornaments that do but deck the house of a state, and* imitatur publicos mores *[it imitates public manners]; hunger is as well satisfied with meat served in pewter as silver. Discretion is the best measure, the rightest foot in what habit soever it run. Erasmus, Reuchlin and More brought no more wisdom into the world with all their new revived words than we find was before; it bred not a profounder divine than Saint Thomas, a greater lawyer than Bartolus, a more acute logician than Scotus; nor are the effects of all this great amass of eloquence so admirable or of that consequence but that* impexa illa antiquitas *[unpolished antiquity] can yet compare with them.*

*But* Musophilus, *first published in 1599, gives powerful expression to humanist ideals, with a fine tribute to the moving power of eloquence. It is a defence of learning, cast in the form of a debate between Musophilus (Lover of the Muses) and Philocosmus (Lover of the world). At times obscure, it contains some magnificent passages.*

*(i) 'Oh blessed letters'*

*Of interest here is the emphasis on the personal nature of poetry; poetry is 'the extract of the soul'. Erasmus had said that style should be expressive of personality; the humanist doctrine of imitation does not involve the suppression of the personal. Surely the idea of continuity, of literature's power to awaken the past, has never been better expressed than in this passage.*

> But yet in all this interchange of all,
>> Virtue, we see, with her fair grace, stands fast;
>> For what high races hath there come to fall,
>> With low disgrace, quite vanishèd and past,
>> Since Chaucer lived, who yet lives and yet shall,
>> Though, which I grieve to say, but in his last.
> Yet what a time hath he wrested from time,
>> And won upon the mighty waste of days,
>> Unto th'immortal honour of our clime,
>> That by his means came first adorned with bays,
>> Unto the sacred relics of whose rhyme
>> We yet are bound in zeal to offer praise.
> And could our lines begotten in this age
>> Obtain but such a blessèd hand of years,
>> And scape the fury of that threat'ning rage,
>> Which in confusèd clouds ghastly appears,
>> Who would not strain his travails to engage,
>> When such true glory should succeed his cares?
> But whereas he came planted in the spring,
>> And had the sun before him of respect,
>> We, set in th'Autumn, in the withering
>> And sullen season of a cold defect,
>> Must taste those sour distastes the times do bring
>> Upon the fullness of a cloyed neglect,
> Although the stronger constitutions shall
>> Wear out th'infection of distempered days,
>> And come with glory to outlive this fall,

Recov'ring of another spring of praise,
        Cleared from th'oppressing humours wherewithal
The idle multitude surcharge their lays.
Whenas perhaps the words thou scornest now
        May live, the speaking picture of the mind,
        The extract of the soul, that laboured how
        To leave the image of herself behind,
        Wherein posterity that love to know
        The just proportion of our spirits may find.
For these lines are the veins, the arteries,
        And undecaying life-strings of those hearts
        That still shall pant, and still shall exercise
        The motion spirit and nature both imparts,
        And shall with those alive so sympathise
        As nourished with their powers enjoy their parts.
Oh blessèd letters, that combine in one
        All ages past, and make one live with all,
        By you we do confer with who are gone,
        And the dead living unto counsel call;
        By you th'unborn shall have communion
        Of what we feel and what doth us befall.
Soul of the world, knowledge, without thee,
        What hath the earth that truly glorious is?
        Why should our pride make such a stir to be
        To be forgot? What good is like to this,
        To do worthy the writing, and to write
        Worthy the reading and the world's delight?

## (ii) 'Oh heavenly eloquence'

*The humanist pope, Pius II, recorded in his commentaries that Giangaleozzo, the tyrant of Milan, used to say that Coluccio's pen did him more harm than thirty troops of Florentine cavalry (Hay,* The Italian Renaissance, *p. 157; Coluccio Salutati was the humanist chancellor of Florence at the time when Milan was threatening to annex it). Daniel's tribute to eloquence starts with a similar thought. By 1599, it may be noted, it is possible to express complete confidence in the vernacular (see further Introduction, above, pp. 30-1).*

Power above powers, oh heavenly eloquence,
        That with the strong rein of commanding words
        Dost manage, guide and master th'eminence

Of men's affections more than all their swords,
  Shall we not offer to thy excellence
  The richest treasure that our wit affords?
Thou that canst do much more with one poor pen
  Than all the powers of princes can effect,
  And draw, divert, dispose and fashion men
  Better than force or rigour can direct!
  Should we this ornament of glory then
  As th'unmaterial fruits of shades neglect?
Or should we careless come behind the rest
  In power of words, that go before in worth,
  Whenas our accent's equal to the best,
  Is able greater wonders to bring forth,
  When all that ever hotter spirits expressed
  Comes bettered by the patience of the North?
And who, in time, knows whither we may vent
  The treasure of our tongue, to what strange shores
  This gain of our best glory shall be sent,
  T'enrich unknowing nations with our stores?
  What worlds in th'yet unformèd Occident
  May come refined with th'accents that are ours?
Or who can tell for what great work in hand
  The greatness of our style is now ordained?
  What powers it shall bring in, what spirits command,
  What thoughts let out, what humours keep restrained,
  What mischief it may powerfully withstand,
  And what fair ends may thereby be attained?
And as for poesy, mother of this force,
  That breeds, brings forth and nourishes this might,
  Teaching it in a loose, yet measured course
  With comely motions how to go upright,
  And fost'ring it with bountiful discourse,
  Adorns it thus in fashions of delight,
What should I say? Since it is well approved
  The speech of heaven, with whom they have commerce
  That only seem out of themselves removed,
  And do with more than human skills converse;
  Those numbers wherewith heaven and earth are moved
  Show weakness speaks in prose but power in verse.
Wherein thou likewise seemest to allow
  That th'acts of worthy men should be preserved,

As in the holiest tombs we can bestow
Upon their glory that have well deserved,
Wherein thou dost no other virtue show
Than what most barb'rous countries have observed;
When all the happiest nations hitherto
Did with no lesser glory speak than do.

## Jonson: Dedication of *Volpone*, and *Discoveries*

*These passages provide various definitions of wisdom and eloquence,
and express several common humanist ideas: the persuasive power of
the word, the close links between style and thought, the importance of
knowledge. The particular slant is towards the writing of poetry,
Jonson's chief interest. Thus, in passage (i) from* Discoveries, *Quintilian's
definition of the orator is applied to the poet; the man who is the true
citizen and can guide the state through oratory becomes the man who
can feign a commonwealth. Or in passage (x), Jonson links a tissue of passages from Quintilian to the contemporary poetic scene, with an attack on
Marlowe's style as bombastic, and a defence of his own writing from
the charges commonly made against it of laboriousness and lack of
invention (see Dekker's amusing portrait, in* Satiromastix, *I. ii. 1-20, of
Jonson, in the guise of Horace, desperately searching for rhymes).
Frequently stressed is the need of the poet for both knowledge of human
life, especially moral knowledge, and for art and care in composition.*

*From the dedication of* Volpone *to the universities of Oxford and
Cambridge*

### The good poet

For if men will impartially and not asquint look toward the offices and
function of a poet, they will easily conclude to themselves the impossi-
bility of any man's being the good poet without first being a good
man.[1] He that is said to be able to inform young men to all good
disciplines, inflame grown men to all great virtues, keep old men in
their best and supreme state, or as they decline to childhood, recover
them to their first strength, that comes forth the interpreter and
arbiter of nature, a teacher of things divine no less than human, a
master in manners, and can alone, or with a few, effect the business of
mankind[2] — this, I take him, is no subject for pride and ignorance to
exercise their railing rhetoric upon.

NOTES

1. Possibly a reference to Strabo, *Geography*, I. ii. 5; more probably to Quintilian, *The education of an orator*, I. Pr. 9.
2. From Minturno, *On the poet* (1559).


*From* Discoveries

## (i) 'De malignitate studentium'[1]

There be some men are born only to suck out the poison of books; 'habent venenum pro victu, imo pro deliciis'.[2] And such are they that only relish the obscene and foul things in poets, which makes the profession taxed. But by whom? Men that watch for it, and had they not had this hint, are so unjust valuers of letters as they think no learning good but what brings in gain. It shows they themselves would never have been of the professions they are but for the profits and fees. But if another learning, well used, can instruct to good life, inform manners, no less persuade and lead men than they threaten and compel, and have no reward, is it therefore the worse study? I could never think[3] the study of wisdom confined only to the philosopher, or of piety[4] to the divine, or of state to the politic. But that he which can feign a commonwealth — which is the poet — can govern[5] it with counsels, strengthen it with laws, correct it with judgements, inform it with religion and morals is all these. We do not require in him mere elocution or an excellent faculty in verse, but the exact knowledge of all virtues and their contraries, with ability to render the one loved, the other hated, by his proper embattling them. The philosophers did insolently to challenge only to themselves that which the greatest generals and gravest counsellors never durst. For such had rather do than promise the best things.


NOTES

1. 'On the malignity of the learned'.
2. 'Poison is their daily bread and their relish too.'
3. *I could never think*: from here to the end of the passage, Jonson adapts Quintilian, *The education of an orator*, I. Pr. 9-14.
4. *Piety*: Gifford's conjecture; the Folio reading is *poetry*.
5. *Govern*: Whalley's conjecture; the Folio reading is *gown*, but Quintilian has *regere*, rule.

## (ii) 'Artium regina'[1]

Now the poesy is the habit or the art, nay rather, the queen of arts, which had her original from heaven, received thence from the Hebrews and had in prime estimation with the Greeks, transmitted to the Latins and all nations that professed civility. The study of it, if we will trust Aristotle,[2] offers to mankind a certain rule and pattern of living well and happily, disposing us to all civil offices of society. If we will believe Tully, it nourisheth and instructeth our youth, delights our age, adorns our prosperity, comforts our adversity, entertains us at home, keeps us company abroad, travels with us, watches, divides the times of our earnest and sports, shares in our country recesses and recreations,[3] insomuch as the wisest and best learned have thought her the absolute mistress of manners and nearest of kin to virtue. And whereas they entitle philosophy to be a rigid and austere poesy, they have, on the contrary, styled poesy a dulcet and gentle philosophy, which leads on and guides us by the hand to action, with a ravishing delight and incredible sweetness.

NOTES

1. 'Queen of arts'.
2. Aristotle never gives so moralistic a definition of poetry, but the doctrines of *The poetics* gained many accretions in the Renaissance.
3. *In defence of Archias*, vii. 16.

## (iii) 'Perspicuitas. Elegantia'[1]

A man should so deliver himself to the nature of the subject whereof he speaks that his hearer may take knowledge of his discipline[2] with some delight, and so apparel fair and good matter that the studious of elegancy be not defrauded; redeem arts from their rough and braky[3] seats, where they lay hid and overgrown with thorns,[4] to a pure, open and flowery light, where they may take[5] the eye and be taken by the hand.

NOTES

1. 'Clarity. Elegance'. Adapted from Vives, preface to *On the transmission of knowledge*.
2. *Discipline*: teaching, instruction.
3. *Braky*: overgrown with brushwood and brambles, rough, tangled.
4. *Thorns*: Jonson seems to have introduced this metaphor into his original. It was a favourite of Erasmus for speaking of the crabbed writing of the scholastic theologians as opposed to the gardens of good literature; for example, in a letter

(Allen no. 1597), he congratulates a friend on having stayed within the enclosure of the Muses and never tangled with the 'thorn hedges' of the theologians.

5. *Take*: charm, delight.


## (iv) 'De orationis dignitate'[1]

Speech is the only benefit man hath to express his excellency of mind above other creatures. It is the instrument of society. Therefore Mercury, who is the president of language, is called 'deorum hominumque interpres'.[2] In all speech, words and sense are as the body and the soul. The sense is as the life and soul of language, without which all words are dead. Sense is wrought out of experience, the knowledge of human life and actions, or of the liberal arts, which the Greeks called *enkuklopaideian*.[3] Words are the people's; yet there is a choice of them to be made. For 'verborum delectus origo est eloquentiae'.[4]


NOTES

1. 'On the dignity of speech'. From Vives, *On the method of speaking*.
2. 'Interpreter of gods and men'; see Virgil, *Aeneid*, IV. 356.
3. Pseudo-Greek for *enkuklios paideia*, general education in the circle of arts, an expression used by Quintilian, *The education of an orator*, I. x. i. (The word is also used by Elyot in this form, see above, p. 178.)
4. 'Choice of words is the foundation of eloquence.' A statement attributed by Cicero, *Brutus*, lxxii. 253, to Julius Caesar in a lost treatise.


## (v) 'Lingua sapientis potius quam loquentis optanda'[1]

Of the two, if either were to be wished, I would rather have a plain downright wisdom than a foolish and affected eloquence.[2] For what is so furious and bedlam-like as a vain sound of chosen and excellent words without any subject of sentence or science mixed?[3]


NOTES

1. 'The tongue of the wise man rather than of the babbler is desirable.'
2. Cicero, *On the orator*, III. xxxv. 142.
3. Ibid., I. xii. 51. 'Without any subject of sentence or science mixed' translates 'nulla subiecta sententia nec scientia', 'without any foundation of thought or knowledge'. Elyot also quotes this sentence from Cicero (see p. 178). The two sentences are quoted together by Aulus Gellius, *Attic nights*, I. xv, the passage on which Jonson is drawing in the rest of the paragraph.

*(vi) 'Lectio'*[1]

But that which we especially require in him is an exactness of study and multiplicity of reading, which maketh a full man, not alone enabling him to know the history or argument of a poem and to report it, but so to master the matter and style as to show he knows how to handle, place or dispose of either with elegancy when need shall be. And not think he can leap forth suddenly a poet by dreaming he hath been in Parnassus or having washed his lips, as they say, in Helicon.[2] There goes more to his making than so. For to nature, exercise, imitation and study, art must be added to make all these perfect. And though these challenge to themselves much in the making up of our maker, it is art only can lead him to perfection and leave him there in possession, as planted by her hand. It is the assertion of Tully, if to an excellent nature there happen an accession or conformation[3] of learning and discipline, there will then remain somewhat noble and singular.[4] For as Simylus saith in Stobaeus . . . without art, nature can ne'er be perfect, and, without nature, art can claim no being.[5] But our poet must beware that his study be not only to learn of himself; for he that shall affect to do that confesseth his ever having a fool to his master. He must read many, but ever the best and choicest; those that can teach him anything he must ever account his masters and reverence, among whom Horace and he that taught him, Aristotle, deserve[6] to be the first in estimation. Aristotle[7] was the first accurate critic and truest judge, nay, the greatest philosopher the world ever had; for he noted the vices of all knowledges in all creatures, and out of many men's perfections in a science he formed still one art. So he taught us two offices together: how we ought to judge rightly of others and what we ought to imitate specially in ourselves. But all this in vain, without a natural wit and a poetical nature in chief. For no man, so soon as he knows this or reads it, shall be able to write the better; but as he is adapted to it by nature, he shall grow the perfecter writer. He must have civil prudence and eloquence, and that whole, not taken up by snatches or pieces, in sentences or remnants, when he will handle business or carry counsels,[8] as if he came then out of the declaimers' gallery[9] or shadow,[10] but furnished[11] out of the body of the state, which commonly is the school of men. The poet is the nearest borderer upon the orator and expresseth all his virtues, though he be tied more to numbers,[12] is his equal in ornament and above him in his strengths.[13]

NOTES

1. 'Reading'. One of the four requisites for the poet; the other three are *ingenium*, goodness of natural wit, *exercitatio*, exercise, and *imitatio*, imitation.

2. An allusion to Persius, *Satires*, *Prologue*, 1-3 (Jonson seems to have confused Helicon, a mountain, with Hippocrene, a spring).

3. *Conformation*: the Folio reading is *confirmation*, but Cicero's phrase is 'conformatio . . . doctrinae', 'moulding through learning'.

4. *In defence of Archias*, vii. 15.

5. The Greek quotation is omitted; Jonson provides a translation. *Simylus*: an obscure writer of moralising poetry, probably of the Hellenistic period. *Stobaeus*: compiler of an anthology probably in the fifth century AD. Jonson seems to have gleaned the quotation from a modern source, Jacobus Pontanus (see further Herford and Simpson, vol. XI, pp. 285-6).

6. *Deserve*: the Folio reading is *deserved*.

7. *Aristotle . . . school of men*: from the Dutch humanist Daniel Heinsius, *On the constitution of tragedy* (1611).

8. *Carry counsels*: Heinsius has *cum consilia tractantur*.

9. *The declaimers' gallery*: i.e. as if he were a mere rhetorician.

10. *Shadow*: i.e. out of the public eye, in an ivory tower.

11. *But furnished*: the Folio reads *furnished but*.

12. *Numbers*: metre.

13. Cicero, *On the orator*, I. xvi. 70; Jonson makes the comparison rather more favourable to the poet.


## (vii) 'De optimo scriptore'[1]

The conceits of the mind are pictures of things, and the tongue is the interpreter of those pictures. The order of God's creatures in themselves is not only admirable and glorious but eloquent; then he who could apprehend the consequence of things in their truth and utter his apprehensions as truly were the best writer or speaker. Therefore Cicero said much when he said, 'Dicere recte nemo potest nisi qui prudenter intellegit.'[2] The shame of speaking unskilfully were small if the tongue only thereby were disgraced, but, as the image of a king in his seal ill-represented is not so much a blemish to the wax or the signet that sealed it as to the prince it representeth, so disordered speech is not so much injury to the lips that give it forth as to the disproportion and incoherence of things in themselves so negligently expressed. Neither can his mind be thought to be in tune whose words do jar, nor his reason in frame whose sentence is preposterous,[3] nor his elocution clear and perfect whose utterance breaks itself into fragments and uncertainties. Were it not a dishonour to a mighty prince to have the majesty of his embassage spoiled by a careless ambassador? And is it not as great an indignity that an excellent conceit and capacity by the indiligence of an idle tongue should be disgraced? Negligent speech doth not only discredit the person of the speaker but it discrediteth the opinion of his reason and judgement; it discrediteth the force and uniformity of the matter and substance. If it be so then in words, which fly and escape censure, and where one good phrase begs pardon for many incongruities and faults, how shall he then be thought wise whose penning is thin and shallow? How shall you look for wit from him whose leisure and head, assisted with the examination of his eyes, yield you no life or sharpness in his writing?

NOTES

1. 'On the best writer'. This passage is taken almost word for word from a manuscript treatise, *Directions for speech and style*, by John Hoskyns, the lawyer who may have been the friend who put Jonson to school at Westminster (Herford and Simpson, vol. I, p. 3).

2. *Brutus*, vi. 23. 'No one can speak aright unless he has sound understanding.'

3. *Preposterous*: back to front, out of order.

## *(viii) 'Oratio imago animi'*[1]

Language most shows a man; speak that I may see thee.[2] It springs out of the most retired and inmost parts of us, and is the image of the parent of it, the mind. No glass renders a man's form or likeness so true as his speech. Nay, it is likened to a man, and as we consider feature and composition in a man, so words in language, in the greatness, aptness, sound, structure and harmony of it. Some men are tall and big, so some language is high and great. Then the words are chosen, their sound ample, the composition full, the absolution[3] plenteous and poured out, all grave, sinewy and strong. Some are little and dwarfs; so of speech it is humble and low, the words poor and flat, the members and periods thin and weak, without knitting or number.[4] The middle are of a just stature. There the language is plain and pleasing, even without stopping, round without swelling, all well turned, composed, elegant and accurate. The vicious language is vast and gaping, swelling and irregular; when it contends to be high, full of rock, mountain and pointedness;[5] as it affects to be low, it is abject, and creeps, full of bogs and holes.

NOTES

1. 'Speech is the image of the soul.' Adapted from Vives, *On the method of speaking*.

2. The alleged saying of Socrates, a favourite quotation of Erasmus; see Introduction, above, p. 32, and p. 49, note 72.

3. *Absolution*: perhaps 'the bringing of sense to a conclusion'. Vives has *absolutiones fusae*. Herford and Simpson gloss as 'the delivery free', but *absolutio* in classical rhetorical contexts has the sense of 'completeness', e.g. *To Herennius*, IV. xix. 27.

4. *Number*: rhythm.

5. *Pointedness*: jaggedness.


## (ix) 'De corruptela morum'[1]

There cannot be one colour of the mind, another of the wit. If the mind be staid, grave and composed, the wit is so; that vitiated, the other is blown and deflowered. Do we not see if the mind languish, the members are dull? Look upon an effeminate person; his very gait confesseth him. If a man be fiery, his motion is so; if angry, 'tis troubled and violent. So that we may conclude: wheresoever manners and fashions are corrupted, language is. It imitates the public riot. The excess of feasts and apparel are the notes of a sick state, and the wantonness of language of a sick mind.


NOTE

1. 'On the corruption of manners'. From Seneca, *Moral letters*, cxiv. 3, 11.


## (x) 'Ingeniorum discrimina'[1]

But the wretcheder are the obstinate contemners[2] of all helps and arts, such as, presuming on their own naturals[3] — which perhaps are excellent — dare deride all diligence, and seem to mock at the terms when they understand not the things, thinking that way to get off wittily with their ignorance. These are imitated often by such as are their peers in negligence, though they cannot be in nature, and they utter all they can think with a kind of violence and indisposition, unexamined, without relation either to person, place or any fitness else; and the more wilful and stubborn they are in it, the more learned they are esteemed of the multitude, through their excellent vice of judgement, who think those things the stronger that have no art, as if to break were better than to open, or to rent asunder gentler than to loose.

It cannot but come to pass that these men, who commonly seek to do more than enough, may sometimes happen on something that is good and great, but very seldom, and when it comes it doth not recompense the rest of their ill. For their jests and their sentences,[4] which they only and ambitiously seek for, stick out and are more eminent because all is sordid and vile about them, as lights are more discerned in a thick darkness than a faint shadow. Now because they speak all they can, however unfitly, they are thought to have the greater copy,[5] where the learned use ever election and a mean;[6] they look back to what they intended at first and make all an even and proportioned body. The true artificer will not run away from nature as he were afraid of her, or depart from life and the likeness of truth, but speak to the capacity of his hearers. And though his language differ from the vulgar somewhat, it shall not fly from all humanity with the Tamburlaines and Tamer-Chams[7] of the late age, which had nothing in them but the scenical strutting and furious vociferation to warrant them to the ignorant gapers. He knows it is his only art so to carry it as none but artificers perceive it. In the meantime, perhaps, he is called barren, dull, lean, a poor writer, or by what contumelious word can come in their cheeks, by these men, who without labour, judgement, knowledge or almost sense are received or preferred before him. He gratulates them and their fortune. Another age or juster men will acknowledge the virtues of his studies, his wisdom in dividing,[8] his subtlety in arguing, with what strength he doth inspire his readers, with what sweetness he strokes them, in inveighing what sharpness, in jest what urbanity he uses. How he doth reign in men's affections, how invade and break in upon them, and makes their minds like the thing he writes. Then, in his elocution, to behold what word is proper, which hath ornament, which height, what is beautifully translated,[9] where figures are fit, which gentle, which strong, to show the composition manly. And how he hath avoided faint, obscure, obscene, sordid, humble, improper or effeminate phrase, which is not only praised of the most but commended, which is worse, especially for that it is naught.

NOTES

1. 'Differences between wits'. This passage is put together from various passages from Book II of Quintilian, *The education of an orator*: xi. 1-3; xii. 1, 5-7; x. 13, 8; xii. 11-12; v. 8-10.

2. *Contemners*: despisers.

3. *Naturals*: mental endowments, natural gifts or powers of mind.

4. *Sentences*: *sententiae*, epigrams, aphorisms.

5. *Copy*: *copia*, abundance.

6. *Election and a mean*: *electio et modus*, discrimination and self-restraint, selection and moderation.

7. *Tamburlaines and Tamer-Chams*: a reference to the play by Marlowe and a lost play modelled on it.

8. *Dividing*: i.e. rhetorical organisation.

9. *Translated*: metaphorical.

## (xi) 'De stylo et optimo scribendi genere'[1]

For a man to write well, there are required three necessaries. To read the best authors, observe the best speakers and much exercise of his own style. In style, to consider what ought to be written and after what manner; he must first think and excogitate his matter, then choose his words and examine the weight of either. Then take care in placing and ranking both matter and words that the composition be comely, and to do this with diligence and often. No matter how slow the style be at first, so it be laboured and accurate; seek the best, and be not glad of the forward conceits or first words that offer themselves to us, but judge of what we invent and order what we approve. Repeat often what we have formerly written, which, beside that it helps the consequence[2] and makes the juncture[3] better, it quickens the heat of imagination, that often cools in the time of setting down, and gives it new strength, as if it grew lustier by the going back. As we see in the contention of leaping, they jump furthest that fetch their race largest;[4] or as in throwing a dart or javelin, we force back our arms to make our loose the stronger. Yet if we have a fair gale of wind, I forbid not the steering out of our sail, so[5] the favour of the gale deceive us not. For all that we invent doth please us in the conception or birth, else we would never set it down. But the safest is to return to our judgement and handle over again those things the easiness of which might make them justly suspected. So did the best writers in their beginnings; they imposed upon themselves care and industry. They did nothing rashly. They obtained first to write well, and then custom made it easy and a habit. By little and little, their matter showed itself to 'em more plentifully, their words answered, their composition followed, and all as in a well-ordered family presented itself in the place. So that the sum of all is: ready writing makes not good writing, but good writing brings on ready writing; yet when we think we have got the faculty, it is even then good to resist it, as to give a horse a check sometimes with [a] bit, which doth not so much stop his course as stir his mettle.

NOTES

1. 'On style and the best way of writing'. From Quintilian, *The education of an orator*, X. iii. 4-10.
2. *Consequence*: sequence.
3. *Juncture*: connection.
4. Take the longest run-up.
5. *So*: provided that.


*(xii) 'Ignorantia animae'*[1]

I know no disease of the soul but ignorance, not of the arts and sciences, but of itself; yet relating to those, it is a pernicious evil, the darkener of man's life, the disturber of his reason and common confounder of truth, with which a man goes groping in the dark, no otherwise than if he were blind.


NOTE

1. 'Ignorance of the soul'.

# 4 MEN AND AFFAIRS: HISTORY AND ETHICS

**Elyot: *The governor***

*(i) 'Of experience which have preceded our time, with a defence of histories' (from Book III)*

*Elyot's defence of history rests on the humanist conviction, supported by the classical historians, of the practical and moral utility of history, which teaches us both what to imitate and what to shun. Livy's definition of the function of history from the preface to his history of Rome is adapted in Elyot's second sentence, and Cicero's definition of history in* On the orator *is also alluded to.*

*Some of Elyot's arguments may seem weak, for example when he defends the truth of ancient histories by saying that far more incredible things are contained in the Bible. The attitude to historical evidence is a long way from the more critical approach of such humanists as Lorenzo Valla. Interestingly, Elyot makes no distinction between history and fiction, and speaks of Homer and Aesop as historians; both history and literature are viewed as the source of moral truths, and no distinction is drawn on the basis of historical accuracy. Similarly Ascham, in the letter to John Astley prefacing his* Report and discourse . . . of the affairs and state of Germany, *speaks of Homer and Chaucer in the same breath as Thucydides (quoted Ryan,* Roger Ascham, *pp. 163-4).*

Experience, whereof cometh wisdom, is in two manner of wise. The one is acts committed or done by other men, whereof profit or damage succeeding, we may, in knowing or beholding it, be thereby instructed to apprehend the thing which to the public weal or to our own persons may be commodious,[1] and to eschew that thing which either in the beginning or in the conclusion appeareth noisome and vicious.[2] The knowledge of this experience is called example and is expressed by history, which of Tully[3] is called the life of memory,[4] and so it agreeth well with the verses of Afranius by me late declared.[5] And therefore, to such persons as do contemn[6] ancient histories, reputing them among leasings[7] and fantasies (these be their words of reproach), it may be said that in contemning histories they frustrate experience, which, as the said Tully saith, is the light of virtue,[8] which they would be seen so much to favour, although they do seldom embrace it. And that shall they perceive manifestly, if they will a little while lay apart their accustomed obstinacy and suffer to be distilled into their ears two or three drops of the sweet oil of remembrance. Let them revolve in their minds generally that there is no doctrine,[9] be it either divine or human, that is not either all expressed in history or at the least mixed with history. But to the intent that there shall be left none ignorance, whereby they might be detained in their error, I will declare unto them what is that that is called an history, and what it comprehendeth. First, it is to be noted that it is a Greek name, and cometh of a word or verb in Greek, *historeo*, which doth signify to know, to see, to ensearch, to enquire, to hear, to learn, to tell or expound unto other. And then must history, which cometh thereof, be wonderful profitable, which leaveth nothing hid from man's knowledge that unto him may be either pleasant or necessary. For it not only reporteth the gests[10] or acts of princes or captains, their counsels and attemptates,[11] enterprises, affairs, manners in living good and bad, descriptions of regions and cities with their inhabitants. But also it bringeth to our knowledge the forms of sundry public weals, with their augmentations and decays, and occasion thereof. Moreover, precepts, exhortations, counsels and good persuasions, comprehended in quick[12] sentences and eloquent orations. Finally, so large is the compass of that which is named history that it comprehendeth all thing that is necessary to be put in memory. Insomuch as Aristotle, where he declareth the parts of man's body with their description and offices, and also the sundry forms and dispositions of all beasts, fowls and fishes, with their generation, he nameth his book an history.[13] Semblably,[14] Theophrastus,[15] his scholar, a noble philosopher, describing all herbs and trees whereof he might have the true knowledge, entitleth his book the history of plants. And finally, Pliny the Elder calleth his most excellent and wonderful work the history of nature;[16] in the which book he nothing omitteth that in the bosom of nature is contained, and may be by man's wit comprehended, and is worthy to be had in remembrance. Which authorities of these three noble and excellent learned men approveth the signification of history to agree well with the exposition of the verb *historeo*, whereof it cometh.

Now let us see what book of Holy Scripture, I mean the Old Testament and the New, may be said to have no part of history. The five books of Moses, the book of Judges, the four books of Kings, Job, Esther, Judith, Ruth, Tobias and also the history of Machabees (which from the other is separate)[17] — I suppose no man will deny but that they be all historical, or, as I might say, entire histories. Also Esdras,[18] Nehemias, Ezechiel and Daniel, although they were prophets, yet be their works compact[19] in form of narrations which by orators be called enunciative,[20] and only pertaineth to histories, wherein is expressed a thing done and persons named. All the other prophets, though they speak of the time future or to come, which is out of the description of an history, yet either in rebuking the sins and enormities past, or bewailing the destruction of their country or captivity of the people, and such like calamity or miserable estate, also in moving or persuading the people, they do recite some circumstance of a narration. But now be we come to the New Testament, and principally the books of the Evangelists, vulgarly called the Gospels, which be one context[21] of an history — do not they contain the temporal life of our saviour Christ, king of kings and lord of the world, until his glorious ascension? And what thing lacketh therein that doth pertain to a perfect history? There lacketh not in things order and disposition, in the context or narration verity, in the sentences gravity, utility in the counsels, in the persuasions doctrine, in expositions or declarations facility. The books of Acts of Apostles, what thing is it else but a plain history? The Epistles of Saint Paul, Saint Peter, Saint John, Saint James and Jude, the apostles, do contain counsels and advertisements[22] in the form of orations, reciting divers places as well out of the Old Testament as out of the Gospels, as it were an abbreviate, called of the Greeks and Latins *epitoma*. This is well known to be true of them that have had any leisure to read Holy Scripture, who, remembering themselves by this my little induction, will leave to neglect history, or contemn it with so general a dispraise as they have been accustomed. But yet some will impugn them with a more particular objection, saying that the histories of the Greeks and Romans be nothing but lies and feigning of poets (some such persons there be between whom and good authors have ever been perpetual hostility). First, how do they know that all the histories of Greeks and Romans be leasings, since they find not that any scripture authentic made about that time that those histories were written do reprove or condemn them? But the most catholic and renowned doctors of Christ's religion, in the corroboration of their arguments and sentences, do allege the same histories, and vouch, as I might say, to their aid the authority of the writers. And yet some of those rabbis,[23] in God's name, which in comparison of the said noble doctors be as who saith petits[24] and uneath[25] lettered, will presume with their own silly wits to disprove that which both by anciency of time and consent of blessed and noble doctors is allowed, and by their works honoured. If they will conject[26] histories to be lies, because they sometime make report of things seen and acts done which do seem to the readers incredible, by that same reason may they not only condemn all Holy Scripture, which containeth things more wonderful than any historian writeth, but also exclude credulity[27] utterly from the company of man. For how many things be daily seen which being reported unto him that never saw them should seem impossible? And if they will allege that all thing contained in Holy Scripture is approbate[28] by the whole consent of all the clergy of Christendom at divers general councils assembled, certes,[29] the same councils never disproved or rejected the histories of Greeks or Romans; but the most catholic and excellent learned men of those congregations embraced their examples, and sowing them in their works, made of them to the Church of Christ a necessary ornament. Admit that some histories be interlaced with leasings, why should we therefore neglect them? Since the affairs there reported nothing concerneth us, we being thereof no partners, nor thereby only may receive any damage. But if by reading the sage counsel of Nestor, the subtle persuasions of Ulysses, the compendious gravity of Menelaus, the imperial majesty of Agamemnon, the prowess of Achilles and valiant courage of Hector, we may apprehend anything whereby our wits may be amended and our personages[30] be more apt to serve our public weal and our prince, what forceth[31] it us though Homer write leasings? I suppose no man thinketh that Aesop wrote gospels, yet who doubteth but that in his fables the fox, the hare and the wolf, though they never spake, do teach many good wisdoms? Which being well considered, men, if they have not avowed to repugn[32] against reason, shall confess with Quintilian that few and uneath one may be found of ancient writers which shall not bring to the readers something commodious[33] — and specially they that do write matters historical, the lesson whereof is as it were the mirror of man's life, expressing actually and as it were at the eye the beauty of virtue, and the deformity and loathliness of vice; wherefore Lactantius saith, 'Thou must needs perish if thou know not what is to thy life profitable, that thou mayest seek for it, and what is dangerous, that thou mayest flee and eschew it.'[34] Which I dare affirm may come soonest to pass by reading of histories and retaining them in continual remembrance.

NOTES

1. *Commodious*: beneficial.
2. Livy, *From the founding of the city*, I. Pr. 10.

3. *Tully*: Cicero.

4. *On the orator*, II. ix. 36.

5. For these lines (preserved by Aulus Gellius, *Attic nights*, XIII. viii) by the Roman comic poet, Afranius, who survives only in fragments, see below, p. 225, where they are quoted by Amyot.

6. *Contemn*: despise.

7. *Leasings*: lies.

8. *On the orator*, II. ix. 36; actually Cicero says 'lux veritatis', the light of truth.

9. *Doctrine*: knowledge.

10. *Gests*: deeds, exploits.

11. *Attemptates*: attempts, endeavours.

12. *Quick*: lively, acute.

13. *Historia animalium* (in Greek *Peri ta zóia historiai*); *historia* here means information obtained by investigation. This is the meaning preserved in the English expression 'natural history' which has no reference to time.

14. *Semblably*: similarly, likewise.

15. *Theophrastus*: c. 370-288/5 BC, Aristotle's pupil, who carried on his investigations into biology; one of his books is entitled *Enquiry into plants* (*Peri phutōn historia*).

16. *Historia naturalis*, a huge collection of scientific facts, written in the first century AD, which was very popular in the Renaissance.

17. I have given the forms of these names as they appear in the Vulgate (the Roman Catholic Bible). Protestants relegate Judith, Tobit (Tobias) and Maccabees to the Apocrypha. In the Vulgate, the two books of Machabees come at the end of the Old Testament as *libri historici novissimi*, after the prophetic books and separate from the *libri historici*, which come first. The five books of Moses are the first five books of the Bible; the four books of Kings include I and II Samuel.

18. *Esdras*: in the Vulgate, what the Authorised Version calls the book of Ezra is called the first book of Esdras.

19. *Compact*: framed, composed.

20. *Enunciative*: Latin, *enuntiativus*, containing factual statements (rather than wishes or commands), narrative (see *Thesaurus linguae latinae*). This term does not belong to Ciceronian rhetoric, but to later Latin; I have not identified Elyot's exact source.

21. *Context*: 'The connected structure of a writing or composition; a continuous text or composition with parts duly connected' (*OED*).

22. *Advertisements*: admonitions, warnings, precepts.

23. *Rabbis*: men learned in religion like the Jewish rabbis; here a term of abuse.

24. *Petits*: junior schoolboys, beginners.

25. *Uneath*: scarcely.

26. *Conject*: conjecture.

27. *Credulity*: belief, faith.

28. *Approbate*: approved formally.

29. *Certes*: assuredly.

30. *Our personages*: ourselves.

31. *Forceth*: concerns.

32. *Repugn*: fight against, resist.

33. *The education of an orator*, X. i. 40.

34. Lactantius, *Divine institutes*, III. v.

*(ii) Reading the classical historians and philosophers (from Book I)*

This passage is the continuation of Elyot's educational programme; after the classical poets (see above, pp. 80-4), the classical historians and philosophers should be read. Elyot is much more enthusiastic about classical history than Erasmus had been in The education of a Christian prince, where he urges a cautious approach; to read about the exploits of Alexander and Julius Caesar and other 'great raging robbers' may incite an impetuous boy to a love of tyranny, unless a Christian perspective is kept before him (see pp. 199-203, Born's translation). Note the high praise given to Erasmus' book at the end of the passage.

Cosmography being substantially perceived, it is then time to induce a child to the reading of histories; but first, to set him in a fervent courage, the master in the most pleasant and elegant wise expressing what incomparable delectation, utility and commodity[1] shall happen to emperors, kings, princes and all other gentlemen by reading of histories, showing him that Demetrius Phalereus, a man of excellent wisdom and learning, and which in Athens had been long exercised in the public weal, exhorted Ptolemy, King of Egypt, chiefly above all other studies to haunt and embrace histories, and such other books wherein were contained precepts made to kings and princes, saying that in them he should read those things which no man durst report unto his person.[2] Also Cicero, father of the Latin eloquence, calleth an history the witness of times, mistress of life, the life of remembrance, of truth the light and messenger of antiquity.[3] Moreover, the sweet Isocrates exhorteth the King Nicocles, whom he instructeth, to leave behind him statues and images that shall represent rather the figure and similitude of his mind than the features of his body, signifying thereby the remembrance of his acts written in histories.[4]

By semblable[5] advertisements[6] shall a noble heart be trained to delight in histories. And then, according to the counsel of Quintilian,[7] it is best that he begin with Titus Livy, not only for his elegancy of writing, which floweth in him like a fountain of sweet milk, but also forasmuch as by reading that author he may know how the most noble city of Rome of a small and poor beginning, by prowess and virtue, little and little came to empire and dominion of all the world.

Also, in that city he may behold the form of a public weal which if the insolency and pride of Tarquin had not excluded kings out of the city, it had been the most noble and perfect of all other.

Xenophon, being both a philosopher and an excellent captain, so invented and ordered his work named *Paidia Cyri*,[8] which may be interpreted 'the childhood' or 'discipline of Cyrus', that he leaveth to the readers thereof an incomparable sweetness and example of living, specially for the conducting and well ordering of hosts or armies. And therefore the noble Scipio who was called Africanus, as well in peace as in war, was never seen without this book of Xenophon.[9]

With him may be joined Quintus Curtius, who writeth the life of King Alexander elegantly and sweetly.[10] In whom may be found the figure of an excellent prince, as he that incomparably excelled all other kings and emperors in wisdom, hardiness, strength, policy, agility, valiant courage, nobility, liberality and courtesy; wherein he was a spectacle or mark for all princes to look on. Contrariwise, when he was once vanquished with volupty[11] and pride, his tyranny and beastly cruelty abhorreth all readers. The comparison of the virtues of these two noble princes, equally described by two excellent writers, well expressed, shall provoke a gentle courage to contend to follow their virtues.

Julius Caesar and Sallust, for their compendious writing, to the understanding whereof is required an exact and perfect judgement, and also for the exquisite[12] order of battle and continuing of the history without any variety, whereby the pain of study should be alleviate, they two would be reserved until he that shall read them shall see some experience in semblable matters. And then shall he find in them such pleasure and commodity as therewith a noble and gentle heart ought to be satisfied. For in them both, it shall seem to a man that he is present and heareth the counsels and exhortations of captains, which be called *conciones*,[13] and that he seeth the order of hosts when they be embattled, the fierce assaults and encounterings of both armies, the furious rage of that monster called war. And he shall ween[14] that he heareth the terrible dints of sundry weapons and ordnance of battle, the conduct and policies of wise and expert captains, specially in the commentaries of Julius Caesar, which he made of his exploiture[15] in France and Britain and other countries, now reckoned among the provinces of Germany; which book is studiously to be read of the princes of this realm of England and their counsellors, considering that thereof may be taken necessary instructions concerning the wars against Irishmen or Scots, who be of the same rudeness and wild disposition that the Swiss and Britons were in the time of Caesar. Semblable utility shall be found in the history of Titus Livy in his third decades, where he writeth of the battles that the Romans had with Hannibal and the Carthaginenses.[16]

Also, there be divers orations, as well in all the books of the said authors as in the history of Cornelius Tacitus, which be very delectable, and for counsels very expedient to be had in memory.

And in good faith, I have often thought that the consultations and orations written by Tacitus do import a majesty with a compendious eloquence therein contained.

In the learning of these authors, a young gentleman shall be taught to note and mark not only the order and elegancy in declaration of the history but also the occasion of the wars, the counsels and preparations on either part, the estimation of the captains, the manner and form of their governance, the continuance of the battle, the fortune and success of the whole affairs. Semblably, out of the wars, in other daily affairs, the estate of the public weal, if it be prosperous or in decay, what is the very occasion of the one or of the other, the form and manner of the governance thereof, the good and evil qualities of them that be rulers, the commodities and good sequel of virtue, the discommodities and evil conclusion of vicious licence.

Surely, if a nobleman do thus seriously and diligently read histories, I dare affirm there is no study or science for him of equal commodity and pleasure, having regard to every time and age.

By the time that the child do come to seventeen years of age, to the intent his courage be bridled with reason, it were needful to read unto him some works of philosophy, specially that part that may inform him unto virtuous manners, which part of philosophy is called moral. Wherefore, there would be read to him for an introduction two the first books of the work of Aristotle called *Ethics* wherein is contained the definitions and proper significations of every virtue, and that to be learnt in Greek; for the translations that we yet have be but a rude and gross shadow of the eloquence and wisdom of Aristotle. Forthwith would follow the work of Cicero called in Latin *De officiis*,[17] whereunto yet is no proper English word to be given, but to provide for it some manner of exposition, it may be said in this form: 'of the duties and manners appertaining to men'. But above all other, the works of Plato would be most studiously read, when the judgement of a man is come to perfection, and by the other studies is instructed in the form of speaking that philosophers used. Lord God, what incomparable sweetness of words and matter shall he find in the said works of Plato and Cicero, wherein is joined gravity with delectation, excellent wisdom with divine eloquence, absolute virtue with pleasure incredible, and every place is so enforced[18] with profitable counsel joined with honesty that those three books be almost sufficient to make a perfect and excellent governor.[19]

The proverbs of Solomon with the books of Ecclesiastes and Ecclesiasticus be very good lessons. All the historical parts of the Bible be right necessary for to be read of a nobleman after that he is mature in years. And the residue, with the New Testament, is to be reverently touched, as a celestial jewel or relic, having the chief interpreter of those books true and constant faith, and dreadfully[20] to set hands thereon, remembering that Oza for putting his hand to the holy shrine that was called *arca foederis*,[21] when it was brought by King David from the city of Gabaa, though it were wavering and in danger to fall, yet was he stricken of God and fell dead immediately.[22] It would not be forgotten that the little book of the most excellent doctor, Erasmus Roterodamus, which he wrote to Charles, now being Emperor and then Prince of Castile,[23] which book is entitled *The institution of a Christian prince*, would be as familiar alway with gentlemen, at all times and in every age, as was Homer with the great King Alexander or Xenophon with Scipio; for, as all men may judge that have read that work of Erasmus, that there was never book written in Latin that in so little a portion contained of sentence, eloquence and virtuous exhortation a more compendious abundance.

## NOTES

1. *Commodity*: profit.
2. Plutarch, *Sayings of kings and commanders, Moralia*, 189D.
3. *On the orator*, II. ix. 36.
4. *To Nicocles*, 36 (this was a popular book).
5. *Semblable*: like, similar.
6. *Advertisements*: precepts.
7. *The education of an orator*, II. v. 19.
8. *Cyropaedia* or *The education of Cyrus*, another popular book.
9. Cicero, *Tusculan disputations*, II. xxvi. 62; *Letters to his brother Quintus*, I. i. 23 (compare Castiglione, above, p. 167).
10. *Quintus Curtius*: see above, p. 96, note 4.
11. *Volupty*: pleasure.
12. *Exquisite*: abstruse, recherché, minute.
13. *Conciones*: *contiones*, speeches made in public.
14. *Ween*: think, suppose.
15. *Exploiture*: exploits, achievements.
16. *Carthaginenses*: Carthaginians.
17. *De officiis*: *On duties*.
18. *Enfarced*: stuffed.
19. Compare Ascham, above, p. 184.
20. *Dreadfully*: fearfully.
21. *Arca foederis*: the ark of the Covenant, the wooden coffer containing the tables of the law (*arca* = chest).

22. II Samuel, 6: 4-7. (Oza and Gabaa are the Vulgate versions of the names.)
23. Charles V, Holy Roman Emperor at the time of the Reformation.


## North: 'Amyot to the readers'

*In praise of history*

The lives of the noble Grecians and Romans *(1579), Sir Thomas North's translation of Plutarch's* Lives, *done from the French version by Jacques Amyot (1559), was a popular book, which continued to be reprinted throughout the seventeenth century; Shakespeare was, of course, its most famous debtor. Plutarch was not a scientific historian; his version of the Alexander story is less accurate than that presented by Arrian. But, with his interest in personal detail and moral anecdote, he was a Renaissance favourite. His appeal is suggested by some remarks in North's letter to the reader. North was as much a man of the world as a scholar; he accompanied his brother on an embassy to the French court in 1574 (where he perhaps got the idea of translating Amyot) and he commanded a troop of three hundred men at the time of the Armada threat; picking up a standard humanist argument in favour of history, he praises Plutarch for writing a book about real life:*

> *All other learning is private, fitter for universities than cities, fuller of contemplation than experience, more commendable in the students themselves than profitable unto others. Whereas stories are fit for every place, reach to all persons, serve for all times, teach the living, revive the dead, so far excelling all other books as it is better to see learning in noble men's lives than to read it in philosophers' writings. Now for the author, I will not deny but love may deceive me, for I must needs love him with whom I have taken so much pain, but I believe I might be bold to affirm that he hath written the profitablest story of all authors. For all other were fain to take their matter as the fortune of the countries whereof they wrote fell out; but this man, being excellent in wit, learning and experience, hath chosen the special acts of the best persons of the famousest nations of the world.*

*Amyot's preface to the reader is a praise of history, using some of the familiar humanist arguments, for example the Livian idea that history teaches us what to avoid and what to follow (compare Elyot, above, p. 211). History is a better teacher than moral philosophy, because it teaches by the force of examples rather than generalities (the standard humanist claim, see Introduction, p. 36). History is a spur to men to act nobly in order to gain fame in writing (compare Castiglione, above, p. 167). History provides knowledge more quickly and safely than experience (compare Erasmus and Ascham, above, pp. 57-8, 180-1). History is especially useful to the prince, because it does not flatter (compare Elyot, above, p. 216).*

The reading of books which bring but a vain and unprofitable pleasure to the reader is justly misliked of wise and grave men. Again, the reading of such as do but only bring profit and make the reader to be in love therewith, and do not ease the pain of the reading by some pleasantness in the same, do seem somewhat harsh to divers delicate wits, that cannot tarry long upon them. But such books as yield pleasure and profit, and do both delight and teach, have all that a man can desire why they should be universally liked and allowed of all sorts of men, according to the common saying of the poet Horace:

> That he which matcheth profit with delight
> Doth win the prize in every point aright.[1]

Either of these yield his effect the better by reason the one runneth with the other, profiting the more because of the delight and delighting the more because of the profit. This commendation, in my opinion, is most proper to the reading of stories, to have pleasure and profit matched together, which kind of delight and teaching, meeting in this wise arm in arm, hath more allowance[2] than any other kind of writing or invention of man. In respect whereof it may be reasonably avowed that men are more beholding to such good wits as by their grave and wise writing have deserved the name of historiographers than they are to any other kind of writers, because an history is an orderly register of notable things said, done or happened in time past, to maintain the continual remembrance of them and to serve for the instruction of them to come.

And like as memory is as a storehouse of men's conceits and devices, without the which the actions of the other two parts[3] should be unperfect and well-near unprofitable, so may it also be said that an history is the very treasury of man's life, whereby the notable doings and sayings of men, and the wonderful adventures and strange cases which the long continuance of time bringeth forth are preserved from the death of forgetfulness. Hereupon it riseth that Plato the wise saith[4] that the name of history was given to this recording of matters to stay the fleeting of our memory, which otherwise would be soon lost and retain little. And we may well perceive how greatly we be beholding unto it if we do no more but consider in how horrible darkness and in how beastly and pestilent a quagmire of ignorance we should be plunged, if the remembrance of all the things that have been done and have happened before we were born were utterly drowned and forgotten. Now therefore, I will overpass the excellency and worthiness of the thing itself, forasmuch as it is not only of more antiquity than any other kind of writing that ever was in the world but also was used among men before there was any use of letters at all, because that men in those days delivered in their lifetimes the remembrance of things past to their successors in songs, which they caused their children to learn by heart, from hand to hand, as is to be seen yet in our days by the example of the barbarous people that inhabit the new found lands in the West, who without any records of writings have had the knowledge of things past well-near eight hundred years afore. Likewise, I leave to[5] discourse that it is the surest, safest and durablest monument that men can leave of their doings in this world, to consecrate their names to immortality. For there is neither picture, nor image of marble, nor arch of triumph, nor pillar, nor sumptuous sepulchre that can match the durableness of an eloquent history, furnished with the properties which it ought to have. Again, I mind not to stand much upon this, that it hath a certain truth in it, in that it always professeth to speak truth, and for that the proper ground thereof is to treat of the greatest and highest things that are done in the world, insomuch that, to my seeming, the great profit thereof is, as Horace saith, that it is commonly called the mother of truth and uprightness,[6] which commendeth it so greatly as it needeth not elsewhere to seek any authority or ornament of dignity but of her very self. For it is a certain rule and instruction, which, by examples past, teacheth us to judge of things present and to foresee things to come, so as we may know what to like of and what to follow, what to mislike and what to eschew. It is a picture, which, as it were in a table, setteth before our eyes the things worthy of remembrance that have been done in old time by mighty nations, noble kings and princes, wise governors, valiant captains and persons renowned for some notable quality, representing unto us the manners of strange nations, the laws and customs of old time, the particular affairs of men, their consultations and enterprises, the means that they have used to compass them withal, and their demeaning[7] of themselves when they were come to the highest or thrown down to the lowest degree of state. So as it is not possible for any case to rise either in peace or war, in public or private affairs, but that the person which shall have diligently read, well conceived and thoroughly remembered histories shall find matter in them whereat to take light, and counsel whereby to resolve himself to take a part, or to give advice unto others how to choose in doubtful and dangerous cases that which may be for their most profit, and in time to find out to what point the matter will come if it be well handled, and how to moderate himself in prosperity, and how to cheer up and bear himself in adversity. These things it doth with much greater grace, efficacy and speed than the books of moral philosophy do, forasmuch as examples are of more force to move and instruct than are the arguments and proofs of reason, or their precise precepts, because examples be the very forms of our deeds and accompanied with all circumstances. Whereas reasons and demonstrations are general, and tend to the proof of things and to the beating of them into understanding; and examples tend to the showing of them in practice and execution, because they do not only declare what is to be done but also work a desire to do it, as well in respect of a certain natural inclination which all men have to follow examples as also for the beauty of virtue, which is of such power that wheresoever she is seen, she maketh herself to be loved and liked. Again, it doth things with greater weight and gravity than the inventions and devices of the poets, because it helpeth not itself with any other thing than with the plain truth; whereas poetry doth commonly enrich things by commending them above the stars and their deserving, because the chief intent thereof is to delight. Moreover, it doth things with more grace and modesty than the civil laws and ordinances do, because it is more grace for a man to teach and instruct than to chastise or punish. And yet, for all this, an history also hath his manner of punishing the wicked, by the reproach of everlasting infamy, wherewith it defaceth their remembrance, which is a great mean to withdraw them from vice who otherwise would be lewdly and wickedly disposed. Likewise, on the contrary part, the immortal praise and glory wherewith it rewardeth well-doers is a very lively and sharp spur for men of noble courage and gentlemanlike nature, to cause them to adventure upon all manner of noble and great things. For books are full of examples of men of high courage and wisdom who, for desire to continue the remembrance of their name by the sure and certain record of histories, have willingly yielded their lives to the service of the common weal, spent their goods, sustained infinite pains both of body and mind in defence of the oppressed, in making common buildings, in stablishing of laws and governments, and in the finding out of arts and sciences necessary for the maintenance and ornament of man's life, for the faithful registering whereof the thank is due to histories. And although true virtue seek no reward of her commendable doings, like a hireling, but contenteth herself with the conscience[8] of her well-doing, yet notwithstanding, I am of opinion that it is good and meet to draw men by all means to good doing, and good men ought not to be forbidden to hope for the honour of their virtuous deeds, seeing that honour doth naturally accompany virtue as the shadow doth the body. For we commonly see, not to feel the sparks of desire of honour is an infallible sign of a base, vile and clownish nature, and that such as account it an unnecessary, needless or unseemly thing to be praised are likewise no doers of any things worthy of praise, but are commonly men of faint courage, whose thoughts extend no further than to their lives, whereof also they have no further remembrance than is before their eyes. But if the counsel of old men be to be greatly esteemed, because they must needs have seen much by reason of their long life, and if they that have travelled long in strange countries, and have had the managing of many affairs, and have gotten great experience of the doings of this world are reputed for sage and worthy to have the reins of great governments put into their hands, how greatly is the reading of histories to be esteemed, which is able to furnish us with more examples in one day than the whole course of the longest life of any man is able to do. Insomuch that they which exercise themselves in reading as they ought to do, although they be but young, become such in respect of understanding of the affairs of this world as if they were old and grey-headed and of long experience. Yea, though they never have removed out of their houses, yet are they advertised,[9] informed and satisfied of all things in the world, as well as they that have shortened their lives by innumerable travels and infinite dangers, in running over the whole earth that is inhabited; whereas, on the contrary part, they that are ignorant of the things that were done and come to pass before they were born continue still as children, though they be never so aged, and are but as strangers in their own native countries. To be short, it may be truly said that the reading of histories is the school of wisdom, to fashion men's understanding by considering advisedly the state of the world that is past, and by marking diligently by what laws, manners and discipline empires, kingdoms and dominions have in old time been stablished and afterward maintained and increased, or contrariwise changed, diminished and overthrown. Also, we read that whensoever the right sage and virtuous Emperor of Rome, Alexander Severus, was to consult of any matter of great importance, whether it concerned wars or government, he always called such to counsel as were reported to be well seen in histories.[10] Notwithstanding, I know there are that will stand against me in this point and uphold that the reading of histories can serve to small purpose, or none at all, towards the getting of skill, because skill consisteth in action, and is engendered by the very experience and practice of things, when a man doth well mark and thoroughly bear away the things that he hath seen with his eyes and found true by proof, according to the saying of the ancient poet Afranius:

> My name is skill, my sire experience hight,[11]
> And memory bred and brought me forth to light.[12]

Which thing was meant likewise by the philosopher that said that the hand is the instrument of skill.[13] By reason whereof it comes to pass, say they, that such as speak of matters of government and state, but specially of matters of war, by the book speak but as book knights, as the French proverb termeth them, after the manner of the Grecians, who call him a book pilot which hath not the sure and certain knowledge of the things that he speaks of; meaning thereby that it is not for a man to trust to the understanding which he hath gotten by reading, in things that consist in the deed-doing, where the hand is to be set to the work, no more than the often hearing of men talk and reason of painting or the disputing upon colours, without taking of the pencil in hand, can stand a man in any stead at all to make him a good painter. But on the contrary part, many have proved wise men and good captains which could neither write nor read. Besides this, they allege further that in matters of war all things alter from year to year, by means whereof the sleights and policies that are to be learned out of books will serve the turn no more than mines that are blown up. According whereunto, Cambyses telleth his son Cyrus in Xenophon that, like as in music the newest songs are commonly best liked of for once, because they were never heard afore, so in the wars those policies that never were practised afore are those that take best success and commonly have the best effect, because the enemies do least doubt[14] of them.[15] Nevertheless, I am not he that will maintain that a wise governor of a commonweal, or a great captain, can be made of such a person as hath never travelled out of his study and from his books, howbeit that which Cicero writeth of Lucius Lucullus[16] is true, that when he departed out of Rome as captain general and lieutenant of the Romans to make war against King Mithridates, he had no experience at all of the wars, and yet afterward he bestowed so great diligence in the reading of histories, and in conferring upon every point with the old captains and men of long experience whom he carried with him, that by the time of his coming into Asia, where he was indeed to put his matters in execution, he was found to be a very sufficient captain, as appeared by his deeds, insomuch that by those ways, clean contrary to the common order of war, he discomfited two of the most puissant and greatest princes that were at that time in the East. For his understanding was so quick, his care so vigilant, and his courage so great, that he needed no long training nor gross instruction by experience. And although I grant there have been divers governors and captains which by the only force of nature, furthered by long continued experience, have done goodly and great exploits, yet can it not be denied me but that if they had matched the gifts of nature with the knowledge of learning and the reading of histories, they might have done much greater things, and they might have become much more perfect. For like as in every other cunning and skill wherein a man intendeth to excel, so also to become a perfect and sufficient person to govern in peace and war, there are three things of necessity required, namely nature, art and practice.[17] Nature, in the case that we treat of, must furnish us with a good mother wit, with a body well disposed to endure all manner of travail,[18] and with a good will to advance ourselves; art must give us judgement and knowledge, gotten by the examples and wise discourses that we have read and double read in good histories; and practice will get us readiness, assuredness and the ease how to put things in execution. For though skill be the ruler of doing the deed, yet it is a virtue of the mind which teacheth a man the mean point between the two faulty extremities of too much and too little, wherein the commendation of all doings consisteth. And whosoever he is that goeth about to attain to it by the only trial of experience, and had liefer[19] to learn it at his own cost than at another man's, he may well be of the number of those that are touched by this ancient proverb, which saith 'Experience is the schoolmistress of fools';[20] because man's life is so short and experience is hard and dangerous, specially in matters of war, wherein, according to the saying of Lamachus, the Athenian captain, a man cannot fault twice,[21] because the faults are so great that most commonly they bring with them the overthrow of the state, or the loss of the lives of those that do them. Therefore, we must not tarry for this wit that is won by experience, which costeth so dear, and is so long a coming that a man is oft-times dead in the seeking of it before he have attained it, so as he had need of a second life to employ it in, because of the over-late coming by it. But we must make speed by our diligent and continual reading of histories both old and new that we may enjoy this happiness which the poet speaketh of:

> A happy wight is he that by mishaps
> Of others doth beware of afterclaps.[22]

By the way, as concerning those that say that paper will bear all things, if there be any that unworthily take upon them the name of historiographers and deface the dignity of the story, for hatred or favour, by mingling any untruth with it, that is not the fault of the history, but of the men that are partial, who abuse that name unworthily to cover and cloak their own passions withal; which thing shall never come to pass if the writer of the story have the properties that are necessarily required in a story writer, as these: that he set aside all affection,[23] be void of envy, hatred and flattery, that he be a man experienced in the affairs of the world, of good utterance and good judgement to discern what is to be said and what is to be left unsaid, and what would do more harm to have it declared than do good to have it reproved or condemned; forasmuch as his chief drift ought to be to serve the common weal and that he is but as a register to set down the judgements and definitive sentences of God's court, whereof some are given according to the ordinary course and capacity of our weak natural reason, and other some go according to God's infinite power and incomprehensible wisdom, above and against all discourse of man's understanding, who being unable to reach to the bottom of his judgements and to find out the first motions and grounds thereof do impute the cause of them to a certain fortune, which is naught else but a feigned device of man's wit, dazzled at the beholding of such brightness and confounded at the gauging of so bottomless a deep; howbeit nothing cometh to pass nor is done without the leave of him that is the very right and truth itself, with whom nothing is past or to come, and who knoweth and understandeth the very original causes of all necessity. The consideration whereof teacheth men to humble themselves under his mighty hand, by acknowledging that there is one first cause which overruleth nature, whereof it cometh that neither hardiness is always happy nor wisdom always sure of good success. These so notable commodities[24] are everywhere accompanied with singular delight, which proceedeth chiefly of diversity and novelty, wherein our nature delighteth and is greatly desirous of, because, we having an earnest inclination towards our best prosperity and advancement, it goeth on still, seeking it in everything which it taketh to be goodly or good in this world. But forasmuch as it findeth not wherewith to content itself under the cope of heaven, it is soon weary of the things that it had earnestly desired afore, and so goeth on wandering in the unskilfulness of her likings, whereof she never ceaseth to make a continual changing, until she have fully satisfied her desires by attaining to the last end, which is to be knit to her chief felicity, where is the full perfection of all goodliness and goodness. This liking of variety cannot be better relieved than by that which is the finder out and the preserver of time, the father of all novelty and messenger of antiquity.[25] For if we find a certain singular pleasure in hearkening to such as be returned from some long voyage, and do report things which they have seen in strange countries, as the manners of people, the natures of places and the fashions of lives differing from ours, and if we be sometime so ravished with delight and pleasure at the hearing of the talk of some wise, discreet and well-spoken old man, from whose mouth there floweth a stream of speech sweeter than honey, in rehearsing the adventures which he hath had in his green and youthful years, the pains that he hath endured and the perils that he hath overpassed, so as we perceive not how the time goeth away, how much more ought we be ravished with delight and wondering, to behold the state of mankind and the true success[26] of things, which antiquity hath and doth bring forth from the beginning of the world, as the setting up of empires, the overthrow of monarchies, the rising and falling of kingdoms and all things else worthy admiration, and the same lively set forth in the fair, rich and true table of eloquence? And that so lively as in the very reading of them we feel our minds to be so touched by them, not as though the things were already done and past, but as though they were even then presently in doing, and we find ourselves carried away with gladness and grief, through fear or hope, well-near as though we were then at the doing of them; whereas, notwithstanding, we be not in any pain or danger, but only conceive in our minds the adversities that other folks have endured, ourselves sitting safe with our contentation and ease, according to these verses of the poet Lucretius:

> It is a pleasure for to sit at ease
> Upon the land and safely thence to see
> How other folks are tossèd on the seas,
> That with the blust'ring winds turmoilèd be.
> Not that the sight of others' miseries
> Doth any way the honest heart delight
> But for because it liketh well our eyes
> To see harms free that on ourselves might light.[27]

Also it is seen that the reading of histories doth so hold and allure good wits that divers times it not only maketh them to forget all other pleasures but also serveth very fitly to turn away their griefs and sometimes also to remedy their diseases. As, for example, we find it written of Alphonsus, King of Naples,[28] that prince so greatly renowned in chronicles for his wisdom and goodness, that being sore sick in the city of Capua, when his physicians had spent all the cunning[29] that they had to recover him his health, and he saw that nothing prevailed, he determined with himself to take no more medicines, but for his recreation caused the story of Quintus Curtius[30] concerning the deeds of Alexander the Great to be read before him; at the hearing whereof he took so wonderful pleasure that nature gathered strength by it and overcame the waywardness of his disease. Whereupon, having soon recovered his health, he discharged his physicians with such words as these, 'Feast me no more with your Hippocrates and Galen,[31] sith they can[32] no skill to help me to recover my health, but well fare Quintus Curtius, that could so good skill to help me to recover my health.' Now if the reading and knowledge of histories be delightful and profitable to all other kind of folk, I say it is much more for great princes and kings, because they have to do with charges of greatest weight and difficulty, to be best stored with gifts and knowledge for the discharge of their duties, seeing the ground of stories is to treat of all manner of high matters of state, as wars, battles, cities, countries, treaties of peace and alliances, and therefore it seemeth more fit for them than for any other kind of degrees of men; because they being bred and brought up tenderly and at their ease, by reason of the great regard and care that is had of their persons, as meet is for so great states to have, they take not so great pains in their youth for the learning of things as behoveth those to take which will learn the noble ancient languages and the painful doctrine comprehended in philosophy. Again, when they come to man's state, their charge calleth them to deal in great affairs, so as there remaineth no exercise of wit more convenient for them than the reading of histories in their own tongue, which without pain is able to teach them even with great pleasure and ease whatsoever the painful works of the philosophers concerning the government of commonweals can show them, to make them skilful in the well ruling and governing of the people and countries that God hath put under their subjection. But the worst is that they ever, or for the most part, have such manner of persons about them as seek nothing else but to please them by all the ways they can, and there are very few that dare tell them the truth freely in all things; whereas, on the contrary part, an history flattereth them not, but layeth open before their eyes the faults and vices of such as were like them in greatness of degree. And therefore Demetrius Phalereus, a man renowned as well for his skill in the good government of a commonweal as for his excellent knowledge otherwise, counselled Ptolemy, first King of Egypt after the death of Alexander the Great, that he should often and diligently read the books that treated of the government of kingdoms, 'because', said he, 'thou shalt find many things there which thy servants and familiar friends dare not tell thee'.[33] Moreover, this is another thing, that such great personages cannot easily travel out of the bounds of their dominions to go view strange countries as private persons do, because the jealousy of their estate and the regard of their dignity requires that they should never be in place where another man might command them. And oftentimes, for want of having seen the countries and known the people and princes that are their neighbours, they have adventured upon attempts without good ground, to avoid the which the instruction they may have by the reading of histories is one of the easiest and fittest remedies that can be found. And though there were none other cause than only this last, surely it ought to induce princes to the often and diligent reading of histories, wherein are written the heroical deeds of wise and valiant men, specially of kings that have been before them, the considering whereof may cause them to be desirous to become like them, specially which were of stately and noble courage; because the seeds of princely virtues that are bred with themselves do then quicken them up with an emulation towards those that have been or are equal in degree with them, as well in respect of nobleness of blood as of greatness of state, so as they be loath to give place to any person, and much less can find in their hearts to be outgone in glory of virtuous doings. Whereof innumerable examples might be alleged, if the thing were not so well known of itself that it were much more against reason to doubt of it than needful to prove it. Therefore a man may truly conclude that an history is the schoolmistress of princes, at whose hand they may without pain, in way of pastime and with singular pleasure, learn the most part of the things that belong to their office.

NOTES

1. *The art of poetry*, 343.
2. *Allowance*: praise, approbation, estimation.
3. *The other two parts*: perhaps understanding and will. Classification of the faculties in the Renaissance is complex and changeable; another trio consists of memory, imagination and the common sense, which interprets the five senses.

4. Probably a reference to *Cratylus*, 437B.

5. *Leave to*: omit, abstain from.

6. *Satires*, I. iii. 98. But Horace is speaking of *utilitas*, expedience, not of history.

7. *Demeaning*: behaviour, conduct, demeanour.

8. *Conscience*: consciousness.

9. *Advertised*: informed, warned.

10. *Lives of the later Caesars* (*Historia Augusta*), 'Lampridius', *Alexander Severus*, xvi. 3.

11. *Hight*: is/was called.

12. Aulus Gellius, *Attic nights*, XIII. viii; see above, p. 215, note 5.

13. Perhaps Aristotle, who in a different context, in *On the soul*, 432A, said that the hand was 'organon organōn', 'a tool of tools'.

14. *Doubt of*: fear, apprehend, suspect.

15. Xenophon, *The education of Cyrus*, I. vi. 38.

16. Cicero, *Academica II* (*Lucullus*), i. 2.

17. Compare Plutarch, *The education of children*, *Moralia*, 2A-B, and Erasmus, above, p. 57.

18. *Travail*: in the sixteenth century, 'travail' (toil) and 'travel' (journeying) were not differentiated as two words; either spelling could imply either sense. The sense of travel is perhaps included here. See also 'travelled' earlier in this paragraph.

19. *Had liefer to*: had rather.

20. See above, p. 182, and note 12.

21. Plutarch, *Sayings of kings and commanders*, *Moralia*, 186F (I have corrected *Tamachus* to *Lamachus*).

22. I have not traced the source of this quotation.

23. *Affection*: emotion, bias.

24. *Commodities*: benefits, useful things.

25. Cicero, *On the orator*, II. ix. 36, calls history 'nuntia vetustatis', 'messenger of antiquity'.

26. *Success*: succession, fortune, outcome.

27. Lucretius, *On the nature of things*, II. 1-4.

28. Alfonso I, King of Naples (Alfonso V of Aragon), 1395-1458, was a patron of art and learning and a classical enthusiast; this story is recounted by the humanist poet Antonio Beccadelli, 'Il Panormita' (1394-1471), in *On the sayings and deeds of King Alfonso*.

29. *Cunning*: skill, knowledge.

30. *Quintus Curtius*: see above, p. 96, note 4.

31. *Hippocrates and Galen*: the two most famous doctors of antiquity, of the fifth century BC and the second century AD respectively.

32. *Can*: know.

33. Plutarch, *Sayings of kings and commanders*, *Moralia*, 189D.

## Erasmus: Letter to Henry VIII

*The prince's need for friends*

*Erasmus sent this letter (Allen no. 272) to Henry VIII in 1513, together with a translation in manuscript of Plutarch's* How to tell a flatterer from a friend; *this was printed in* Little works by Plutarch *in 1514. I have discussed the importance of Plutarch's essay in the Introduction (see above, p. 38). In his letter, Erasmus cites examples from Herodotus and others to support his point about the prince's need for good counsel.*

Nothing is so agreeable in day-to-day life and nothing so important in the conduct of affairs as a true and genuinely frank friend; but there's nothing that a man is blessed with less often (just as, in general, the best things tend to be the rarest). And as Xenophon's Hiero cleverly observes,[1] no one else has quite such need of this essential ingredient in good fortune as do princes, who are thoroughly fortunate in other respects; no one else requires so many and such true friends. The individual who looks ahead on behalf of thousands needs to see more than others. And so it is important for a prince to have many eyes, that is, many shrewd and faithful friends.[2] The Persian king Darius, understood this, and once said, when offered a pomegranate of unusual size, that he wished he had as many Zopyruses as the pomegranate contained seeds.[3] This Zopyrus was a man of outstanding integrity and devotion to the king; Darius rightly valued him so highly that he said he would rather have one Zopyrus unmutilated than capture a thousand Babylons[4] – a clear declaration that no treasure is as precious as a friend. When Darius' son, Xerxes, was about to invade Greece, and had assembled an army so vast that no one since has been able to believe it, Demaratus was the only man among them all who gave him frank and friendly advice; and he didn't appreciate how honest Demaratus was until bitter experience proved it.[5] The Lydian King Croesus had the same experience with Solon.[6] Similarly, we read that amid all Alexander the Great's associates the only honest counsellor he had was Aristotle's pupil, Callisthenes, and even he was a frank critic rather than a friend.[7] Dionysius of Syracuse only had Dion and Plato,[8] Nero only Seneca; but if he had listened to Seneca's advice, he would have reigned for longer and could have been counted among the good emperors.

Perhaps these rulers' tastes and dispositions left no room for free-spirited friends. But even when a prince is naturally easy and approachable, and (one can say no more) just like you, the very splendour of his position, which attracts a swarm of friends, also makes it harder to distinguish a true friend from a counterfeit. 'Prosperity wins friends, adversity tests them'[9] isn't a silly saying. And just as a true friend is a precious possession, anyone who insinuates himself under a mere mask of friendship is a bane. We carefully test with touchstones whether gold is pure or not, and there are indications by which one can tell natural from artificial gems; wouldn't it be thoroughly ridiculous not to take the same amount of trouble over an issue that's so much more important, namely how to distinguish a flatterer from a friend, the worst of banes from the greatest of goods? And so that one needn't rely on trial and error in assessing friends (a costly method, like testing poison by tasting), the writer who's undeniably the most learned of the Greeks, Plutarch, has presented a remarkable system, which makes it easy to tell the difference between true, honest friends and fraudulent impostors. But in advising friends, just as in giving them medical treatment, discretion is needed as well as honesty, since there's a danger of our destroying the friendship itself by clumsy attempts to correct our friend's mistakes; so Plutarch added a final section on the tact that's needed in advising a friend where advice is necessary. I have rendered this most valuable work in Latin for your Majesty's sake, as a way of giving proof once again, now that you are the most splendid of kings, of the same loyal devotion that I displayed when you were a most promising boy. Farewell.

NOTES

1. Xenophon, *Hiero*, iii.
2. See Aristotle, *Politics*, 1287B.
3. Plutarch, *Sayings of kings and commanders*, *Moralia*, 173A.
4. Ibid., 173A. See also Herodotus, *Histories*, III. 160.
5. Herodotus, *Histories*, VII. 101-4, 209, 234-7.
6. Ibid., I. 29-33, 86.
7. Plutarch, *Lives*, *Alexander*, lii-lv.
8. Dionysius II of Syracuse repudiated the attempts of Dion and Plato to make him into a philosopher king.
9. Pseudo-Seneca, *On conduct*, no. 51. (*De moribus* is a collection of *sententiae* by Seneca and others put together in late antiquity, which was believed to be genuine in the Middle Ages; a text will be found in volume III of the Teubner edition of Seneca.)

## Castiglione: *The courtier*

### (i) How to request and receive favours (from Book II)

*In this passage, Castiglione gives practical guidance on the handling of matters important to the courtier: how to ask for favours and how to receive them. Here, we are very much in the world of actualities, where a man needs all his cleverness to manipulate the patronage system in order to advance himself and his family. Castiglione knew about this from personal experience. He became head of his family when he was only 21, on his father's death; in 1504-6, he was trying to get prefer-ment for his brother Girolamo in the entourage of Cardinal Sigismondo Gonzaga, the brother of his former prince, Francesco Gonzaga. Unfor-tunately, Castiglione had offended Francesco when he moved from Mantua to Urbino, and the Cardinal was unwilling to risk annoying his brother; then Girolamo died in 1506.*

*The speaker is Federico Fregoso, a courtier, diplomat and friend of Castiglione.*

Very seldom or, in manner, never shall he crave anything of his lord for himself, lest the lord, having respect to[1] deny it him for himself, should happen to grant it him with displeasure, which is far worse. Again, in suing for others, he shall discreetly observe the times, and his suit shall be for honest and reasonable matters, and he shall so frame his suit, in leaving out those points that he shall know will trouble him and in making easy after a comely sort the lets,[2] that his lord will evermore grant it him, and though he deny it, he shall not think to have offended him whom he meant not to do; for because great men oftentimes, after they have denied request to one that hath sued to them with great instance,[3] think the person that laboured to them so earnestly for it was very greedy of it, and therefore in not obtaining it, hath cause to bear him ill will that denied him it, and upon this suspicion, they conceive an hatred against that person, and can never afterward brook him nor afford him good countenance. He shall not covet to press into the chamber or other secret places where his lord is withdrawn unless he be bid, for all he be of great authority with him; because great men often-times, when they are privately gotten alone, love a certain liberty to speak and do what they please, and therefore will not be seen or heard of any person that may lightly deem of them, and reason willeth no less. Therefore, such as speak against great men for making of their chamber persons of no great quality in other things but in knowing how to attend about their person, methink, commit an error, because I cannot see why they should not have the liberty to refresh their minds which we ourselves would have to refresh ours. But in case[4] the courtier that is inured with weighty affairs happen to be afterward secretly in chamber with him, he ought to change his coat and to defer grave matters till another time and place, and frame himself to pleasant communication and such as his lord will be willing to give ear unto, lest he hinder that good mood of his. But herein and in all other things let him have an especial regard that he be not cumbrous to him. And let him rather look to have favour and promotion offered him than crave it so openly, in the face of the world, as many do that are so greedy of it that a man would ween the not obtaining it grieveth them as much as the loss of life; and if they chance to enter into any displeasure, or else see other in favour, they are in such anguish of mind that they can by no means dissemble the malice, and so make all men laugh them to scorn, and many times they are the cause that great men favour some-one only to spite them withal. And afterward, if they happen to enter in favour that passeth a mean, they are so drunken in it that they know not what to do for joy, and a man would ween that they wist not what were become of their feet and hands, and, in a manner, are ready to call company to behold them and to rejoice with them as a matter they have not been accustomed withal. Of this sort I will not have our courtier to be. I would have him esteem favour and promotion, but, for all that, not to love it so much that a man should think he could not live without it. And when he hath it, let him not show himself new or strange in it, nor wonder at it when it is offered him, nor refuse it in such sort as some that, for very ignorance, receive it not, and so make men believe that they acknowledge themselves unworthy of it. Yet ought a man always to humble himself somewhat under his degree, and not receive favour and promotions so easily as they be offered him, but refuse them modestly, showing he much esteemeth them, and after such a sort that he may give him an occasion that offereth them to offer them with a great deal more instance; because the more resistance a man maketh in such manner to receive them, the more doth he seem to the prince that giveth them to be esteemed, and that the benefit which he bestoweth is so much the more as he that receiveth it seemeth to make of it, thinking himself much honoured thereby. And these are the true and perfect promotions that make men esteemed of such as see them abroad, because when they are not craved every man conjectureth they arise of true virtue, and so much the more as they are accompanied with modesty.

NOTES

1. *Having respect to*: being reluctant to.
2. *Lets*: hindrances, impediments, difficulties.
3. *Instance*: earnestness, urgency, persistence.
4. *In case*: if.

*(ii) The good counsellor (from Book IV)*

*The fourth book of* The courtier *treats of good government and then of the Platonic ascent to contemplation of divine beauty; it reveals fully its author's humanism and ethical idealism. Ottaviano Fregoso (who in real life was to become Doge of Genoa and then to die in Imperial custody) has been asked to complete the description of the courtier; in a speech which is perhaps intended to startle the reader who has been thinking that he is reading a book about courtly frivolity, he states that all the attributes and accomplishments of the courtier described so far are only valuable as a means to an end. The end he proposes is the thoroughly humanistic one of giving the prince good counsel, which Elyot was to call 'the end of all doctrine and study'. The courtier is to model himself on the Greek philosophers, Aristotle, who induced Alexander to love philosophy, so that he brought civilisation to savages, and Plato, who tried to educate Dionysius of Syracuse (Everyman edition, pp. 299-301). Fregoso's speech draws on two essays from Plutarch's* Moralia *which are both concerned with counsel and princely rule,* Philosophers and men in power *and* To an uneducated ruler.

Thus, continuing in the talk that these lords have ministered, which I full and wholly allow and confirm, I say that, of things which we call good, some there be that simply and of themselves are always good, as temperance, valiant courage, health and all virtues that bring quietness to men's minds. Other be good for divers respects and for the end they be applied unto, as the laws, liberality, riches and other like. I think therefore that the courtier, if he be of the perfection that Count Lewis and Sir Frederick have described him, may indeed be a good thing and worthy praise, but, for all that, not simply, nor of himself, but for respect of the end whereto he may be applied. For, doubtless, if the courtier with his nobleness of birth, comely behaviour, pleasantness, and practice in so many exercises should bring forth no other fruit but to be such a one for himself, I would not think to come by this perfect trade of courtiership that a man should of reason bestow so much study and pains about it, as whoso will compass it must do. But I would say rather that many of the qualities appointed him, as dancing, singing and sporting, were lightness and vanity, and in a man of estimation rather to be dispraised than commended; because those precise fashions, the setting forth oneself, merry talk and such other matters belonging to entertainment of women and love, although perhaps many other be of a contrary opinion, do many times nothing else but womanish the minds, corrupt youth and bring them to a most wanton trade of living; whereupon afterward ensue these effects that the name of Italy is brought into slander, and few there be that have the courage I will not say to jeopard[1] their life but to enter once into a danger. And, without peradventure,[2] there be infinite other things that if a man bestow his labour and study about them would bring forth much more profit both in peace and war than this trade of courtiership of itself alone. But in case[3] the courtier's doings be directed to the good end they ought to be and which I mean, methink then they should not only not be hurtful or vain but most profitable and deserve infinite praise. The end, therefore, of a perfect courtier, whereof hitherto nothing hath been spoken, I believe is to purchase him, by the mean of the qualities which these lords have given him, in such wise the good will and favour of the prince he is in service withal that he may break his mind[4] to him and always inform him frankly of the truth of every matter meet for him to understand, without fear or peril to displease him. And when he knoweth his mind is bent to commit anything unseemly for him, to be bold to stand with[5] him in it, and to take courage after an honest sort at the favour which he hath gotten him through his good qualities, to dissuade him from every ill purpose and to set him in the way of virtue. And so shall the courtier, if he have the goodness in him that these lords have given him, accompanied with readiness of wit, pleasantness, wisdom, knowledge in letters and so many other things, understand how to behave himself readily in all occurrents[6] to drive into his prince's head what honour and profit shall ensue to him and to his by justice, liberality, valiantness of courage, meekness, and by the other virtues that belong to a good prince, and contrariwise what slander and damage cometh of the vices contrary to them. And therefore, in mine opinion, as music, sports, pastimes and other pleasant fashions are, as a man would say, the flower of courtliness, even so is the training and the helping forward of the prince to goodness, and the fearing him from evil, the fruit of it. And because the praise of well-doing consisteth chiefly in two points, whereof the one is in choosing out an end that our purpose is directed unto that is good indeed, the other the knowledge to find out apt and meet means to bring it to the appointed good end, sure it is that the mind of him which thinketh to work so that his prince shall not be deceived, nor led with flatterers, railers and liars, but shall know both the good and the bad, and bear love to the one and hatred to the other, is directed to a very good end. Methink, again, that the qualities which these lords have given the courtier may be a good means to compass it, and that because, among many vices that we see nowadays in many of our princes, the greatest are ignorance and self-liking; and the root of these two mischiefs is nothing else but lying, which vice is worthily abhorred of God and man, and more hurtful to princes than any other, because they have more scarcity than of anything else of that which they need to have more plenty of than of any other thing: namely, of such as should tell them the truth and put them in mind of goodness;[7] for enemies be not driven of love to do these offices, but they delight rather to have them live wickedly and never to amend; on the other side, they dare not rebuke them openly for fear they be punished. As for friends, few of them have free passage to them, and those few have a respect[8] to reprehend their vices so freely as they do private men's; and many times, to curry favour and to purchase good will, they give themselves to nothing else but to feed them with matters that may delight and content their mind, though they be foul and dishonest. So that of friends they become flatterers, and to make a hand[9] by that strait[10] familiarity they speak and work always to please, and for the most part open the way with lies, which in the prince's mind engender ignorance not of outward matters only but also of his own self. And this may be said to be the greatest and foulest lie of all other, because the ignorant mind deceiveth himself and inwardly maketh lies of himself. Of this, it cometh that great men, beside that they never understand the truth of anything, drunken with the licentious liberty that rule bringeth with it, and with abundance of delicacies drowned in pleasures, are so far out of the way, and their mind is so corrupted in seeing themselves always obeyed and, as it were, worshipped with so much reverence and praise, without not only any reproof at all but also gainsaying, that through this ignorance they wade to an extreme self-liking, so that afterward they admit no counsel nor advice of others. And because they believe that the understanding how to rule is a most easy matter, and to compass it there needeth neither art nor learning but only stoutness, they bend their mind and all their thoughts to the maintenance of that port they keep, thinking it the true happiness to do what a man listeth. Therefore do some abhor reason and justice, because they ween it a bridle, and a certain mean to bring them in bondage and to minish in them the contentation and heart's ease that they have to bear rule, if they should observe it, and their rule were not perfect nor whole if they should be compelled to obey unto duty and honesty, because they have an opinion that whoso obeyeth is no right lord indeed.[11] Therefore, taking these principles for a precedent,[12] and suffering themselves to be led with self-liking, they wax lofty, and with a stately countenance, with sharp and cruel conditions, with pompous garments, gold and jewels, and with coming, in a manner, never abroad to be seen, they think to get estimation and authority among men, and to be counted almost gods; but they are, in my judgement, like the colosses that were made in Rome the last year, upon the feast-day of the place of Agone,[13] which outwardly declared a likeness of great men and horses of triumph, and inwardly were full of tow and rags. But the princes of this sort are so much worse, as the colosses by their own weighty peise[14] stand upright of themselves, and they, because they be ill counterpoised and without line or level placed upon unequal ground, through their own weightiness overthrow themselves, and from one error run into infinite.[15] Because their ignorance, being annexed with this false opinion that they cannot err and that the port they keep cometh of their knowledge, leadeth them every way by right or by wrong to lay hand upon possessions boldly, so[16] they may come by them. But in case they would take advisement[17] to know and to work that that they ought, they would as well strive not to reign as they do to reign, because they should perceive what a naughty and dangerous matter it were for subjects that ought to be governed to be wiser than the princes that should govern. You may see that ignorance in music, in dancing, in riding hurteth no man, yet he that is no musician is ashamed and afeared to sing in the presence of others, or to dance he that cannot, or he that sitteth not well a horse to ride; but of the unskilfulness to govern people arise so many evils, deaths, destructions, mischiefs and confusions that it may be called the deadliest plague upon the earth. And yet some princes most ignorant in government are not bashful nor ashamed to take upon them to govern I will not say in the presence of four or half a dozen persons but in the face of the world; for their degree is set so on loft[18] that all eyes behold them,[19] and therefore not their great vices only but their least faults of all are continually noted. As it is written that Cimon was ill spoken of because he loved wine, Scipio sleep, Lucullus banquetings.[20] But would God the princes of these our times would couple their vices with so many virtues as did they of old time, which, if they were out of the way in any point, yet refused they not the exhortations and lessons of such as they deemed meet to correct those faults; yea they sought with great instance[21] to frame their life by the rule of notable personages, as Epaminondas by Lysis of Pythagoras' sect, Agesilaus by Xenophon, Scipio by Panaetius,[22] and infinite others. But in case a grave philosopher should come before any of our princes, or whoever beside that would show them plainly and without any circumstance the horrible face of true virtue, and teach them good manners and what the life of a good prince ought to be, I am assured they would abhor him at the first sight as a most venomous serpent, or else they would make him a laughing-stock as a most vile matter. I say therefore that since nowadays princes are so corrupt through ill usages, ignorance and false self-liking, and that it is so hard a matter to give them the knowledge of the truth and to bend them to virtue, and men with lies and flattery and such naughty[23] means seek to curry favour with them, the courtier, by the mean of those honest qualities that Count Lewis and Sir Frederick have given him, may soon and ought to go about so to purchase him the good will and allure unto him the mind of his prince that he may make him a free and safe passage to commune with him in every matter without troubling him. And if he be such a one as is said, he shall compass it with small pain, and so may he always open unto him the truth of every matter at ease. Beside this, by little and little distil into his mind goodness, and teach him continency, stoutness of courage, justice, temperance, making him to taste what sweetness is hid under that little bitterness which at the first sight appeareth unto him that withstandeth vices, which are always hurtful, displeasant and accompanied with ill report and shame, even as virtues are profitable, pleasant and praisable, and enflame him to them with the examples of many famous captains and of other notable personages, unto whom they of old time used to make images of metal and marble and sometime of gold, and to set them up in common-haunted places, as well for the honour of them as for an encouraging of others, that with an honest envy they might also endeavour themselves to reach unto that glory. In this wise may he lead him through the rough way of virtue, as it were, decking it about with boughs to shadow it and strewing it over with sightly flowers, to ease the grief of the painful journey in him that is but of a weak force. And sometime with music, sometime with arms and horses, sometime with rhymes and metre, otherwhile with communication of love, and with all those ways that these lords have spoken of, continually keep that mind of his occupied in honest pleasure, imprinting notwithstanding therein always beside, as I have said, in company with these flickering provocations[24] some virtuous condition, and beguiling him with a wholesome craft, as the wary physicians do who many times, when they minister to young and tender children in their sickness a medicine of a bitter taste, anoint the cup about the brim with some sweet liquor.[25] The courtier therefore applying to such a purpose this veil of pleasure in every time, in every place and in every exercise, he shall attain to his end, and deserve much more praise and recompense than for any other good work that he can do in the world; because there is no treasure that doth so universally profit as doth a good prince, nor any mischief so universally hurt as an ill prince. Therefore is there also no pain so bitter and cruel that were a sufficient punishment for those naughty and wicked courtiers that make their honest and pleasant manners and their good qualities a cloak for an ill end, and by mean of them seek to come in favour with their princes for to corrupt them, and to stray them from the way of virtue, and to lead them to vice. For a man may say that such as these be do infect with deadly poison not one vessel whereof one man alone drinketh, but the common fountain that all the people resorteth to.[26]

## NOTES

1. *Jeopard*: hazard, put in jeopardy.
2. *Without peradventure*: without doubt.
3. *In case*: if.
4. *Break his mind*: reveal what is in his mind.
5. *Stand with*: withstand, argue with.
6. *In all occurrents*: in all circumstances.
7. Compare Isocrates, *To Nicocles*, 1-4.
8. *Have a respect*: are wary, reluctant.
9. *To make a hand*: to make profit for oneself.
10. *Strait*: close.
11. Plutarch, *To an uneducated ruler*, *Moralia*, 779E.
12. *Precedent*: a model to be followed.
13. Piazza d'Agone, now Piazza Navona.
14. *Peise*: weight.
15. Plutarch, *To an uneducated ruler*, *Moralia*, 780A-B.
16. *So*: provided that.
17. *Take advisement*: take thought, decide.
18. *On loft*: high.
19. Cicero, *On duties*, II. xiii. 44.
20. Plutarch, *To an uneducated ruler*, *Moralia*, 782F. On Cimon and Lucullus, see also *Lives*, *Cimon*, iii. 3, iv. 3; *Lucullus*, xxxviii. 2 – xl.
21. *Instance*: earnestness, persistence.
22. Cicero, *On the orator*, III. xxxiv. 139 mentions the first two examples. On Epaminondas and Lysis, see also Cornelius Nepos, *On famous men*, *Epaminondas*, ii. 2. For Scipio and Panaetius, see e.g. Cicero, *Tusculan disputations*, I. xxxiii. 81; *On the republic*, I. xxi. 34; *On the ends of goods and evils*, IV. ix. 23; *On behalf of Murena*, xxxi. 66; Plutarch, *Philosophers and men in power*, *Moralia*, 777A.
23. *Naughty*: wicked.
24. *Flickering provocations*: the Italian means allurements, beguilements; *flickering*: perhaps coaxing, caressing.
25. For the image, see Lucretius, *On the nature of things*, I. 936f.
26. Plutarch, *Philosophers and men in power*, *Moralia*, 778D-E.

## (iii) The good prince (from Book IV)

*Assisted by good counsel, the ruler will become the promoter of good government. Castiglione's political idealism has been set against the realpolitik of Machiavelli's* The prince *and criticised for its naïvety. However, it was a vision shared by many in the period; and it is against such an ideal that the deviations presented in plays by Shakespeare and the Jacobean dramatists should be viewed, if we are to feel their full impact.*

Then said the Lord Gaspar, 'In what manner wise be they then to be commanded that be discreet and virtuous, and not by nature bound?' The Lord Octavian answered, 'With that tractable commandment kingly and civil. And to such it is well done otherwhile[1] to commit the bearing of such offices as be meet for them, that they may likewise bear sway and rule over others of less wit than they be, yet so that the principal government may full and wholly depend upon the chief prince. And because you have said that it is an easier matter to corrupt the mind of one than of a great sort,[2] I say that it is also an easier matter to find one good and wise than a great sort. Both good and wise ought a man to suppose a king may be, of a noble progeny, inclined to virtue of his own natural motion and through the famous memory of his ancestors, and brought up in good conditions. And though he be not of another kind than man, as you have said is among the bees, yet if he be helped forward with the instructions, bringing up and art of the courtier, whom these lords have fashioned so wise and good, he shall be most wise, most continent, most temperate, most manly and most just, full of liberality, majesty, holiness and mercy; finally, he shall be most glorious and most dearly beloved both to God and man, through whose grace he shall attain unto that heroical and noble virtue that shall make him pass the bounds of the nature of man, and shall rather be called a demigod than a man mortal. For God delighteth in and is the defender, not of those princes that will follow and counterfeit him in showing great power and make themselves to be worshipped of men, but of such as, beside power, whereby they are mighty, endeavour themselves to resemble him also in goodness and wisdom, whereby they may have a will and a knowledge to do well and to be his ministers, distributing for the behoof of man the benefits and gifts that they receive of him. Therefore, even as in the firmament the sun and the moon and the other stars show to the world, as it were, in a glass a certain likeness of God, so upon the earth a much more liker image of God are those good princes that love and worship him, and show unto the people the clear light of his justice, accompanied with a shadow of the heavenly reason and understanding; and such as these be doth God make partners of his true dealing, righteousness, justice and goodness, and of those other happy benefits which I cannot name, that disclose unto the world a much more evident proof of the Godhead than doth the light of the sun or the continual turning of the firmament with the sundry course of the stars.[3] It is God therefore that hath appointed the people under the custody of princes, which ought to have a diligent care over them, that they may make him account of it, as good stewards do their lord, and love them, and think their own all the profit and loss that happeneth to them, and principally above all thing provide for their good estate and welfare. Therefore ought the prince not only to be good but also to make others good,[4] like the carpenter's square, that is not only straight and just itself but also maketh straight and just whatsoever it is occupied about. And the greatest proof that the prince is good is when the people are good, because the life of the prince is a law and ringleader[5] of the citizens, and upon the conditions of him must needs all others depend; neither is it meet for one that is ignorant to teach, nor for him that is out of order to give order, nor for him that falleth to help up another. Therefore, if the prince will execute these offices aright, it is requisite that he apply all his study and diligence to get knowledge, afterward to fashion within himself and observe unchangeably in everything the law of reason, not written in papers or in metal but graven in his own mind, that it may be to him always not only familiar but inward, and live with him as a parcel of him, to the intent it may night and day, in every time and place, admonish him and speak to him within his heart, ridding him of those troublous affections that untemperate minds feel, which because, on the one side, they be, as it were, cast into a most deep sleep of ignorance, on the other, overwhelmed with the unquietness which they feel through their wayward and blind desires, they are stirred with an unquiet rage, as he that sleepeth otherwhile with strange and horrible visions; heaping then a greater power upon their naughty desire, there is heaped also a greater trouble withal.

NOTES

1. *Otherwhile*: sometimes.
2. *Sort*: number.
3. Plutarch, *To an uneducated ruler*, *Moralia*, 780F-781A.
4. Aristotle, *Nicomachean Ethics*, 1102A.
5. *Ringleader*: leader, authority, without pejorative connotations.

### Elyot: *The governor*

*'The election of friends and the diversity of flatterers' (from Book II)*

*Elyot draws many of the details in this chapter from Plutarch's popular essay,* How to tell a flatterer from a friend *(see above, pp. 38-9). Erasmus had also used this essay for a chapter on the evils of flattery in* The education of a Christian prince, *and Elyot probably had this in mind as well.*

*The linked themes of counsel and flattery seem to have been of especial interest to Elyot, perhaps because of his experience of political life under Henry VIII. There are further chapters on counsel, which Elyot calls 'the end of all doctrine and study', at the end of* The governor, *and the themes are also handled in two later works,* Pasquil the plain *and* Of the knowledge which maketh a wise man. *In the former, Pasquil, the plain man like Kent in* King Lear, *accuses Gnatho, the loquacious flatterer, and Harpocrates, who assents by silence, of causing disasters to the kingdom and dilates on the evils of flattery; 'a knock on the head, though it be to the skull, is not so dangerous to be healed as an evil affection thrust into thy master's brains by false opinion' (quoted in Lehmberg,* Sir Thomas Elyot, *p. 117). In the second work, Plato debates whether he was right to speak the truth to Dionysius, tyrant of Sicily, with Aristippus, here the type of the shape-changing flatterer. Both works probably hint that Henry VIII has been ill advised in his break with Rome.*

A nobleman above all things ought to be very circumspect in the election[1] of such men as should continually attend upon his person at times vacant from busy affairs, whom he may use as his familiars and safely commit to them his secrets. For, as Plutarch saith, whatsoever he be that loveth, he doteth and is blind in that thing which he doth love, except by learning he can accustom himself to ensue[2] and set more price by those things that be honest and virtuous than by them that he seeth in experience and be familiarly used.[3] And surely, as the worms do breed most gladly in soft wood and sweet, so the most gentle and noble wits, inclined to honour, replenished[4] with most honest and courteous manners, do soonest admit flatterers and be by them abused;[5] and it is no marvel. For, like as the wild corn, being in shape and greatness like to the good, if they be mingled, with great difficulty will be tried out,[6] but either in a narrow-holed sieve they will still abide with the good corn, or else where the holes be large they will issue out with the other, so flattery from friendship is hardly[7] severed, forasmuch as in every motion and affect of the mind they be mutually mingled together.[8] Of this perverse and cursed people be sundry kinds: some which apparently[9] do flatter, praising and extolling everything that is done by their superior, and bearing him on hand[10] that in him it is of every man commended which of truth is of all men abhorred and hated; to the affirmance thereof they add to oaths, adjurations and horrible curses, offering themselves to eternal pains except their report be true. And if they perceive any part of their tale mistrusted, then they set forth suddenly an heavy and sorrowful countenance, as if they were abject and brought into extreme desperation. Other there be which in a more honest term may be called assentators[11] or followers, which do await diligently what is the form of the speech and gesture of their master, and also other his manners and fashion of garments, and to the imitation and resemblance thereof they apply their study, that for the similitude of manners they may the rather be accepted into the more familiar acquaintance. Like to the servants of Dionysius, King of Sicily, which although they were inclined to all unhappiness[12] and mischief, after the coming of Plato, they perceiving that for his doctrine[13] and wisdom the king had him in high estimation, they then counterfeited the countenance and habit of the philosopher, thereby increasing the king's favour towards them, who then was wholly given to study of philosophy. But after that Dionysius by their incitation had expelled Plato out of Sicily, they abandoned their habit and severity, and eftsoons[14] returned to their mischievous and voluptuous living.[15]

The great Alexander bore his head some part on the one side more than the other, which divers of his servants did counterfeit;[16] semblably[17] did the scholars of Plato, the most noble philosopher, which forasmuch as their master had a broad breast and high shoulders and for that cause was named Plato, which signifieth broad or large, they stuffed their garments and made on their shoulders great bolsters to seem to be of like form as he was,[18] whereby he should conceive some favour towards them for the demonstration of love that they pretended[19] in the ostentation of his person; which kind of flattery I suppose Plato could right well laugh at. But these manner of flatterers may be well found out and perceived by a good wit which sometime by himself diligently considereth his own qualities and natural appetite. For the company or communication of a person familiar which is alway pleasant and without sharpness, inclining to inordinate favour and affection, is alway to be suspected. Also, there is in that friend small commodity[20] which followeth a man like his shadow, moving only when he moveth and abiding where he list to tarry. These be the mortal enemies of noble wits and specially in youth, when commonly they be more inclined to glory than gravity; wherefore that liberality which is on such flatterers employed is not only perished but also spilt[21] and devoured; wherefore, in mine opinion, it were a right necessary law that should be made to put such persons openly to tortures, to the fearful example of other, since in all princes' laws, as Plutarch saith,[22] not only he that hath slain the king's son and heir but also he that counterfeiteth his seal or adulterateth his coin with more base metal shall be judged to die as a traitor. In reason, how much more pain (if there were any greater pain than death) were he worthy to suffer that with false adulation doth corrupt and adulterate the gentle and virtuous nature of a nobleman, which is not only his image but the very man himself. For without virtue man is but in the number of beasts. And also by perverse instruction and flattery such one slayeth both the soul and good renown of his master. By whose example and negligence perisheth also an infinite number of persons, which damage to a realm neither with treasure nor with power can be redubbed.[23]

But hard it is alway to eschew these flatterers, which like to crows do pick out men's eyes ere they be dead. And it is to noblemen most difficile,[24] whom all men covet to please, and to displease them it is accounted no wisdom perchance lest there should ensue thereby more peril than profit. Also Carneades, the philosopher, was wont to say that the sons of noblemen learned nothing well but only to ride.[25] For whiles they learned letters their masters flattered them, praising every word that they spake. In wrestling their teachers and companions also flattered them, submitting themselves and falling down to their feet. But the horse or courser, not understanding who rideth him, nor whether he be a gentleman or yeoman, a rich man or a poor, if he sit not surely and can skill[26] of riding, the horse casteth him quickly. This is the saying of Carneades.

There be other of this sort which more covertly lay their snares to take the hearts of princes and noblemen. And as he which intendeth to take the fierce and mighty lion pitcheth his hay[27] or net in the wood, among great trees and thorns, whereas is the most haunt of the lion, that being blinded with the thickness of the covert, ere he be ware, he may suddenly tumble into the net; where the hunter, seeing[28] both his eyes and binding his legs strongly together, finally daunteth his fierceness and maketh him obedient to his ensigns[29] and tokens. Semblably, there be some that by dissimulation can ostent or show a high gravity mixed with a sturdy entertainment[30] and fashion, exiling themselves from all pleasure and recreation, frowning and grudging[31] at everything wherein is any mirth or solace, although it be honest, taunting and rebuking immoderately them with whom they be not contented; naming themselves therefore plain men, although they do the semblable and oftentimes worse in their own houses. And by a simplicity and rudeness of speaking, with long deliberation used in the same, they pretend the high knowledge of counsel to be in them only, and in this wise pitching their net of adulation, they entrap the noble and virtuous heart, which only beholdeth their feigned severity and counterfeit wisdom; and the rather because this manner of flattery is most unlike to that which is commonly used.[32] Aristotle, in his *Politics*,[33] exhorteth governors to have their friends for a great number of eyes, ears, hands and legs, considering that no one man may see or hear all thing that many men may see and hear, nor can be in all places or do as many things well at one time as many persons may do. And oftentimes a beholder or looker on espieth a default that the doer forgetteth or skippeth over; which caused the Emperor Antoninus[34] to enquire of many what other men spake of him, correcting thereby his defaults which he perceived to be justly reproved.

NOTES

1. *Election*: choice.
2. *Ensue*: seek after, follow.
3. *How to tell a flatterer from a friend*, *Moralia*, 48F.
4. *Replenished*: furnished.
5. *How to tell a flatterer from a friend*, *Moralia*, 49B-C.
6. *Tried out*: sifted out.
7. *Hardly*: with difficulty.
8. *How to tell a flatterer from a friend*, *Moralia*, 51A.
9. *Apparently*: openly.
10. *Bearing him on hand*: leading him to believe, deluding him.
11. *Assentators*: assenters.
12. *Unhappiness*: evil, mischief.
13. *Doctrine*: learning.
14. *Eftsoons*: again, a second time.
15. *How to tell a flatterer*, 52D-E.
16. Ibid., 53D.
17. *Semblably*: similarly.
18. Developed from *How to tell a flatterer*, 53C?
19. *Pretented*: pretended.
20. *Commodity*: benefit.
21. *Spilt*: destroyed, spoiled, squandered.
22. This notion seems to derive from Erasmus, *The education of a Christian prince* (Born's translation, pp. 194-5), rather than from Plutarch. See also Plutarch, *Philosophers and men in power*, *Moralia*, 778D-E.

23. *Redubbed*: repaired, remedied.
24. *Difficile*: difficult.
25. *How to tell a flatterer*, 58F.
26. *Can skill*: have skill (can = know).
27. *Hay*: net.
28. *Seeling*: making blind, preventing from seeing.
29. *Ensigns*: tokens.
30. *Entertainment*: manner of social behaviour.
31. *Grudging*: complaining.
32. *How to tell a flatterer*, 59D-E.
33. *Politics*, 1287B.
34. *Marcus Aurelius Antoninus*, the Stoic philosopher.

## Machiavelli: *The prince*

*Niccolò Machiavelli (1469-1527) was given a humanist education by his father. Then, like many Florentine humanists, he entered the chancery, carrying out diplomatic and administrative duties for the newly restored Republic (the Medici had lost power after the French had occupied Florence). The prince was written when Machiavelli had been forced to retire from political life after the collapse of the Republic in 1512, in an attempt to gain the favour of the restored Medici; Machiavelli suppressed his republicanism in order to become the adviser to princes. The book takes the common humanist form of the advice-book, and in the introductory letter to Lorenzo de' Medici (grandson of the famous Lorenzo), Machiavelli says that it is based on the proper humanist sources, experience of contemporary affairs and study of the ancient world. But these traditional materials were put to novel and iconoclastic ends. (On the relation of* The prince *to the humanist tradition, see the discussions by Skinner,* The foundations of modern political thought, *vol. I, pp. 113-38;* Machiavelli, *pp. 21-47.)*

*Some of his advice does follow conventional humanist lines: in the first passage given here, he urges that the prince study ancient history in order to learn how to behave (though the lessons Machiavelli was to draw from Herodian's history of the Roman emperors after Marcus Aurelius in chapter 19 were far from conventional); and in the second, he gives advice on the choice of counsellors and how to avoid flatterers. (This section met with the approval of Edward Dacres, who published the first printed translation of* The prince *into English in 1640.) However, in the third and fourth passages given here, Machiavelli boldly and deliberately stands on its head the humanist ideal of the good prince which so many treatises had elaborated. The third is the preface to the* section in which he discusses the virtues appropriate to the prince; he states clearly that he is going to depart from tradition. Cicero had argued in On duties *that expediency could never conflict with moral rectitude (III. iii. 11; vii. 34 – viii. 36; II. iii. 9-10). But Machiavelli asserts blandly that always to practise the virtues would lead to the prince's downfall. In the fourth passage, he again overturns Ciceronian precedent. In* On duties, *Cicero had said that fraud and force were the opponents of justice and belonged to the fox and the lion; both were unworthy of a man, but fraud was the more contemptible (I. xiii. 41). All humanist treatises had stressed that the prince must keep his word. Machiavelli, backing up his argument in true humanist fashion with an allusion to Greek myth, but drawing from it a most unhumanistic lesson, says that the prince must know how to play the parts of the fox and the lion, and should break his word if it is to his advantage to do so.*

Machiavelli's prince does not, of course, show the unbridled licence of a Tamburlaine or the gloating tyranny of a Richard III. Machiavelli condemns the excessive cruelty of Agathocles, ruler of Syracuse, and the prince's exercise of power has as its aim the political stability that the Italian states had so obviously failed to attain; the book ends with a plea for Italy to unite under a strong ruler, who will bring order and prosperity and expel foreign invaders. Nevertheless, Machiavelli set out to shock, and, as we know, he succeeded, becoming linked with the devil and fathering a whole race of tyrants on the Elizabethan and Jacobean stage. Many later humanist discussions of the same topics restate the old beliefs, with a glance in Machiavelli's direction. Elyot's chapter on fraud in* The governor *(Book III, chapter 4), which reiterates the Ciceronian condemnation of the fox and says that the devil is the father of lies, reads like an attack on Machiavelli; although* The prince *was not published till 1532, it had been circulating in manuscript before that, and Thomas Cromwell may have owned a copy (see Lehmberg,* Sir Thomas Elyot, *pp. 86-8). Similarly, the passage from Daniel's* Musophilus *given below, with its linking of success with honesty, could well be directed against Machiavelli, while Ben Jonson's section on clemency from* Discoveries *mentions Machiavelli by name. A subtle use of Machiavelli is made by Marvell in* An Horatian Ode *upon Cromwell's return from Ireland, where, in contrast to the more conventional panegyric of Cromwell's present and future leadership, he portrays Cromwell's past career in terms of the Machiavellian prince who carves out for himself a new state – a somewhat equivocal compliment.*

*The extracts from* The prince *are given here in Dacres' translation, together with his comments on them. His diffuse prose does not do justice to the punch of the original.*

### (i) 'Touching the exercise of the mind' (from chapter 14)

But touching the exercise of the mind, a prince ought to read histories, and in them consider the actions of the worthiest men, mark how they have behaved themselves in the wars, examine the occasions of their victories and their losses — whereby they may be able to avoid these and obtain those — and above all, do as formerly some excellent man hath done, who hath taken upon him to imitate, if anyone that hath gone before him hath left his memory glorious, the course he took, and kept always near unto him the remembrances of his actions and worthy deeds; as it is said that Alexander the Great imitated Achilles,[1] Caesar Alexander[2] and Scipio Cyrus.[3] And whoever reads the life of Cyrus written by Xenophon may easily perceive afterwards in Scipio's life how much glory his imitation gained him, and how much Scipio did conform himself in his chastity, affability, humanity and liberality with those things that are written by Xenophon of Cyrus.

NOTES

1. See Plutarch, *Lives, Alexander*, viii. 2; xv. 8-9; Quintus Curtius, *History of Alexander* IV. vi. 29.
2. See Plutarch, *Lives, Caesar*, xi. 5-6; Suetonius, *The deified Julius, Lives of the Caesars*, I. vii; Lucan, *The civil war*, X. 17ff.
3. See Cicero, *Tusculan disputations*, II. xxvi. 62; *Letters to his brother Quintus*, I. i. 23.

### (ii) 'Touching princes' secretaries' and 'That flatterers are to be avoided' (chapters 22 and 23)

It is no small importance to a prince the choice he makes of servants, being ordinarily good or bad as his wisdom is. And the first conjecture one gives of a great man and of his understanding is upon the sight of his followers and servants he hath about him,[1] when they prove able and faithful, and then may he always be reputed wise, because he hath known how to discern those that are able and to keep them true to him. But when they are otherwise, there can be no good conjecture made of him; for the first error he commits is in this choice. There was no man that had any knowledge of Antony of Venafro, the servant of

Pandulfus Petrucci, prince of Siena, who did not esteem Pandulfus for a very discreet man, having him for his servant.[2] And because there are three kinds of understandings: the one that is advised by itself, the other that understands when it is informed by another, the third that neither is advised by itself nor by the demonstration of another[3] — the first is best, the second is good, and the last quite unprofitable. Therefore it was of necessity that if Pandulfus attained not the first degree, yet he got to the second; for whenever anyone hath the judgement to discern between the good and the evil that anyone does and says, however that he hath not this invention from himself, yet still comes he to take notice of the good or evil actions of that servant, and those he cherishes and these he suppresses, insomuch that the servant, finding no means to deceive his master, keeps himself upright and honest. But how a prince may thoroughly understand his servant, here is the way that never fails. When thou seest the servant study more for his own advantage than thine and that in all his actions he searches most after his own profit, this man thus qualified shall never prove good servant, nor canst thou ever rely upon him; for he that holds the stern of the state in hand ought never call home his cares to his own particular, but give himself wholly over to his prince's service, nor ever put him in mind of anything not appertaining to him. And on the other side, the prince, to keep him good to him, ought to take a care for his servant, honouring him, enriching and obliging him to him, giving him part both of dignities and offices, to the end that the many honours and much wealth bestowed on him may restrain his desires from other honours and other wealth, and that those many charges cause him to fear changes that may fall, knowing he is not able to stand without his master. And when both the princes and the servants are thus disposed, they may rely the one upon the other; when otherwise the end will ever prove hurtful for the one as well as for the other.

I will not omit one principle of great importance, being an error from which princes with much difficulty defend themselves, unless they be very discreet and make a very good choice, and this is concerning flatterers, whereof all writings are full; and that because men please themselves so much in their own things and therein cozen themselves that very hardly can they escape this pestilence, and desiring to escape it, there is danger of falling into contempt; for there is no other way to be secure from flattery but to let men know that they displease thee not in telling thee truth, but when everyone hath this leave thou losest thy reverence. Therefore ought a wise prince take a third course, making choice of some understanding men in his state, and give only to them a free liberty of speaking to him the truth,[4] and touching those things only which he inquires of and nothing else; but he ought to be inquisitive of everything and hear their opinions, and then afterwards advise himself after his own manner, and in these deliberations and with every one of them so carry himself that they all know that the more freely they shall speak, the better they shall be liked of; and besides those not give ear to anyone, and thus pursue the thing resolved on and thence continue obstinate in the resolution taken. He who does otherwise either falls upon flatterers or often changes upon the varying of opinions, from whence proceeds it that men conceive but slightly of him. To this purpose I will allege you a modern example. Peter Lucas,[5] a servant of Maximilian's, the present Emperor, speaking of his majesty, said that he never advised with anybody nor never did anything after his own way, which was because he took a contrary course to what we have now said; for the Emperor is a close man, who communicates his secrets to none, nor takes counsel of anyone, but as they come to be put in practice, they begin to be discovered and known, and so contradicted by those that are near about him, and he, as being an easy man, is quickly wrought from them. Whence it comes that what he does today he undoes on the morrow, and that he never understands himself what he would nor what he purposes, and that there is no grounding upon any of his resolutions. A prince, therefore, ought always to take counsel, but at his own pleasure and not at other men's, or rather should take away any man's courage to advise him of anything but what he asks; but he ought well to ask at large, and then touching the things inquired of be a patient hearer of the truth, and perceiving that for some respect the truth were concealed from him be displeased thereat. And because some men have thought that a prince that gains the opinion to be wise may be held so not by his own natural endowments but by the good counsels he hath about him, without question they are deceived; for this is a general rule and never fails, that a prince who of himself is not wise can never be well advised unless he should light upon one alone wholly to direct and govern him who himself were a very wise man. In this case, it is possible he may be well governed, but this would last but little, for that governor in a short time would deprive him of his state; but a prince not having any parts of nature, being advised of more than one, shall never be able to unite these counsels; of himself shall he never know how to unite them, and each one of the counsellors probably will follow that which is most properly his own, and he shall never find the means to amend or discern these things, nor can they fall out otherwise, because men always prove mischievous unless upon some necessity they be forced to become good. We conclude therefore that counsels, from whence-soever they proceed, must needs take their beginning from the prince's wisdom, and not the wisdom of the prince from good counsels.

## Dacres' comment

In this chapter, our author prescribes some rules how to avoid flattery and not to fall into contempt. The extent of these two extremes is so large on both sides that there is left but a very narrow path for the right temper to walk between them both; and happy were that prince who could light on so good a pilot as to bring him to port between those rocks and these quicksands. Where majesty becomes familiar, unless endued with a supereminent virtue, it loses all awful[6] regards, as the light of the sun because so ordinary, because so common, we should little value, were it not that all creatures feel themselves quickened by the rays thereof. On the other side, 'omnis insipiens arrogantia et plausibus capitur'.[7] Every fool is taken with his own pride and others' flatteries; and this fool keeps company so much with all great wise men that hardly with a candle and lantern can they be discerned betwixt. The greatest men are more subject to gross and palpable flatteries, and especially the greatest of men, who are kings and princes; for many seek the ruler's favour (Proverbs, 29: 26). For there are divers means whereby private men are instructed; princes have not that good hap, but they whose instruction is of most importance, so soon as they have taken the government upon them, no longer suffer any reprovers; for but few have access unto them, and they who familiarly converse with them do and say all for favour (Isocrates to Nicocles).[8] All are afraid to give him occasion of displeasure, though by telling him truth. To this purpose therefore says one,[9] a prince excels in learning to ride the great horse rather than in any other exercise, because his horse, being no flatterer, will show him he makes no difference between him and another man, and unless he keep his seat well will lay him on the ground. This is plain dealing. Men are more subtle, more double-hearted; they have a heart and a heart, neither is their tongue their heart's true interpreter. Counsel in the heart of man is like deep waters, but a man of understanding will draw it out (Proverbs, 20: 5). This understanding is most requisite in a prince, inasmuch as the whole globe is in his hand, and the inferior orbs are swayed by the motion of the highest. And therefore, surely it is the honour of a king to search out such a secret (Proverbs, 25: 2). His counsellors are his eyes and ears;[10] as they ought to be dear to him, so they ought to be true to him and make him the true report of things without disguise. If they prove false eyes, let him pluck them out; he may, as they use glass eyes, take them forth without pain and see never a whit the worse for it. The wisdom of a prince's counsellors is a great argument of the prince's wisdom. And being the choice of them imports the prince's credit and safety, our author will make him amends for his other errors by his good advice in his 22 chapter, whither I refer him.


NOTES

1. Compare Isocrates, *To Nicocles*, 27.
2. A contemporary example; Machiavelli had dealings with both Pandolfo Petrucci, the ruler of Siena, and his adviser and ambassador, Antonio da Venafro.
3. See Livy, *From the founding of the city*, XXII. xxix. 8, drawing on Hesiod, *Works and days*, 293ff.
4. Compare Isocrates, *To Nicocles*, 28.
5. Bishop Luca Rainaldi, ambassador to the Emperor Maximilian.
6. *Awful*: reverential, filled with awe.
7. A translation follows.
8. Isocrates, *To Nicocles*, 2-4.
9. Carneades, according to Plutarch, *How to tell a flatterer from a friend*, 58F.
10. Aristotle, *Politics*, 1287B.


*(iii) 'Of those things in respect whereof men, and especially princes, are praised or dispraised' (chapter 15)*

It now remains that we consider what the conditions of a prince ought to be and his terms of government over his subjects and towards his friends. And because I know that many have written hereupon, I doubt lest I, venturing also to treat thereof, may be branded with presumption, especially seeing I am like enough to deliver an opinion different from others. But my intent being to write for the advantage of him that understands me, I thought it fitter to follow the effectual truth of the matter than the imagination thereof, and many principalities and republics have been in imagination which neither have been seen nor known to be indeed; for there is such a distance between how men do live and how men ought to live that he who leaves that which is done for that which ought to be done learns sooner his ruin that his preservation; for that man who will profess honesty in all his actions must needs go to ruin among so many that are dishonest. Whereupon it is necessary for a prince desiring to preserve himself to be able to make use of that honesty and to lay it aside again as need shall require. Passing by, then, things that are only in imagination belonging to a prince, to discourse upon those that are really true, I say that all men whensoever mention is made of them, and especially princes, because they are placed aloft in the view of all, are taken notice of for some of these qualities which procure them either commendations or blame, and this is that some one is held liberal, some miserable (miserable I say, not covetous; for the covetous desire to have though it were by rapine, but a miserable man is he that too much forbears to make use of his own), some free givers, others extortioners, some cruel, others piteous, the one a league breaker, another faithful, the one effeminate and of small courage, the other fierce and courageous, the one courteous, the other proud, the one lascivious, the other chaste, the one of fair dealing, the other wily and crafty, the one hard, the other easy, the one grave, the other light, the one religious, the other incredulous, and such like. I know that everyone will confess it were exceedingly praiseworthy for a prince to be adorned with all these above named qualities that are good, but because this is not possible, nor do human conditions admit such perfection in virtues, it is necessary for him to be so discreet that he know how to avoid the infamy of those vices which would thrust him out of his state, and if it be possible, beware of those also which are not able to remove him thence, but where it cannot be, let them pass with less regard. And yet let him not stand much upon[1] it though he incur the infamy of those vices without which he can very hardly save his state; for if all be thoroughly considered, some things we shall find which will have the colour and very face of virtue and following them, they will lead thee to thy destruction, whereas some others that shall as much seem vice, if we take the course they lead us, shall discover unto us the way to our safety and well-being.

## Dacres' comment

The second blemish in this our author's book I find in his fifteenth chapter, where he instructs his prince to use such an ambidexterity as that he may serve himself either of virtue or vice according to his advantage, which in true policy is neither good in attaining the principality nor in securing it when it is attained. For politics presuppose ethics, which will never allow this rule, as that a man might make this small difference between virtue and vice that he may indifferently lay aside or take up the one or the other, and put it in practice as best conduceth to the end he propounds himself. I doubt our author would have blamed David's regard to Saul, when (I Samuel, 24) in the cave he cut off the lap of Saul's garment and spared his head, and afterwards in the 26th [chapter] when he forbade Abishai to strike him as he lay sleeping. Worthy of a prince's consideration is that saying of Abigail to David (I Samuel, 25: 30), 'It shall come to pass when the Lord shall have done to my lord according to all that he hath spoken concerning thee, and shall have appointed thee ruler over Israel, that this shall be no grief to thee, nor offence of heart unto my lord, that thou hast forborn to shed blood' etc. For surely the conscience of this evil ground whereupon they have either built or underpropped their tyranny causes men as well *metus* as *spes in longum proicere*,[2] which sets them awork on further mischief.

NOTES

1. *Stand upon*: allow oneself to be influenced by, attach importance to.
2. 'To extend far ahead their fears as well as their hopes'.

## (iv) 'In what manner princes ought to keep their words' (chapter 18)

How commendable in a prince it is to keep his word and live with integrity, not making use of cunning and subtlety, everyone knows well; yet we see by experience in these our days that those princes have effected great matters who have made small reckoning of keeping their words, and have known by their craft to turn and wind men about, and in the end have overcome those who have grounded upon the truth. You must then know there are two kinds of combating or fighting: the one by right of the laws, the other merely by force. That first way is proper to men, the other is also common to beasts, but because the first many times suffices not, there is a necessity to make recourse to the second;[1] wherefore it behoves a prince to know how to make good use of that part which belongs to a beast as well as that which is proper to a man. This part hath been covertly showed to princes by ancient writers, who say that Achilles and many others of those ancient princes were entrusted to Chiron, the centaur, to be brought up under his discipline;[2] the moral of this, having for their teacher one that was half a beast and half a man, was nothing else but that it was needful for a prince to understand how to make his advantage of the one and the other nature, because neither could subsist without the other. A prince, then, being necessitated to know how to make use of that part belonging to a beast, ought to serve himself of the conditions of the fox and the lion;[3] for the lion cannot keep himself from snares, nor the fox defend himself against the wolves. He had need then be a fox that he may beware of the snares and a lion that he may scare the wolves. Those that stand wholly upon the lion understand not well themselves. And therefore, a wise prince cannot nor ought not keep his faith given, when the observance thereof turns to disadvantage and the occasions that made him promise are past. For if men were all good, this rule would not be allowable; but being they are full of mischief and would not make it good to thee, neither art thou tied to keep it with them, nor shall a prince ever want lawful occasions to give colour to this breach. Very many modern examples hereof might be alleged, wherein might be showed how many peaces concluded and how many promises made have been violated and broken by the infidelity of princes; and ordinarily things have best succeeded with him that hath been nearest the fox in condition. But it is necessary to understand how to set a good colour upon this disposition, and to be able to feign and dissemble thoroughly; and men are so simple and yield so much to the present necessities that he who hath a mind to deceive shall always find another that will be deceived. I will not conceal any one of the examples that have been of late. Alexander the Sixth[4] never did anything else than deceive men and never meant otherwise, and always found whom to work upon; yet never was there man would protest more effectually, nor aver anything with more solemn oaths and observe them less than he; nevertheless, his cozenages all thrived well with him, for he knew how to play this part cunningly. Therefore is there no necessity for a prince to be endued with all these above-written qualities, but it behoves well that he seem to be so, or rather I will boldly say this, that having these qualities and always regulating himself by them, they are hurtful, but seeming to have them, they are advantageous; as to seem pitiful, faithful, mild, religious and of integrity, and indeed to be so, provided withal thou beest of such a composition that if need require thee to use the contrary, thou canst and know'st how to apply thyself thereto. And it suffices to conceive this, that a prince, and especially a new prince, cannot observe all those things for which men are held good, he being often forced for the maintenance of his state to do contrary to his faith, charity, humanity and religion, and therefore it behoves him to have a mind so disposed as to turn and take the advantage of all winds and fortunes; and as formerly I said, not forsake the good while he can, but to know how to make use of the evil upon necessity. A prince, then, ought to have a special care that he never let fall any words but what are all seasoned with the five above-written qualities, and let him seem to him that sees and hears him all pity, all faith, all integrity, all humanity, all religion; nor is there anything more necessary for him to seem to have than this last quality;[5] for all men in general judge thereof rather by the sight than by the touch — for every man may come to the sight of him, few come to the touch and feeling of him; every man may come to see what thou seemest, few come to perceive and understand what thou art; and those few dare not oppose the opinion of many who have the majesty of state to protect them; and in all men's actions, especially those of princes, wherein there is no judgement to appeal unto, men forbear to give their censures till the events[6] and ends of things. Let a prince therefore take the surest courses he can to maintain his life and state, the means shall always be thought honourable, and commended by everyone; for the vulgar is overtaken with the appearance and event of a thing, and, for the most part of people, they are but the vulgar; the others, that are but few, take place where the vulgar have no subsistence. A prince there is[7] in these days, whom I shall not do well to name, that preaches nothing else but peace and faith, but had he kept the one and the other, several times had they taken from him his state and reputation.

*Dacres' comment*

In the eighteenth chapter, our author discourses how princes ought to govern themselves in keeping their promises made; whereof he says they ought to make such small reckoning as that rather they should know by their craft how to turn and wind men about, whereby to take advantage of all winds and fortunes. To this I would oppose that in the fifteenth psalm, verse 5, 'He that sweareth to his neighbour and disappointeth him not, though it were to his own hindrance'. It was a king[8] that writ it, and methinks the rule he gave should well befit both king and subject; and surely this persuades against all taking of advantages. A man may reduce all the causes of faith-breaking to three heads. One may be because he that promised had no intention to keep his word, and this is a wicked and malicious way of dealing. A second may be because he that promised repents of his promise made, and that is grounded on unconstancy and lightness, in that he would not be well resolved before he entered into covenant. The third may be when it so falls out that it lies not in his power that made the promise to perform it. In which case a man ought to imitate the good debtor, who having not wherewithal to pay hides not himself but presents his person to his creditor, willingly suffering imprisonment. The first and second are very vicious and unworthy of a prince; in the third, men might well be directed by the examples of those two famous Romans, Regulus and Posthumius.[9] I shall close this with that answer of Charles the Fifth, when he was pressed to break his word with Luther for his safe return from Worms: 'Fides rerum promissarum etsi toto mundo exulet, tamen apud imperatorem eam consistere oportet.' (Though truth be banished out of the whole world, yet should it always find harbour in an emperor's breast.)

NOTES

1. Taken from Cicero, *On duties*, I. xi. 34, but altering the spirit of Cicero's words.
2. On Achilles' upbringing by Chiron, see Homer, *Iliad*, XI. 831-2; Pindar, *Pythian* VI. 21ff; *Nemean* III. 43ff; and for a Latin source, Statius, *Achilleid*, II. 86-167. In *The advancement of learning*, Bacon says that Machiavelli expounds the myth 'ingeniously but corruptly'.
3. Again in contrast to Cicero, *On duties*, I. xiii. 41; and see Plutarch, *Lives*, *Lysander*, vii.
4. The Borgia pope, 1492-1503.
5. Aristotle, *Politics*, 1314B-1315A.
6. *Events*: outcome.
7. Ferdinand of Aragon (1452-1516), grandfather of the Emperor Charles V.
8. King David.
9. Discussed by Cicero, *On duties*, III. xxvi. 99 – xxxi. 111: Regulus, captured by the Carthaginians, was sent to Rome on parole to negotiate the return of some Carthaginian prisoners in exchange for his own release (the version in Horace, *Odes*, III. v, is slightly different), advised against accepting the deal and returned to Carthage to face torture and death; Posthumius was handed over to the Samnites on his own advice to cancel the peace he had made with them after the battle of the Caudine Forks.

## Daniel: *Musophilus*

*'No state stands sure but on the grounds of right'*

*This rather difficult passage from* Musophilus *displays humanist idealism to the full. Daniel argues that the state will find its best support in cultivating learning, because successful action must be grounded in knowledge – a familiar humanist argument. Though unlettered action may prosper for a while, it will eventually collapse; fraud will yield to truth and honesty. The emphasis on fraud and deceit may well be in response to Machiavelli; we may note the sentence about leaving faith and respect beyond the Alps.*

> Whiles other gifts than of the mind shall get
>     Under our colours that which is our dues,
>     And to our travails neither benefit,

Nor grace, nor honour, nor respect accrues,
This sickness of the state's soul, learning, then
The body's great distemp'rature ensues.[1]
For if that learning's rooms to learned men
Were as their heritage distributed,
All this disordered thrust would cease, for when
The fit were called, th'unworthy frustrated,
These would b'ashamed to seek, those to b'unsought,
And stay'ng their turn were sure they should be sped.
Then would our drooping Academies brought
Again in heart regain that reverend hand
Of lost opinion, and no more be thought
Th'unnecessary furnish of the land,
Nor disencouraged with their small esteem
Confused, irresolute and wavering stand,
Caring not to become profound, but seem
Contented with a superficial skill,
Which for a slight reward enough they deem
When th'one succeeds as well as th'other will,
Seeing shorter ways lead sooner to their end,
And others' longer travails thrive so ill.
Then would they only labour to extend
Their now unsearching spirits beyond these bounds
Of others' powers, wherein they must be penned,
As if there were besides no other grounds,
And set their bold *plus ultra* far without
The pillars of those axioms age propounds;[2]
Discov'ring daily more and more about
In that immense and boundless ocean
Of nature's riches never yet found out
Nor foreclosed with the wit of any man;
So far beyond the ordinary course
That other unindustrious ages ran,
That these more curious times they might divorce
From the opinion they are linked unto
Of our disable[3] and unactive force,
To show true knowledge can both speak and do,
Armed for the sharp,[4] which in these days they find,
With all provisions that belong thereto;
That their experience may not come behind
The time's conceit, but leading in their place

May make men see the weapons of the mind
　Are states' best strengths and kingdoms' chiefest grace,
　And rooms of charge, charged full with worth and praise,
　Makes majesty appear with her full face,
Shining with all her beams, with all her rays,
　Unscanted of her parts, unshadowèd
　In any darkened point, which still[5] bewrays[6]
　The wane of power, when power's unfurnishèd
　And hath not all those entire complements
　Wherewith the state should for her state be sped.
And though the fortune of some age consents
　Unto a thousand errors grossly wrought,
　Which flourished over[7] with their fair events[8]
　Have passed for current,[9] and good courses thought,
　The least whereof in other times again
　Most dangerous inconveniences[10] have brought,
Whilst to the times not to men's wits pertain
　The good successes of ill-managed deeds,
　Though th'ignorant, deceived with colours vain,
　Miss of the causes whence this luck proceeds;
　Foreign defects, giving home faults the way,
　Make ev'n that weakness sometimes well succeeds.
I grant that some unlettered practic[11] may,
　Leaving beyond the Alps faith and respect
　To God and man, with impious cunning sway
　The courses fore-begun with like effect,
　And without stop maintain the turning on
　And have his errors deemed without defect;
But when some powerful opposition
　Shall with a sound encount'ring shock disjoint
　The fore-contrived frame, and thereupon
　Th'experience of the present disappoint,
　And other stirring spirits and other hearts
　Built-huge for action, meeting in a point,
Shall drive the world to summon all their arts
　And all too little for so real might,
　When no advantages of weaker parts
　Shall bear out shallow counsels from the light,
　And this sense-opening action, which doth hate
　Unmanly craft, shall look to have her right,
Who then holds up the glory of the state,

Which lettered arms and armèd letters won,
Who shall be fittest to negotiate
Contemned[12] Justinian or else Littleton?[13]
When it shall not be held wisdom to be
Privately made and publicly undone,
But sound designs that judgement shall decree
Out of a true discern of the clear ways
That lie direct, with safe-going equity[14]
Embroiling not their own and others' days;
Extending forth their providence beyond
The circuit of their own particular,[15]
That even the ignorant may understand
How that deceit is but a caviller,
And true unto itself can never stand,
But still must with her own conclusions war.
Can truth and honesty, wherein consists
The right repose on earth, the surest ground
Of trust, come weaker armed into the lists
Than fraud or vice, that doth itself confound?
Or shall presumption that doth what it lists,
Not what it ought, carry her courses sound?
Then what safe place out of confusion
Hath plain-proceeding honesty to dwell?
What suit of grace hath virtue to put on
If vice shall wear as good and do as well?
If wrong, if craft, if indiscretion
Act as fair parts with ends as laudable?
Which all this mighty volume of events,
The world, the universal map of deeds,
Strongly controls, and proves from all descents[16]
That the directest courses best succeeds,[17]
When craft, wrapped still in many cumberments,
With all her cunning thrives not, though it speeds.
For should not grave and learn'd experience
That looks with th'eyes of all the world beside,
And with all ages holds intelligence,
Go safer than deceit without a guide,
Which in the by-paths of her diffidence[18]
Crossing the ways of right still runs more wide?
Who will not grant? And therefore this observe:
No state stands sure but on the grounds of right,

Of virtue, knowledge, judgement to preserve,
And all the powers of learnings requisite;
Though other shifts a present turn may serve,
Yet in the trial they will weigh too light.

## NOTES

1. *Ensues*: transitive, follows as a result or consequence from ('the body's great distemp'rature' is the subject of the sentence).
2. These lines allude to the famous device of the Emperor Charles V, a pair of columns with the motto *plus oultre* or *plus ultra*, signifying that his empire, which included Latin America, went beyond the pillars of Hercules (the straits of Gibraltar), which bounded the Roman empire (see Frances Yates, *Astraea* (Penguin, 1977), p. 23). Daniel hopes that learning will go beyond the pillars of tradition. This expansionist approach to learning is perfectly in accordance with humanism (see above, pp. 153-4).
3. *Disable*: impotent.
4. *The sharp*: an unbuttoned rapier in fencing; to fight at the sharp means to play with unbated swords, i.e. in earnest.
5. *Still*: always.
6. *Bewrays*: exposes, reveals.
7. *Flourished over*: adorned, embellished.
8. *Events*: outcomes.
9. *Current*: genuine.
10. *Inconveniences*: harms, troubles, misfortunes.
11. *Practic*: man of action.
12. *Contemned*: despised.
13. This line seems to allude to the conflict in the sixteenth century between common law and equity, as administered in the court of chancery – a conflict which was to be subsumed in the seventeenth century under the struggle between king and Parliament over the royal prerogative. The equitable jurisdiction of the chancellor, deriving from the king, had come into being so that the subject could obtain redress in cases for which the common law had no remedy or against the rigour of the common law. The chancellor administered equity, following his own discretion, very much in the spirit of Roman or civil law. Thus equity is symbolised here by Justinian, who consolidated Roman law, while the common law is symbolised by Thomas Littleton, whose *Treatise on tenures* was to be called the ornament of the common law by Sir Edward Coke, the scourge of the Stuarts. Daniel takes the court side.
14. See previous note.
15. *Particular*: noun; personal interest, concern.
16. *Descents*: a descent in logic was a particular kind of inference.
17. *Succeeds*: singular verb with plural subject.
18. *Diffidence*: distrust, lack of faith.

## Jonson: *Discoveries*

*It will come as no surprise, in view of the humanist interest in the topic, that* Discoveries *contains several trenchant paragraphs on the importance of counsel. In the third passage given here, following Vives, Jonson stresses the need for honesty in the counsellor, as well as giving some practical advice on how to present counsel to princes in a palatable way.*

*In the last passage given here, on the theme of clemency, Jonson reaffirms the traditional ideal of the good prince, with direct reference to Machiavelli. Seneca in his moral essay* On mercy *had said that the prince only resorts to punishment with extreme reluctance; and clemency was one of the virtues all the humanist treatises ascribed to the prince. In* The prince, *Machiavelli asserts that reluctance to punish may lead to the need for greater acts of cruelty in the future; in chapter 17,* On cruelty and piety, *contradicting Cicero (*On duties, *II. vii. 23-4), he says that it is better to be feared than loved, because fear keeps men obedient. Returning to Seneca's views, Jonson says that cruelty belongs to the beast and that it is self-perpetuating; the good prince is safe in the love of his subjects. He stresses the importance of religion as the basis of rule (contrast Machiavelli, above, p. 257), and paints a dark picture of tyranny, reminiscent of Erasmus' portrait of princes in his essay on the adage* The beetle searches for the eagle.

### (i) 'Consilia'[1]

No man is so foolish but may give another good counsel sometimes, and no man is so wise but may easily err if he will take no other's counsel but his own. But very few men are wise by their own counsel or learned by their own teaching. For he that was only taught by himself had a fool to his master.

NOTE

1. 'Counsels'.

### (ii) 'Illiteratus princeps'[1]

A prince without letters is a pilot without eyes. All his government is groping. In sovereignty, it is a most happy thing not to be compelled, but so it is the most miserable not to be counselled. And how can he be counselled that cannot see to read the best counsellors? — which are books; for they neither flatter us nor hide from us.[2] He may hear, you will say. But how shall he always be sure to hear truth? Or be counselled the best things, not the sweetest? They say princes learn no art truly but the art of horsemanship. The reason is the brave beast is no flatterer. He will throw a prince as soon as his groom.[3] Which is an argument that the good counsellors to princes are the best instruments of a good age. For though the prince himself be of most prompt inclination to all virtue, yet the best pilots have need of mariners beside sails, anchor and other tackle.

NOTES

1. 'An unlettered prince'.
2. Also quoted by Bacon, *Of counsel*. This sentence and the one before are from Justus Lipsius, *Politics*.
3. Plutarch, *How to tell a flatterer from a friend*, *Moralia*, 58F.

## (iii) 'Mutua auxilia'[1]

Learning needs rest; sovereignty gives it. Sovereignty needs counsel; learning affords it. There is such a consociation[2] of offices[3] between the prince and whom his favour breeds that they may help to sustain his power as he their knowledge. It is the greatest part of his liberality, his favour; and from whom doth he hear discipline[4] more willingly or the arts discoursed more gladly than from those whom his own bounty and benefits have made able and faithful?

In being able to counsel others, a man must be furnished with an universal store in himself, to the knowledge of all nature; that is the matter and seed-plot, there are the seats of all argument and invention. But especially, you must be cunning[5] in the nature of man; there is the variety of things, which are as the elements and letters which his art and wisdom must rank and order to the present occasion. For we see not all letters in single words, nor all places[6] in particular discourses. That cause seldom happens wherein a man will use all arguments.

The two chief things that give a man reputation in counsel are the opinion of his honesty and the opinion of wisdom; the authority of those two will persuade when the same counsels uttered by other persons less qualified are of no efficacy or working.

Wisdom without honesty is mere craft and cozenage. And therefore the reputation of honesty must first be gotten, which cannot be but by living well. A good life is a main[7] argument.

Next a good life, to beget love in the persons we counsel, by dissembling our knowledge of ability in ourselves and avoiding all suspicion of arrogance, ascribing all to their instruction, as an ambassador to his master or a subject to his sovereign, seasoning all with humanity[8] and sweetness, only expressing care and solicitude. And not to counsel rashly or on the sudden, but with advice and meditation; 'dat nox consilium'.[9] For many foolish things fall from wise men if they speak in haste or be extemporal.[10] It therefore behoves the giver of counsel to be circumspect, especially to beware of those with whom he is not thoroughly acquainted, lest any spice of rashness, folly or self-love appear, which will be marked by new persons and men of experience in affairs.

And to the prince or his superior to behave himself modestly and with respect. Yet free from flattery or empire.[11] Not with insolence or precept, but as the prince were already furnished with the parts he should have, especially in affairs of state. For in other things they will more easily suffer themselves to be taught or reprehended; they will not willingly contend. But hear with Alexander the answer the musician gave him, 'Absit, o rex, ut tu melius haec scias quam ego.'[12]

NOTES

1. 'Mutual aid'. This paragraph is drawn from Vives, dedication of *On the transmission of knowledge* to John III of Portugal, the rest of the passage from his *On consultation*.

2. *Consociation*: union, alliance, close association.

3. *Offices*: services, obligations.

4. *Discipline*: instruction, teaching.

5. *Cunning*: knowledgeable, versed in.

6. *Places*: the places of rhetoric, topics, i.e. the appropriate materials on which to base an argument or theme.

7. *Main*: strong, powerful.

8. *Humanity*: courtesy, politeness.

9. 'Night gives counsel.' Proverbial. Also quoted by Bacon, *Of counsel*.

10. *Extemporal*: speaking extempore.

11. *Empire*: dictatorial or bullying behaviour.

12. 'God forbid, your majesty, that you should know more about these things than me.' From Plutarch, *On the fortune or the virtue of Alexander*, II, *Moralia*, 334C-D. Plutarch tells the story of Philip, but Jonson follows Vives in applying it to Alexander. The point of the story lies in the clever way in which the musician contradicts the king.

## (iv) 'Clementia'[1]

A prince should exercise his cruelty not by himself but by his ministers; so he may save himself and his dignity with his people by sacrificing those when he list, saith the great doctor of state, Machiavel.[2] But I say, he puts off man and goes into a beast that is cruel. No virtue is a prince's own or becomes him more than his[3] clemency, and no glory is greater than to be able to save with his power. Many punishments sometimes and in some cases as much discredit a prince as many funerals a physician. The state of things is secured by clemency; severity represseth a few, but it irritates more. The lopping of trees makes the boughs shoot out thicker, and the taking away of some kind of enemies increaseth the number. It is then most gracious in a prince to pardon when many about him would make him cruel, to think then how much he can save when others tell him how much he can destroy, not to consider what the impotence of others hath demolished but what his own greatness can sustain. These[4] are a prince's virtues, and they that give him other counsels are but the hangman's factors.

He that is cruel to halves,[5] saith the said St Nicolas,[6] loseth no less the opportunity of his cruelty than of his benefits; for then to use his cruelty is too late and to use his favours will be interpreted fear and necessity, and so he loseth the thanks.[7] Still the counsel is cruelty. But princes by hearkening to cruel counsels become in time obnoxious to[8] the authors, their flatterers and ministers, and are brought to that, that when they would they dare not change them; they must go on and defend cruelty with cruelty, they cannot alter the habit. It is then grown necessary they must be as ill as those have made them, and in the end they will grow more hateful to themselves than to their subjects. Whereas, on the contrary, the merciful prince is safe in love, not in fear. He needs no emissaries, spies, intelligencers to entrap true subjects. He fears no libels, no treasons. His people speak what they think, and talk openly what they do in secret. They have nothing in their breasts that they need a cipher for. He is guarded with his own benefits.

The strength of empire is in religion. What else is the Palladium[9] with Homer that kept Troy so long from sacking?[10] Nothing more commends the sovereign to the subject than it. For he that is religious must be merciful and just necessarily. And they are two[11] strong ties upon mankind. Justice is the virtue that innocence rejoiceth in. Yet even that is not always so safe but it may love to stand in the sight of mercy. For sometimes misfortune is made a crime, and then innocence is succoured no less than virtue. Nay, oftentimes virtue is made capital,[12] and through the condition of the times it may happen that that may be punished with our praise. Let no man therefore murmur at the actions of the prince, who is placed so far above him. If he offend, he hath his discoverer. God hath a height beyond him. But where the prince is good, Euripides saith, 'God is a guest in a human body.'[13]

There is nothing with some princes sacred above their majesty, or profane but what violates their sceptres. But a prince with such counsel is like the God Terminus[14] of stone, his own landmark, or, as it is in the fable,[15] a crowned lion. It is dangerous offending such an one, who being angry knows not how to forgive. That cares not[16] to do anything for maintaining or enlarging of empire; kills not men or subjects but destroyeth whole countries, armies, mankind, male and female, guilty or not guilty, holy or profane, yea, some that have not seen the light. All is under the law of their spoil and licence. But princes that neglect their proper office thus, their fortune is oftentimes to draw a Sejanus[17] to be near about 'em;[18] who will at last affect to get above 'em,[19] and put them in a worthy fear of rooting both them out and their family. For no men hate an evil prince more than they that helped to make him such. And none more boastingly weep his ruin than they that procured and practised it. The same path leads to ruin which did to rule, when men profess a licence in governing. A good king is a public servant.

## NOTES

1. 'Mercy'. This passage makes use of Seneca, *On mercy*, I. xxiv. 1; xxv. 1; iii. 3; viii. 6-7; x. 4; xiii. 2-5; i. 9 (Loeb numeration).

2. See Machiavelli's account of Cesare Borgia's treatment of his governor, Remirro de Orco, *The prince*, chapter 7.

3. *His*: the Folio reads *this*.

4. *These*: the Folio reads *there*.

5. *To halves*: incompletely.

6. *St Nicolas*: ironic name for Niccolò Machiavelli.

7. See *The prince*, chapter 8, where Machiavelli says that a new ruler must determine what injuries he needs to inflict and inflict them once and for all.

8. *Obnoxious to*: subject to, dependent on.

9. *Palladium*: the sacred image of Pallas Athene, which protected the city of Troy, until stolen by Diomedes and Odysseus (this legend does not actually come in Homer).

10. The interpretation of H. Farnese, *Jove's skin, or On the ancient glory of the ruler* (1607), pp. 105-6.

11. *Two*: the Folio reads *too*.

12. *Capital*: punishable by death, as in a capital offence.

13. *Euripides*: actually one of Menander's monostichs, gnomic sayings in single lines ascribed to the Greek comic poet in antiquity but mostly not authentic.

14. *Terminus*: Roman god of boundaries, symbolised by the boundary mark.

15. *The fable*: of Reynard the fox.

16. *Cares not*: does not mind.

17. *Sejanus*: the ambitious and powerful minister eventually suppressed by the Emperor Tiberius, about whom Jonson wrote a play (the Folio reads *Scianus*).

18. *'em*: the Folio reads *him*.

19. Ditto.

# 5  RELIGION AND VERNACULAR SCRIPTURE

**Erasmus: the *Paraclesis***

*'I would to God the ploughman would sing a text of the Scripture at his ploughbeam'*

*The* Paraclesis *(*Exhortation*) was the preface to Erasmus' edition of the New Testament in Greek first published in 1516. Almost the whole of it is given here. Apart from its famous plea for the diffusion of the Bible in the vernacular, it contains many themes found elsewhere in Erasmus' writings: the quarrelsomeness and hyper-subtlety of scholastic theology (there are many jibes at the scholastics), the natural inclination of men to goodness, the closeness of many pagan ideas to Christian teaching, the worthlessness of monastic rules and of images in comparison with the word of God. The argument moves in the characteristic Erasmian way, returning to points made earlier and restating them with new epigrams.*

*The translation used here is an anonymous one, perhaps by William Roy, first published in Antwerp in 1529 and entitled* An exhortation to the diligent study of scripture.

Neither do I count it best at this time to revocate[1] and call to memory the sorrowful complaint (although it be not new, yet alas it is too true, and I think it could never be more justly verified than at this present time) that sith with such great diligence all men's inventions are studied and commended, yet only this immortal fountain of Christ's pure philosophy is despised and mocked of so many — yea and chiefly of them which profess to be the heads and examples of the Christian, few there are that seek these wholesome springs of health. And yet they that seek them do so unfruitfully look upon them, adding their own glosses and opinions, that they seem rather to trouble and defile these springs of life than to drink of them sweetly, that they might have in themself floods of living water running into everlasting life, which both should be to the glory of God and profit of the Christian.

We see that in all other sciences[2] which by man's policy have been invented, there is no mystery so dark and secret but that the quickness of our wit hath attained it, there is nothing so hard but that diligent labour hath subdued it unto him. How chanceth it then that we embrace not with faithful hearts, as it is convenient,[3] this pure philosophy, sith we profess the holy name of Christ? Plato's adherents, Pythagoras' scholars, the Academics, Stoics, Epicures, the fautors[4] of Aristotle and disciples of Diogenes[5] know groundly,[6] yea, and by heart, the traditions of their own sect, and fight most fiercely for them, ready rather to die than to forsake their patron and author. And why do not we much more give our minds and studies unto our master and prince, Christ? Who would not count it a foul thing, yea, and a great rebuke, to him that professeth Aristotle's philosophy, if he be ignorant what his master judgeth concerning the causes of the thunder, of the rainbow, of the earthquakes and of such other natural causes? — which though they were known or unknown make not them that labour to know them happy nor unhappy. And should we, which are so many ways consecrated and with so many sacraments bound unto Christ, think it no shame a whit to be ignorant in his Scripture and doctrine, which give us most sure comfort and felicity, and which are the anchor of the soul both sure and stable, preserving us from perishing in all tempests of temptation? Howbeit,[7] for what intent use we this comparison, sith it is extreme madness to compare Christ with Zeno[8] and Aristotle, and his heavenly doctrine with their trifling traditions?

Let them feign and imagine unto the captains of their sect as much as they may, yea, as much as they will. Yet truly, only this master and teacher came from heaven, which alone could teach sure things, being the everlasting wisdom of the father, which alone hath taught wholesome things, being the foundation of all man's health, which alone hath fulfilled to the uttermost point all that he hath taught, and which alone may perform whatsoever he hath promised. If anything had been brought from the Chaldes[9] or the Egyptians, we would the more greedily desire to know it, because it came far and from a strange country — yea, it is the more dear and precious that cometh from afar. And we are oftentimes so grievously vexed about the dream and fantasy of a foolish fellow, not only with small profit but also with great loss of time, that it is shame to rehearse it. I wonder that this desire doth not likewise tickle[10] and entice the Christian hearts, which know well enough, as the thing is indeed, that this wholesome doctrine came not from Egypt or Syria, but from the very heaven and seat of God. Why do we not think with ourselves on this manner? — it must needs be a new and marvellous kind of learning, sith that God himself, which was immortal, became a natural man and mortal, descending from the right hand of his father into this wretched world to teach it unto us. It must needs be a high and excellent thing and no trifle which that heavenly and marvellous master came to teach openly. Why do we not go about to know, search and try out with a godly curiosity this fruitful philosophy? Sith that this kind of wisdom, being so profound and inscrutable that utterly it damneth and confoundeth as foolish all the wisdom of this world, may be gathered out of so small books as out of most pure springs, and that with much less labour than the doctrine of Aristotle out of so many brawling and contentious books, or of such infinite commentaries, which do so much dissent — besides the incomparable fruit which needeth not here to be spoken of. Neither is it needful that thou be clogged with so many irksome and babbling sciences. The means to this philosophy are easy and at hand. Do only thy diligence to bring a godly and ready mind, chiefly endued with plain and pure faith. Be only desirous to be instruct[11] and confirmable[12] to this meek doctrine, and thou hast much profited. Thy master and instructor, that is the spirit of God, will not from thee be absent, which is never more gladly present with any than with simple and plain hearts. Men's doctrines and traditions, besides the promising of false felicity, do confound many men's wits, and make them clean to despair, because they are so dark, crafty and contentious. But this delectable doctrine doth apply herself equally to all men, submitting herself unto us while we are children, tempering her tune after our capacity, feeding us with milk, forbearing, nourishing, suffering and doing all things, until we may increase and wax greater in Christ. And contrariwise, it is not so low and depressed[13] unto the weak but it is as high and marvellous to the perfect — yea the more thou wadest in the treasures of this science, the further thou art from attaining her majesty. To the children she is low and plain, and to greater she seemeth above all capacity. She refuseth no age, no kind, no fortune, no state and condition.

Insomuch that the sun is not more common and indifferent[14] to all men than this doctrine of Christ. She forbiddeth[15] no man at all, except he abstain willingly, envying his own profit. And truly, I do greatly dissent from those men which would not that the Scripture of Christ should be translated into all tongues, that it might be read diligently of the private and secular men and women, either as though Christ had taught such dark and insensible things that they could scant[16] be understood of a few divines, or else as though the pith and substance of the Christian religion consisted chiefly in this, that it be not known. Peradventure it were most expedient that the counsels of kings should be kept secret, but Christ would that his counsels and mysteries should be spread abroad as much as is possible. I would desire that all women should read the Gospel and Paul's Epistles, and I would to God they were translated into the tongues of all men, so that they might not only be read and known of the Scots and Irishmen but also of the Turks and Saracens. Truly, it is one degree to good living, yea the first – I had almost said the chief – to have a little sight in the Scripture, though it be but a gross knowledge, and not yet consummate (be it in case that[17] some would laugh at it, yea, and that some should err and be deceived).[18] I would to God the ploughman would sing a text of the Scripture at his ploughbeam, and that the weaver at his loom with this would drive away the tediousness of time; I would the wayfaring man with this pastime would expel the weariness of his journey, and, to be short, I would that all the communication of the Christian should be of the Scripture; for, in a manner, such are we ourselves as our daily tales[19] are. Let every man prosper and attain that he may, and declare effectuously[20] his mind unto his neighbour; let not him that cometh behind envy the foremost; let also the foremost allect[21] him that followeth, ever exhorting him not despair. Why do we apply only to certain the profession which is indifferent and common to all men? Neither truly is it meet – sith that baptism is equally common unto all Christian men, wherein consisteth the first profession of the Christian religion, sith other sacraments are not private, and, to conclude, sith the reward of immortality pertaineth indifferently unto all men – that only the doctrine should be banished from the secular and possessed only of a few whom the commonalty call divines or religious persons. And yet I would that these, although they be but a small company in comparison to the whole number which bear the name of Christ and are called Christian – I would, I say, desire with all mine heart that they were indeed such as they are called; for I am afraid that a man may find some among the divines which are far unworthy their name and title, that is to say, which speak worldly things and not godly – yea, and among the religious, which profess the poverty of Christ and to despise the world, thou shalt find more worldly pleasure and vanity than in all the world besides. Him do I count a true divine which not with crafty and subtle reasons, but that in heart, countenance, eyes and life, doth teach to despise riches, and that a Christian ought not to put confidence in the succour and help of this world, but only whole to hang on heaven; not to avenge injury; to pray for them that say evil by us; to do good against evil; that all good men should be loved and nourished indifferently as the members of one body; that evil men, if they cannot be reformed and brought into a good order, ought to be suffered; that they which are despoiled of their goods and put from their possessions and mourn in this world are very blessed and not to be lamented; that death is to be desired of the Christian, sith it is nothing else but a going to immortality. If any man being inspired with the Holy Ghost do preach and teach these and such other things, if any man exhort, entice and bolden[22] his neighbour unto these things, he is a very and true divine, though he be a weaver, yea, though he dig and delve. But he that accomplisheth and fulfilleth these things in his life and manners, he verily is a great doctor. Peradventure another which is not Christian shall more subtly dispute by what manner the angels understand.[23] Howbeit, to persuade and exhort that we may here live pure and immaculate from all vices and iniquities, and to lead an angel's life, that is the office and duty of a Christian and divine. If any man would object and say that these are gross and unsavoury things, to him would I none otherwise answer but that Christ chiefly hath taught these things, and that the Apostles to these have us exhorted. This learning and doctrine be it never so unsavoury hath brought us forth so many good Christian and so thick swarms of faithful martyrs. This unlearned (as they call it) philosophy hath subdued under her laws the most noble princes, so many kingdoms, so many nations, which thing no king's power, neither learning of the philosophers was ever able to bring to pass. Neither will I resist them but that they may dispute their profound and subtle questions if it please them among the more perfect. Howbeit, the rude multitude of the Christian may be comforted, because truly the Apostles did never teach such things. Whether they knew them or no, I would other men should judge.

But truly if that the princes for their part would remember themselves and go about to fulfil with pureness of living this humble and rude learning (as they call it); if the preachers in their sermons would advance this doctrine, exhorting all men unto it and not to their own fantasies and imaginations; if schoolmasters would instruct their children rather with this simple science than with the witty[24] traditions of Aristotle and Averroës,[25] then should the Christianity[26] be more at quietness, and not be disturbed with such perpetual storms of dissension and war. Then should this unreasonable desire of avarice, which appeteth[27] riches insatiably, whether it be right or wrong, be somedeal[28] assuaged and cease of his rage. Then should these contentious pleadings which now in all things admixt[29] themselves have an end; for no man would resist evil.[30] And to be short, then should we not differ only in title and certain ceremonies from the heathen and unfaithful but rather in the pure conversation of our life. And no doubt in these three degrees of men, that is to say, in princes and officers which are in their stead, in bishops and other priests which are their vicars, and in them that bring up the tender youth, which are formed and reformed even as their master enticeth them, doth chiefly consist the whole power either to increase the Christian religion or else to restore it again, which hath long been in decay. Now if these would a while seclude[31] their own private business and lift up their hearts with a pure intent unto Christ, seeking only his glory and the profit of their neighbour, we should see verily within few years a true and godly kind of Christian spring up in every place, which would not only in ceremonies, dispicions[32] and titles profess the name of Christ, but in their very heart and true conversation of living. By this armour should we much sooner prevail against the unfaithful and enemies of Christ than with strength, violence and threatenings. Let us join together all armies, powers and might of sword, yet is there nothing stronger than the truth. We cannot call any man a Platonist, unless he have read the works of Plato. Yet call we them Christian, yea, and divines, which never have read the Scripture of Christ. Christ sayeth, 'He that loveth me doth keep my sayings'; this is the knowledge and mark which he hath prescribed. Therefore if we be true Christian men in our hearts, if we believe unfeignedly that he was sent down from heaven to teach us such things as the wisdom of the philosophers could never attain, if faithfully we trust or look for such things of him as no worldly prince, be he never so rich, can give unto us, why have we anything in more reverence and authority than his Scripture, word and promise, which he left here among us to be our consolation? Why recount[33] we anything of gravity or wisdom which dissenteth from his doctrine? Why in this heavenly and mystical learning do we counter[34] and descant, running more at riot than the common and profane interpreters in the civil law or books of physic, winding ourselves in it as in a trifling game or matter of small substance, commenting, tossing and wresting it, even as it cometh to our tongue's end? We apply and draw this heavenly and unspotted doctrine unto our life, and measure it after our vain conversation, according unto the manner of the Lesbes,[35] which bend their rule to the fashion of their stone or timber, and cut not their stone or timber to the rule. And because we will not be seen ignorant in anything, but rather that we have read and know much, we do, I dare not say corrupt these fruitful springs, but that no man can deny we appropriate unto a few men that thing which Christ would have most common. And this kind of philosophy doth rather consist in the affects of the mind than in subtle reasons; it is a life rather than a disputation; it is an inspiration rather than a science; and rather a new transformation than a reasoning. It is a seldom[36] thing to be a well learned man, but it is leeful[37] for every man to be a true Christian; it is leeful for every man to live a godly life, yea, and I dare be bold to say it is leeful for every man to be a pure divine. Now doth every man's mind incline unto that which is wholesome and expedient for his nature. And what other thing is this doctrine of Christ which he calleth the new regeneration but a restoring or repairing of our nature, which in his first creation was good? A man may find very many things in the gentiles' books which are agreeable unto[38] this doctrine, although no man hath showed it so absolutely, neither yet with such efficacity, as Christ himself. For there was never such a rude and gross sect of philosophy which did teach that man's felicity rested on money; there was none so shameless to affirm that the chief point and ground of goodness consisted in this worldly honour and pleasures. The Stoics did knowledge[39] that no man might worthily be called wise except he were a good and virtuous liver, neither that anything was verily good and honest but only virtue, and that nothing was evil and to be abhorred but only vice and sin. Socrates, as Plato maketh mention, did teach by many reasons that injury ought not to be avenged with injury. He taught also that, sith the soul is immortal, they are not to be mourned for which depart hence, if they have lived well, because they are gone into a more prosperous life. Finally, he taught and exhorted all men to subdue the affections of their bodies, and to apply their souls to the contemplation of those things which truly are immortal, although they be not seen with these bodily eyes. Aristotle writeth in his *Politics* that there can nothing be so sweet and delicious to man but that at sometime it doth displease him, only virtue except. The Epicure[40] granteth that there can be nothing delectable and pleasant in this life except the mind and conscience, from whence all pleasure spring, be clear and without grudge[41] of sin — besides that there have been some that have fulfilled a great part of this doctrine, and chiefly of all Socrates, Diogenes and Epictetus.[42] Howbeit, sith Christ himself hath both taught and also done these things more consummately than any other, is it not a marvellous thing that these things are not only unknown of them which profess the name of Christ but also to be despised of them, yea, and to be made a laughing stock? If there be anything that goeth more near to Christianity, let us then disannul these things and follow them. But sith there is no nother[43] thing that can make a true Christian man, why then do we recount this immortal doctrine more abrogate[44] and out of use than the books of Moses? The first point of Christianity is to know what Christ hath taught. The next is to do thereafter and to fulfil it as nigh as God giveth us grace.

Neither think I that any man will count himself a faithful Christian because he can dispute with a crafty and tedious perplexity of words of relations, quiddities and formalities,[45] but in that he knowledgeth and expresseth in deeds those things which Christ both taught and accomplished. Neither speak I this to discommend their study and labour which have exercised their wits in these subtle inventions (for I would offend no man) but rather because I believe, as the matter is indeed, that the very pure and natural philosophy of Christ can be gathered out so fruitfully of no place as out of the Gospels and Epistles of the Apostles; in which if a man will study devoutly, attending more to prayer than arguing, desiring rather to be made a new man than to be armed with Scriptures unto contention, he without doubt shall find that there is nothing pertaining unto man's felicity, other[46] else unto any operation expedient unto this present life, but it is declared, discussed and absolutely touched.[47] If we go about to learn anything, wherefore shall another master and instructor more please us than Christ himself? If we require a rule and form to live after, why do we rather embrace another example than the very first copy and patron, which is Christ himself? If we desire an wholesome medicine against the grievous and noisome lusts or appetites of our minds, why seek we not here the most fruitful remedy? If we appete to quicken and refresh with reading our dull and fainting mind, I pray thee where shall we find such quick[48] and firy sparkles? If we covet to withdraw our minds from the tedious cares of this life, why seek we any other delectable pastimes? Why had we liefer[49] learn the wisdom of Christ's doctrine out of men's books than of Christ himself, which in this Scripture doth chiefly perform that thing which he promised unto us when he said that he would continue with us unto the end of [the] world? For in this his testament, he speaketh, breatheth and liveth among us in a manner more effectually than when his body was presently conversant in this world. The Jews neither saw nor heard so much as thou mayst daily both hear and see in the Scripture of Christ; there wanteth nothing but that thou bring the ears and eyes of faith, wherewith he may be heard and perceived. What a marvellous world is this! We keep the letters which are written from our friend; we kiss them and bear them about with us; we read them over twice or thrice. And how many thousands are there among the Christian which are esteemed of great literature[50] and yet have not once in their lives read over the Gospels and Epistles of the Apostles? Mahomet's adherents are all well instruct in their own sect, and the Jews unto this day, even from their tender age, study diligently their Moses. Why do not we such honour unto Christ, embracing his precepts, which bring eternal life? They that profess Saint Benedict's institution (which is a rule both made of a man that was but of small learning and also written unto the secular, rude and unlearned) observe their example, learn it by heart and drink it into their hearts. Saint Austin's[51] adherents are not ignorant in their rule, Saint Francis' friars do know, observe and advance their patron's precepts, yea, and carry them about with them whithersoever they go, insomuch that they think not themselves in safety except their book be with them. Why set they more by their rule, which was written of a man, than the whole Christianity by the holy Scripture, which Christ did equally preach unto all men, which we have all professed in baptism, and, to conclude, which is most holy among all other doctrines and none to be compared with it, although thou heap six hundred together? And I would to God that, as Paul did write that the law of Moses had no glory in comparison to the glory of the Gospel that succeeded after it, that even so the Evangelies[52] and Epistles were esteemed of the Christian so holy, or had in such reverence, that the doctrines of men in respect of them might seem nothing holy. I am content that every man advance his doctor at his own pleasure. Let them extol Albert, Alexander, Saint Thomas, Aegidius, Richard and Occam.[53] I will diminish no man's fame nor glory, neither yet resist and reprove the old manner of study. Let them be witty, subtle and, in a manner, above capacity or angelical,[54] yet truly must they needs knowledge that these are most true, undoubted and fruitful. Paul and Saint John will that we judge the spirits of prophets whether they are of God or not; and Saint Augustine, reading all other men's books with judgement, requireth none nother authority to his books. Only in the Scripture when he cannot attain a thing, he submitteth himself unto it.[55] And our doctor, which is Christ, was not allowed by the schools of divines, but of the heavenly father, his own and goodly voice bearing witness, and that twice: first at Jordan, as he was baptised, and after in his transfiguration on the mount Thabor,[56] saying, 'This is my well-beloved son, in whom I am pleased. Hear you him.'[57] Oh this sure authority, which, as they say, hath no contradiction![58] What signifieth this 'Hear you him'? Truly that he is only the true teacher and instructor, and that we ought only to be his disciples. Now let every man with their whole affection praise their authors as much as they will; yet was this voice without nay only spoken of Christ our Saviour, upon whom descended the Holy Ghost in likeness of a dove, which did confirm the testimony of the heavenly father. With this spirit was Peter endued, unto whom the high shepherd Christ committed his sheep, once, twice, yea thrice, to be fed and nourished, meaning truly no nother thing but that he should instruct them with the heavenly food of Christian doctrine.[59] In Paul, Christ seemed in a manner new born again, whom he himself called a chosen vessel and a pure preacher of his name and glory.[60] Saint John expressed in his learning that thing which he had sucked or drunk out of the holy fountain of Christ's bosom. What like thing is there in Duns[61] (I would not you should think that I speak it of envy), what like thing is there in Saint Thomas? Howbeit, I commend this man's holiness, and marvel at the subtle wit and judgement of the other. Why do we not all apply our diligent study in these great authors, I mean Christ, Peter, Paul and John? Why bear we not about these in our bosoms? Why have we them not ever in our hands? Why do we not hunt, seek and search out these things with a curious diligence? Why give we a greater portion of our life to the study of Averroës than to the Evangely of Christ? Why do we, in a manner, consume all our age in the decrees of men and vain opinions which are so contrary and dissenting among themselves? Be it in case they be great divines that made such constitutions, yet notwithstanding, only in Christ's word consisteth the exercise and inurance[62] of him which before God is reputed for a great divine. It is meet that we all which have professed the name of Christ (at the least, if we have promised with mind and heart) that we be instruct with the doctrine of Christ, being yet tender infants in our parents' arms and wanton children at our nurse's teat; for it is imprinted most deep and cleaveth most surely which the rude and unformed shell of our soul doth first receive and learn.[63] I would our first and unformed speech should sound of Christ. I would our ignorant childhood should be informed with Christ's Evangely; and to them I would Christ should be so sweetly taught that they might be enflamed to love him, and that after they should proceed by a little and a little, creeping by the ground, until that by insensible increments they spring up to be strong in Christ. Other men's traditions are such that many repent themselves because they have spent so much study and labour upon them. And often it chanceth that they which have most manfully fought through all their life, even unto the death, to defend men's doctrines and decrees, yet in the point of death have cast away their shield and have clean dissented from their author's sect. But blessed is he whom death assaileth, if his heart be whole occupied in this wholesome doctrine. Let us therefore all with fervent desire thirst after these spiritual springs; let us embrace them; let us be studiously conversant with them; let us kiss these sweet words of Christ with a pure affection; let us be new transformed into them; for such are our manners as our studies be; yea, and to be short, let us die in them. He that cannot attain them (but who is he that cannot if he will himself?), yet at the least let him submit himself unto them, recounting them very holy and as the storehouse or treasury of God's own mind, from whence cometh forth all goodness. If a man would show us a step of Christ's foot, Good lord, how would we kneel and worship it! And why do we not rather honour his quick and lively image, which is most expressly contained in these books? If a man would bring unto us Christ's coat, whither would we not run headlong that we might once kiss it? Howbeit, if thou bring out his coat, shirt, shoes and all his household stuff, yet is there nothing that doth more truly and expressly represent Christ than the Gospels and Epistles. We garnish or adorn an image of wood or stone with gold and precious stones for the love of Christ. But why are not these things rather garnished with gold and gems, yea, and more preciously, if so anything can be more precious than they, sith they represent much more presently Christ unto us than any image can do? As for images, what thing can they express but the figure of his body? — if they express that. But the Evangely doth represent and express the quick and living image of his most holy mind, yea, and Christ himself, speaking, healing, dying, rising again, and, to conclude, all parts of him, insomuch that thou couldest not so plain and fruitfully see him although he were present before thy bodily eyes.

NOTES

1. *Revocate*: recall.
2. *Sciences*: branches of study.
3. *Convenient*: appropriate, proper, due.
4. *Fautors*: adherents, partisans.
5. *Diogenes*: the founder of the Cynic sect in the fourth century BC.
6. *Groundly*: thoroughly.
7. *Howbeit*: adverb, however.
8. *Zeno*: probably the founder of Stoicism is meant here.
9. *Chaldes*: Babylonians.
10. *Tickle*: excite agreeably.
11. *Instruct*: instructed.
12. *Confirmable*: in the sixteenth century, this was confused with 'conformable', i.e. compliant — the sense here.
13. *Depressed*: lowered, humbled.
14. *Indifferent*: impartial, i.e. shining on all alike.
15. *Forbiddeth*: excludes.
16. *Scant*: scarcely, hardly.
17. *Be it in case that*: even though.
18. A mistranslation of the Latin, which means 'Never mind that many would mock; others would be caught.'
19. *Tales*: conversation, discourse. (A christianisation of the idea of speech

being the mirror of the mind.)

20. *Effectuously*: effectually.
21. *Allect*: entice, allure.
22. *Bolden*: encourage, embolden.
23. A jibe at the scholastics.
24. *Witty*: clever, subtle.
25. *Averroës*: the Arabic commentator on Aristotle (*c*. 1126-*c*. 1198).
26. *Christianity*: Christendom, the body of Christians.
27. *Appeteth*: seeks after, desires.
28. *Somedeal*: somewhat.
29. *Admixt*: admix.
30. I am puzzled by this phrase, which is an addition to the Latin.
31. *Seclude*: set aside, banish, exclude.
32. *Dispicions*: disputations.
33. *Recount*: consider, account.
34. *Counter*: dispute, contradict.
35. *Lesbes*: Lesbians (the inhabitants of Lesbos). Aristotle mentions the Lesbian rule in the *Nicomachean Ethics*, V. x. 6-7 (1137B), discussing the principle of equity: 'There are some cases for which it is impossible to lay down a law, so that a special ordinance becomes necessary. For what is itself indefinite can only be measured by an indefinite standard, like the leaden rule used by Lesbian builders; just as that rule is not rigid but can be bent to the shape of the stone, so a special ordinance is made to fit the circumstances of the case' (Loeb translation). Erasmus reapplies the simile in a pejorative sense.
36. *Seldom*: adjective, rare.
37. *Leeful*: permissible (leave + ful).
38. *Agreeable unto*: in accordance with.
39. *Knowledge*: recognise, acknowledge.
40. *Epicure*: Epicurean.
41. *Grudge*: murmuring of conscience, uneasiness.
42. *Epictetus*: freed slave and Stoic philosopher; see above, p. 96, note 17.
43. *No nother*: no other.
44. *Abrogate*: annulled, cancelled.
45. Scholastic methods of logical definition. *Quiddity* = essence.
46. *Other*: or.
47. *Touched*: treated.
48. *Quick*: live.
49. *Liefer*: more willingly.
50. *Literature*: humane learning, literary culture.
51. *Austin*: Augustine.
52. *Evangelies*: Gospels.
53. The medieval theologians, Albertus Magnus, Alexander of Hales, Thomas Aquinas, Giles of Rome, Richard of St Victor and William of Occam.
54. A jibe at the scholastics: *seraphicus*, 'angelical', was one of their favourite terms of commendation.
55. A mistranslation of the Latin, which is in the first person: 'In these writings alone I revere even what I do not follow.'
56. *Thabor*: Mount Thabor (the Vulgate spelling; Tabor in the Authorised Version) was believed by St Jerome and others to be the mountain on which the Transfiguration took place, although in the gospel accounts the mountain is not named (see Matthew, 17: 1; Mark, 9: 2).
57. Matthew, 3: 17; 17: 5.
58. A jibe at scholastic jargon; the Latin word is *irrefragabilis*, a non-classical term.

59. John, 21: 15-17.
60. Acts of the Apostles, 9: 15.
61. *Duns*: Duns Scotus, the scholastic theologian, see above, p. 113, note 7.
62. *Inurance*: habituation.
63. Compare Horace, *Epistles*, I. ii. 64-70.

# SELECT BIBLIOGRAPHY

A full bibliography on humanism and its influence on English literature would be immense; the following is highly selective, and is intended as an introduction to the subject. It contains books referred to in this volume and some others.

## I Primary texts

*Collections*

Cassirer, Ernst, Kristeller, Paul Oskar and Randall, John Herman (eds.) *The Renaissance philosophy of man: selections in translation* (University of Chicago Press, 1948). Contains translations of *On his own ignorance and that of many others* and other works by Petrarch

Ross, James Bruce, and McLaughlin, Mary Martin (eds.) *The portable Renaissance reader* (Viking Portable Library, Penguin, 1977). Contains short extracts in translation from Italian humanists and others

Woodward, William Harrison *Vittorino da Feltre and other humanist educators: essays and versions* (Cambridge University Press, 1897). Contains translations from humanist educational works

*Ascham, Roger*

*English works: Toxophilus, Report of the affaires and state of Germany, The scholemaster*, ed. William Aldis Wright (Cambridge University Press, 1904)

*The scholemaster*, ed. John E. B. Mayor (Bell and Daldy, 1863). An edition with detailed notes

*The schoolmaster (1570)*, ed. Lawrence V. Ryan (Folger Documents of Tudor and Stuart Civilization, Cornell University Press for the Folger Shakespeare Library, 1967). An edition in modernised spelling

*Castiglione, Baldesar*

*Il cortegiano*, ed. Vittorio Cian, 3rd edn (Sansoni, 1929). Standard Italian edition, with notes

*The book of the courtier*, trans. George Bull, rev. edn (Penguin Classics, 1976)

*The book of the courtier*, trans. Sir Thomas Hoby, introduction by Walter Raleigh (Tudor Translations, ed. W. E. Henley, no. 23, David Nutt, 1900)

*The book of the courtier*, trans. Sir Thomas Hoby, introduction by J. H. Whitfield (Everyman's University Library, Dent, 1974)

*Colet, John*

*An exposition of St Paul's Epistle to the Romans*, ed. with a translation by J. H. Lupton (Bell and Daldy, 1873)

*An exposition of St Paul's First Epistle to the Corinthians*, ed. with a translation by J. H. Lupton (George Bell, 1874)

*Daniel, Samuel*

*Poems and A defence of ryme*, ed. Arthur Colby Sprague (University of Chicago Press, 1965). Contains *Musophilus*

*Elyot, Sir Thomas*

*The boke named the gouernour*, ed. Henry Herbert Stephen Croft (2 vols., Kegan Paul, 1880). Full annotation

*The book named the governor*, ed. S. E. Lehmberg (Everyman's Library, Dent, 1962). Modernised spelling

*Of the knowledge which maketh a wise man*, ed. Edwin Johnston Howard (Anchor Press, 1946)

*Erasmus, Desiderius*

There are two editions of the complete works of Erasmus in Latin: the Leyden edition, which was done in the eighteenth century by Joannes Clericus (Jean Leclerc, 1657-1736), of which there is a modern reprint, and the Amsterdam edition, a new scholarly edition with full annotation, which is still in progress. There is also the complete edition of Erasmus' letters in Latin by Percy Allen. The complete works of Erasmus in English translation are currently coming out from the University of Toronto Press; the volumes so far published are listed below.

*Opera omnia emendatiora et auctiora* (10 vols. in 11, Gregg Press, 1962). Facsimile of the edition by Clericus, published by Petrus van der Aa, Leyden, 1703-7

*Opera omnia ... recognita et adnotatione critica instructa notisque illustrata* (North-Holland, 1969- ). The Amsterdam edition, in progress. Vol. I. i contains *The antibarbarians*, vol. I. ii *On giving children an early and a liberal education*, *On abundance*, *On the proper system of study* and *Ciceronianus*, vol. I. iii the *Colloquies*

*Opus epistolarum*, ed. P. S. Allen, H. M. Allen and H. W. Garrod (12 vols., Clarendon Press, 1906-58). Complete edition of the letters in Latin

*The collected works of Erasmus* (University of Toronto Press, 1974- ). In progress. Vols. I-VI contain *Letters*, vol. XXIII *The antibarbarians* and the *Parallels*, vol. XXIV *On abundance* and *On the proper system of study*, vol. XXXI *Adages* I. i. 1 to I. v. 100

*Christian humanism and the Reformation: selected writings of Erasmus*, ed. John C. Olin, rev. edn (Fordham University Press, 1975). Contains a translation of the *Paraclesis*

*Erasmus*, ed. Richard L. DeMolen (Documents of Modern History, Edward Arnold, 1973). A selection of letters etc. in translation

[*Ciceronianus*] A translation will be found in Izora Scott, *Controversies over the imitation of Cicero* (Teachers College, Columbia University, 1910)

*Colloquies*, trans. Craig R. Thompson (University of Chicago Press, 1965)

*Ten colloquies*, trans. Craig R. Thompson (Library of Liberal Arts, Bobbs-Merrill, 1957). Contains a translation of *The pious feast*

*The education of a Christian prince*, trans. Lester K. Born (Records of Civilization, no. XXVII, Columbia University Press, 1936, reprinted Octagon Books, 1973)

*Enchiridion*, trans. and ed. Raymond Himelick (Indiana University Press, 1963)

[*On giving children an early and a liberal education*] A full précis will be found in William Harrison Woodward, *Desiderius Erasmus concerning the aim and method of education* (Cambridge University Press, 1904)

*Praise of folly and Letter to Martin Dorp 1515*, trans. Betty Radice, introduction A. H. T. Levi (Penguin Classics, 1971)

*Harvey, Gabriel*

*Gabriel Harvey's Ciceronianus*, introduction and notes by Harold S. Wilson, trans. Clarence A. Forbes (Studies in the Humanities, no. 4, University of Nebraska, 1945)

*Hoole, Charles*

*A new discovery of the old art of teaching schoole*, ed. E. T. Campagnac
(Liverpool University Press, 1913)

*Jonson, Ben*

*Works* , ed. C. H. Herford, Percy and Evelyn Simpson, corrected edn
(Clarendon Press, 1954-63), 11 vols. Text of *Discoveries* in vol.
VIII, notes in vol. XI
*The complete poems*, ed. George Parfitt (Penguin English Poets, 1975).
Contains a text of *Discoveries* in modernised spelling

*Machiavelli, Niccolò*

*Il principe*, ed. L. Arthur Burd (Clarendon Press, 1891). Italian text,
English notes
*The prince*, trans. George Bull, rev. edn (Penguin Classics, 1981)
*The prince 1640*, trans. Edward Dacres (Scolar Press, 1969). A Scolar
Press facsimile
*The discourses*, ed. Bernard Crick, trans. L. J. Walker (Penguin Classics,
1983)

*More, Thomas*

*Complete works* (Yale University Press, 1963- ). In progress. Vol. III
Part 1 contains *Translations of Lucian*, ed. Craig R. Thompson,
vol. IV *Utopia*, ed. Edward Surtz and J. H. Hexter
*Utopia*, trans. Paul Turner (Penguin Classics, 1965)

*Mulcaster, Richard*

*Mulcaster's Elementarie*, ed. E. T. Campagnac (Clarendon Press, 1925)

*North, Sir Thomas*

*Plutarch's Lives of the noble Grecians and Romans,* trans. Sir Thomas
North, introduction by George Wyndham (Tudor Translations,
ed. W. E. Henley, nos. VII-XII, 6 vols., David Nutt, 1895-6)
*Shakespeare's Plutarch: the Lives of Julius Caesar, Brutus, Marcus
Antonius, and Coriolanus in the translation of Sir Thomas North*,
ed. T. J. B. Spencer (Penguin, 1964)

*Vives, Juan Luis*

*Vives On education: a translation of the De tradendis disciplinis of Juan
Luis Vives*, Foster Watson (Cambridge University Press, 1913)

*Wilson, Thomas*

*Wilson's Arte of rhetorique 1560*, ed. G. H. Mair (Clarendon Press, 1909)

## II Secondary works

Bainton, Roland H. *Erasmus of Christendom* (Fontana, 1972)

Baldwin, T. W. *William Shakspere's small Latine and lesse Greeke* (2 vols., University of Illinois Press, 1944). Contains a detailed account of English Renaissance education

Bolgar, R. R. *The classical heritage and its beneficiaries* (Cambridge University Press, 1954)

Boyle, Marjorie O'Rourke *Christening pagan mysteries: Erasmus in pursuit of wisdom* (University of Toronto Press, 1981)

— *Erasmus on language and method in theology* (University of Toronto Press, 1977)

Bradshaw, Brendan 'The Christian humanism of Erasmus', *Journal of theological studies*, n.s., XXXIII (1982), pp. 411-47

Brower, Reuben, A. *Hero and saint: Shakespeare and the Graeco-Roman heroic tradition* (Clarendon Press, 1971)

Bruce, F. F. *The English Bible: a history of translations* (University Paperbacks, Methuen, 1963)

Bush, Douglas *The Renaissance and English humanism*, The Alexander Lectures (University of Toronto Press, 1939)

Campana, Augusto 'The origin of the word "humanist" ', *Journal of the Warburg and Courtauld Institutes*, IX (1946), pp. 60-73

Caspari, Fritz *Humanism and the social order in Tudor England* (University of Chicago Press, 1954)

Cave, Terence *The Cornucopian text: problems of writing in the French Renaissance* (Clarendon Press, 1979). Contains a section on Erasmus

Charlton, Kenneth *Education in Renaissance England* (Routledge and Kegan Paul, 1965)

Dickens, A. G. *The age of humanism and Reformation: Europe in the fourteenth, fifteenth and sixteenth centuries* (Prentice-Hall, 1977)

Dresden, Sem *Humanism in the Renaissance*, trans. Margaret King (World University Library, Weidenfeld and Nicolson, 1968)

Doran, Madeleine *Endeavours of art: a study of form in Elizabethan drama* (University of Wisconsin Press, 1954). Opening chapters contain an interesting discussion of Renaissance classicism, the ideal of eloquence, etc.

Duncan, Douglas *Ben Jonson and the Lucianic tradition* (Cambridge University Press, 1979)

Eisenstein, Elizabeth L. *The printing press as an agent of change: communications and cultural transformations in early-modern Europe* (2 vols., Cambridge University Press, 1979)

Erskine-Hill, Howard *The Augustan idea in English literature* (Edward Arnold, 1983)

Gray, Hanna H. 'Renaissance humanism: the pursuit of eloquence' in Paul Oskar Kristeller and Philip P. Wiener (eds.), *Renaissance essays from the Journal of the history of ideas* (Harper and Row, 1968), pp. 199-216

Hale, J. R. (ed.) *A concise encyclopaedia of the Italian Renaissance* (Thames and Hudson, 1981)

Hall, B. 'Erasmus: biblical scholar and reformer' in T. A. Dorey (ed.), *Erasmus* (Studies in Latin Literature and its Influence, Routledge and Kegan Paul, 1970), pp. 81-113

Hay, Denys *The Italian Renaissance in its historical background*, The Wiles Lectures, 2nd edn (Cambridge University Press, 1977)

Hunter, G. K. *John Lyly: the humanist as courtier* (Routledge and Kegan Paul, 1962). Chapter 1, 'Humanism and courtship', contains an interesting discussion on the clash between humanist ideals and life at court

Jacobsen, Eric *Translation, a traditional craft: an introductory sketch with a study of Marlowe's Elegies* (Classica et Mediaevalia, Dissertationes, VI, Copenhagen, Gyldendalske Boghandel, Nordisk Forlag, 1958). Includes useful material on education

Jones, Emrys (ed.) *Henry Howard, Earl of Surrey: poems* (Clarendon Press, 1964). Brief but excellent introduction on how humanist ideas affected Surrey

— *The origins of Shakespeare* (Clarendon Press, 1977)

— 'Pope and dullness', Chatterton Lecture on an English Poet, *Proceedings of the British Academy,* LIV (1968), pp. 231-63

Jones, Richard Foster *The triumph of the English language: a survey of opinions concerning the vernacular from the introduction of printing to the Restoration* (Stanford University Press, 1953)

Kaiser, Walter *Praisers of folly: Erasmus, Rabelais, Shakespeare* (Gollancz, 1964)

Kelley, Donald R. *Foundations of modern historical scholarship:*

*language, law and history in the French Renaissance* (Columbia University Press, 1970)

Kristeller, Paul Oskar *Eight philosophers of the Italian Renaissance* (Chatto and Windus, 1965)

—— *Renaissance thought and its sources*, ed. Michael Mooney (Columbia University Press, 1979)

Lehmberg, Stanford E. *Sir Thomas Elyot: Tudor humanist* (University of Texas Press, 1960)

Lewis, C. S. *English literature in the sixteenth century excluding drama*, *Oxford history of English literature* (Clarendon Press, 1954)

McConica, James Kelsey *English humanists and Reformation politics under Henry VIII and Edward VI* (Clarendon Press, 1965)

Major, John M. *Sir Thomas Elyot and Renaissance humanism* (University of Nebraska Press, 1964)

Mason, H. A. *Humanism and poetry in the early Tudor period* (Routledge and Kegan Paul, 1959)

Miola, Robert S. *Shakespeare's Rome* (Cambridge University Press, 1983)

Panofsky, Erwin *Renaissance and renascences in Western art* (Paladin, 1970)

Pfeiffer, Rudolf *History of classical scholarship from 1300 to 1850* (Clarendon Press, 1976)

Phillips, Margaret Mann *The 'Adages' of Erasmus: a study with translations* (Cambridge University Press, 1964)

—— 'Erasmus and the classics' in T. A. Dorey (ed.), *Erasmus* (Studies in Latin Literature and its Influence, Routledge and Kegan Paul, 1970), pp. 1-30

—— *Erasmus and the Northern Renaissance*, rev. edn (Boydell Press, 1981)

Reynolds, L. D. and Wilson, N. G. *Scribes and scholars: a guide to the transmission of Greek and Latin literature*, 2nd edn (Clarendon Press, 1974)

Rice, Eugene F. *The Renaissance idea of wisdom* (Harvard University Press, 1958)

Robinson, Christopher *Lucian and his influence in Europe* (Classical Life and Letters, Duckworth, 1979)

Russell, D. A. *Plutarch* (Classical Life and Letters, Duckworth, 1973)

Ryan, Lawrence V. *Roger Ascham* (Stanford University Press, 1963)

Scott, Izora *Controversies over the imitation of Cicero* (Teachers College, Columbia University, 1910)

Screech, M. A. *Ecstasy and the praise of folly* (Duckworth, 1980)

Seigel, Jerrold E. *Rhetoric and philosophy in Renaissance humanism: the union of eloquence and wisdom, Petrarch to Valla* (Princeton University Press, 1968)

Simon, Joan *Education and society in Tudor England* (Cambridge University Press, 1966)

Skinner, Quentin *The foundations of modern political thought*, vol. I, *The Renaissance* (Cambridge University Press, 1978)

— *Machiavelli* (Past Masters, Oxford University Press, 1981)

Trousdale, Marion *Shakespeare and the rhetoricians* (Scolar Press, 1982)

Watson, Foster *The English grammar schools to 1660: their curriculum and practice* (Cambridge University Press, 1908)

— *The old grammar schools* (Frank Cass, 1968)

Weiss, R. *Humanism in England during the fifteenth century*, 3rd edn (Blackwell, 1967)

Woodhouse, J.R. *Baldesar Castiglione: a reassessment of 'The courtier'* (Edinburgh University Press, 1978)

Woodward, William Harrison *Desiderius Erasmus concerning the aim and method of education* (Cambridge University Press, 1904)

— *Studies in education during the age of the Renaissance 1400-1600* (Cambridge University Press, 1906)

— *Vittorino da Feltre and other humanist educators: essays and versions* (Cambridge University Press, 1897)

# INDEX

The reader is referred to the list of *Contents* for a list of the anthologised extracts.